SEARCH AND RESCUE

THE LIFE AND LOVE THAT IS LOOKING FOR YOU

SEARCH AND RESCUE

THE LIFE AND LOVE THAT IS LOOKING FOR YOU

MICHAEL THOMPSON

HEART & LIFE
PUBLISHERS

Search and Rescue: The Life and Love that Is Looking for You

Copyright © 2010 by Michael Thompson
All rights reserved.

Published by Heart & Life Publishers, Grand Rapids, Michigan.
www.heartandlife.com

ISBN-10: 0-615-40749-4
ISBN-13: 978-0-615-40749-4

Unless otherwise noted, Scripture quotations are from The Holy Bible, New International Version®.

Copyright © 1973, 1978, 1984 by International Bible Society. Used by permission of Zondervan. All rights reserved.

Cover design: Nole Design, www.noledesign.com
Interior design: Nole Design, www.noledesign.com
Author photo: Paul Liggitt, www.plphoto.com
Map illustrations: M. Brad Aderhold

Printed in the United States of America

For Robin, Ashley, Hannah and Abbey—
There is nobody I'd rather be journeying with than you. Thank you for teaching me everyday how to Love and what Life is really about.

For Mom and Dad—
Thank you for loving God and loving me and the years of support, encouragement and orientation. You both love well.

CONTENTS

PART I	LOST	17
CHAPTER 1	SEARCH AND RESCUE	20
CHAPTER 2	ORIENTATION	36
CHAPTER 3	PACKING UP	53
PART II	WHERE ARE WE?	72
CHAPTER 4	GETTING OUR BEARINGS	78
CHAPTER 5	TWO REALMS AND THE REALM THAT MATTERS MOST	98
CHAPTER 6	TWO KINGDOMS	120
CHAPTER 7	THE ECONOMY OF KINGDOM: WAR	139
PART III	THE SEARCH	157
CHAPTER 8	SEARCH FOR THE HEART	163
CHAPTER 9	WE'RE NOT THE ONLY ONES SEARCHING	180
CHAPTER 10	ONE TO SHOW THE WAY	198
PART IV	REORIENTED	211
CHAPTER 11	RESTORATION: LIVING NEWLY	215
CHAPTER 12	OVERWHELMED	232
CHAPTER 13	TRAINING: THE GOOD THAT GOD US UP TO IN OUR LIVES	252
EPILOGUE	WHERE DO WE GO FROM HERE?	273

ACKNOWLEDGMENTS

Thank you Kevin Miles from Heart & Life Publishers for trusting God and believing I had something to say and going the distance with me. Scott Stankavage, Anthony Dilweg, Molly Detweiler, Nolan Abney, Dawn Stuart, Susan Hale, Rick Zyczkiewicz, Justin Johns and the Z Creative Team for you significant contributions and tremendous talents. I'm honored to be your teammate.

To my brothers, Tom Benner, Jim Chenet and Jay Stott and the many good men on the Z team (Rick, Keith, JB, Michael, Chris, Ken and Kelly), for standing with me on the front lines of the battle. A man couldn't have better men to fight with and fight for. Thanks for assisting the Father in rescuing me again and again.

To all the Zoweh men and women, thank you for walking with Robin and me and letting us walk with you. You know who you are and so does the Father.

With deep gratitude and appreciation to the Eastern Allies, what a force for the Kingdom you've become. I truly love that you're out there searching and rescuing the lives around you. You fight well.

To Gary from The Noble Heart, Craig, Bart, John and the Ransomed Heart team, you dug me out of the rubble and I am forever grateful.

Because this Life is wonderfully overwhelming, thank you most of all Jesus— for searching for me, rescuing me, and saving me in every way a person can be saved and restoring me into more than I ever thought possible. You are my King, and I know we're not done. This gets me out of bed every day.

INTRODUCTION

SEARCH and RESCUE

Fate Has Chosen Him.

A Fellowship Will Protect Him.

Evil Will Hunt Them.

These words invite us to travel along with ordinary little Frodo Baggins on his extraordinary journey in the film *The Lord of the Rings: The Fellowship of the Ring*. As these bold words flash across the screen, we find our hearts quickening. We watch with anticipation the images of peril and adventure accompanying these declarations. Why does this tale and others like it touch so many of us so deeply?

These stories stir us because they are reflections, images and echoes of our own. Frodo's story is our story. We are all engaged in a great mission, a crucial quest, *for Life*. A Life that has meaning; a Life that matters. Much depends on our choices along the way. Each step we take, each choice we make in our lives, is *always* connected to the previous one as well as the succeeding one. We must have our eyes opened to the battle around us and to the evil that indeed threatens to thwart us at every turn—attempting to steal our lives. But more importantly than the evil that hunts us, we need to see and know that something, *Someone*, who is far greater than all the evil in the world, is also searching for us, guiding us, reaching out His hand to us. He is the One offering us the Life for which we long. And just like Frodo and his fellowship, we will need faithful friends, vital equipment and a true orientation to lead us on this grand adventure. *There is so much more going on in this life than we have been led to believe.*

When I look back at my life's journey over the past decade, it's not hard for me to see my "lostness." I maintain a journal with a couple of weekly entries, and so many of them contain phrases like, *What am I going to do? How can I get out of this? When are things going to change?*

I know I'm not alone. When I look at the Scriptures and read the "journal entries" in the Psalms, David and the other authors cry out from a place of uncertainty, hurting, loneliness and pain.

> *Oh Lord, how long will you look on? Rescue my life from their ravages, my precious life from these lions.*
> Psalm 35:17

> *God, for your sake, help me! Use your influence to clear me. Listen, God–I'm desperate. Don't be too busy to hear me.*
> Psalm 54:1 (MSG)

> *Hear my prayer, O Lord; let my cry for help come to you.*
> *Do not hide your face from me when I am in distress.*
> Psalm 102:1-2a

In the past 10 years or so, I have lived a Christian life, but all too often, I still have felt a deep, nagging sense of lostness—the sense that *something is missing*. It's like putting together one of those 1,000-piece puzzles. You get to the end and almost have the complete picture, only to discover there are no more pieces left on the table. You look in the box, around the table, under the couch...*what the heck?*

It's the same feeling Neo must have felt in the beginning of the film, *The Matrix*, when Morpheus says to him:

> *Let me tell you why you're here. You're here because you know something. What you know you can't explain, but you feel it. You've felt it your entire life, that there's something wrong with the world. You don't know what it is, but it's there, like a splinter in your mind, driving you mad. It is this feeling that has brought you to me. Do you know what I'm talking about?*

I know what he's talking about. I've been there...moving through life trying to assemble all the pieces and follow all the rules of the good Christian life. As with Neo, something needed to change. I needed to be rescued and have the splinter removed. And that is exactly what happened. Don't misunderstand...I still have moments in life where I'm confused or disoriented. The story we're living in is way too big not to. *But now* I'm less prone to the lostness I once felt so deeply.

There is a life I've found or, maybe better said, a Life that has found me—and it's a Life of *more*. I truly believe that if it can happen to me, if I can be found, then it can happen to anyone and everyone. I want you to understand...I am not writing about something I've already accomplished, but rather a life I'm still in the middle of building. Not a day goes by that I don't interact with the lives and stories of others who are stuck at the bottom of some well, a pit they've either fallen down or been sucked into. And they are struggling, losing heart, scared and feeling alone. If that is you, I want you to know you are not alone. There are many in that same frustrating and painful spot. The problem is that most of us have not yet reached the end of ourselves where we are too tired to do anything but admit we are lost. Some of us are more determined than others to hold to our own program and do all we can to arrange our own lives.

One more try. This time will be different.

If it is to be it's up to me.
Everything happens for a reason.
When life gives you lemons make lemonade.
When the going gets tough, the tough get going.

How's that going by the way?

The time for bumper sticker theology and mega-doses of positive thinking is over. If you feel it too—the irritation that comes from the "splinter in your mind" and seems to be an epidemic, if you know there is more, but the program you're running continues to find you retracing your steps, I know how you feel. I believe wholeheartedly that what I'm sharing in these pages is going to be life-changing for you, because it was for me. It won't keep you from ever hitting the bottom of a well again or getting pulled into difficult situations, but it will equip you not to *live* there.

To quote Morpheus again, "*Be patient Neo, the answers are coming.*"

So how do we find our way through this uncertain, and often times painful, life journey? Where do we begin? Author and counselor John Eldredge said it like this: "Life is not a bunch of problems to be solved, it is a great story to be entered into." And so I invite you to begin there—to take the first step into a new story...your story. It was Frodo's uncle, Bilbo, who once gave him this piece of advice:

It's a dangerous business, Frodo, going out your front door. You step onto the road, and if you don't keep your feet, there's no knowing where you might be swept off to.

How did the little hobbit know to declare both *a warning* and *an invitation*? Clearly he knew from his own experience, from the time he was first swept up into the larger story. So this is where we start, with both a warning and an invitation. The journey will not be easy or comfortable—but it will be worth it.

Will you join me?

PART I

LOST

CHAPTER 1 SEARCH AND RESCUE
CHAPTER 2 ORIENTATION
CHAPTER 3 PACKING UP

I'm lost.

We've all been lost at one time or another, and it's a scary place to be. Nothing is familiar. We don't want to admit our lostness, and we surely don't want anyone else to know about it. Yet, admitting it is the first step to turning the situation around. What if we took some time to explore this state of "lostness," if for no other reason than to seek momentary clarity and the opportunity it affords us to take our first steps toward being found? What if we pressed into the gamut of uncomfortable and disheartening emotions this declaration stirs up?

Let's take a little inventory. What can "I'm lost" mean? Perhaps bad directions, a wrong turn, uncertainty, momentary confusion, or a long-term misunderstanding. We mostly associate the phrase with travel and directions. Seldom do we see it as the condition of *our lives*. Being lost is a shared condition—we all are, or have been, lost in one way or another.

When you look at the stories and films we love (both fiction and non-fiction), it's hard to find a story that at some point doesn't find the main characters declaring how lost they are or have been. They will often say *Those were dark days. We didn't know how we were going to make it. I would still be there if it weren't for...*

And yet, this experience of being lost is also a deeply personal one. Our lives are not one-size-fits-all, and our "lostness" can never be resolved with a one-formula-solves-all equation. My experience of being lost and yours might have a common theme, but the variables are so vastly different that your rescue will not look the same as mine. I may want many of the same things you do, and yet our paths may lead us to many different stops along the way. While it can seem comforting to know we're all in this together, to make support groups and to encourage one another through some kind of misery-loves-company fellowship... this is not a way to freedom but rather a way to stay and cope. *Freedom, not coping,* must be our course of action, our way of life. Coping causes an endless turnstile of motion without gaining any ground.

This shared experience of lostness is a dangerous one and often leads us down the wrong path in our search for direction, freedom and life. It is kind of like the blind leading the blind. In the short-term, we find it so tempting to see the attractiveness of someone else's journey and try to make it our own. What is dangerous is that it can work... for a time. Then the reality of our situation surfaces and we find ourselves lost *again* and wondering: *Where Am I?*

Asking the question *Where Am I?* might be your first step toward breaking the cycle. What I'm not offering in these pages is an *answer*. I discovered that was a major part of my problem; I was treating my life like a problem that needed an answer. What I really needed was a perspective that would offer my life an *orientation*, a long-term remedy that would take my life into a whole new cosmos.

For many, the life we are living and the Life we are seeking often seem galaxies apart. But as I have found, the Life that is *looking for you* can narrow the distance from galaxies to an arm's length. The Source of Life has overcome obstacles and brought down hurdles unknown to this world. God, through Jesus, is setting the world right and redeeming it all for His name's sake and for those He has set in His heart to love: you and me. *Pack up* and buckle up, for this Life is more wild and more glorious, more dangerous and more significant, than we've been led to believe.

But before we get there, there is some work we have to do. We have to examine our lives and find out how we got off track and lost our way. This is possible and important even while we call ourselves Christians, doing the "church thing" and being a part of a "small group." It was Socrates who said, "The unexamined life is not worth living." Let's take a look under the hood and see what's going on.

CHAPTER 1

SEARCH and RESCUE

For the Son of Man came to seek and to save what was lost.

-Jesus of Nazareth (Luke 19:10)

We search and search and search for life, then we are found.

-C.S. Lewis

He saved me in every way a person could be saved.

-Rose, from the movie *Titanic*

Back in 1987, there was a 58-hour dramatic rescue in Midland, Texas, of a baby girl named Jessica McClure. Most of the country was captured by the news reports of a little girl who was lost and then found, rescued and recovered. Working around the clock for two and a half days, rescuers finally pulled 18-month-old Jessica from an abandoned well shaft, where she had been trapped 22 feet below the surface.

What started as an innocent children's game at the home of the family babysitter turned into a terrifying ordeal. But before Jessica's fateful fall, the scene was one filled with the playful shouts and laughter of a fun game of hide-and-seek. In a funny voice, a grown-up would announce (after a good long count to 20 and the usual *ready or not, here I come*), "Where's Jessica? I'm going to find you! Where's little Jessica?" These are words every parent, grandparent, big brother, big sister, uncle, aunt or babysitter has sung out when walking about, looking for little ones who have disappeared into their favorite hiding spots.

That fall day in Midland, the *Where are you?* song soon turned into shouts of concern. Concern gave way to more desperate, frantic cries and then turned to *panic*. When little Jessica was finally located, the reality set in. She was found, but she was not safe. She had fallen down an old well and was trapped in its shaft, 22 feet below.

Soon the entire community was mobilized, for it would take a community to rescue Baby Jessica. Police, firefighters, EMTs and engineers came to offer help. The nation tuned in to watch, hope and pray for her safe rescue and recovery. It was the early days of cable television, and this was one of the first times that "national news coverage" took over nearly every channel (all 36 of them)—all "broadcasting live" from Midland, Texas.

Now that Jessica was found, the question turned to how to rescue her. The rescuers quickly realized that they couldn't go into the same shaft Jessica had fallen into due to risk of a cave-in that would fatally bury the baby girl. Instead, they changed the plan to creating a shaft adjacent to the one that held Jessica. The trick was going to be keeping a safe distance so as not to disturb the old 22-foot well where Jessica lay and thereby risking a cave-in. So digging began some eight to ten feet from the hole where Jessica was. Now, West Texas is not known for its deep rich soils, so the heavy equipment used for drilling had to be stopped when the rescue workers hit rock just a few feet into the new hole. If they continued to drill with the heavy equipment, they would once again risk collapsing the dirt into Jessica's hole. The rescue tunnel would now have to be dug by hand. For more than two days, rescuers painstakingly chipped away at the rock, battling the earth and the clock to free Jessica. All the while, live news coverage brought the whole drama into homes and offices across the nation and the world.

On the morning of October 16, 1987, after 58 hours of meticulous digging, the wait was over, and Baby Jessica was handed into loving and caring hands. She was rescued. She was safe. All over the world, those who looked on broke into applause and cheers, *She's safe; She made it; Oh, thank God!* We all celebrated with shouts of gladness and reached for the tissues or our shirt sleeves to wipe away tears of joyful relief. Baby Jessica remarkably escaped the ordeal with minor injuries. The search was over. The rescue was complete and the recovery a success!

Similarly, the world celebrated on October 12, 2010, when the first of 33 Chilean miiners emerged from his underground prison after 69 days. Amazingly, all the miners survived the extended entrapment half a mile underground without life-threatening injuries or illness. Like Baby Jessica's, their successful rescue and recovery were deemed miraculous.

In all our lives, things get lost. Tools, clothes, papers, reports and assignments, to name a few. So do people. In responding to what is lost, our emotions can range from the low-grade nagging and frustration we feel about a small inconvenience to the frantic and deep sense of loss or despair we experience when what is lost is precious. I know personally the guilt, fear, shame, regret and resentment that can accompany lost *things*.

But when *people* get lost there is a shock wave released within a family or a community, and the *all-points bulletins* mobilize anyone and everyone to join in the massive search and rescue. Why so large an emotional upgrade when it's people who are lost? I believe it is because of the priceless *value* of relationships and the significance they hold for Life.

Who in their lifetime hasn't lost keys, a planner, a cell phone, jewelry, tomorrow's big presentation notes or the family dog? These are the moments in life that bring with them varying degrees of panic and quickly lead to a frantic search with hope for a recovery. You know what it looks like—the retracing of steps, the probing of your own memory, quick interrogations of all family members, "Did you see my wallet?!?" These are inconvenient and stressful moments to say the least.

But on the dashboard of life with its *gauges of significance*, keys, cell phones and purses register in the *minimal* or *less significant* categories. Those moments of searching for wallets or tomorrow's presentation papers are stressful and can have us moving about the house frantically. As consuming as these moments are, we hope that in a few short minutes things will be recovered and, with a big sigh of relief, life can return to normal. We also carry with us the real sense that, though it will be inconvenient, these smaller things are *replaceable.* With a trip to the store, things can be set right.

Wouldn't it be great if everything and anything we might lose along our life's journey could be replaced and recovered as simply as that? *Things* can be replaced, but there is another category of things that get lost. These are different; these losses leave holes, brokenness and pain that won't be filled, fixed or relieved with anything of this earth. Becoming lost or losing a loved one can often lead to a loss of heart and eventually even a loss of life. There isn't a question of *if* we will lose heart in our lifetime; there are only questions of *how* and *when* we will lose heart and, most importantly, *can* or *will we* recover.

A LIFE OF FIRSTS

I am amazed when I look at my life and realize how many *firsts* I have experienced. For example, I've recently experienced the first time I've been the father of a 15-year-old daughter. It won't be the last time though because I have three girls, and yet the experience will be different when the others turn 15. Each daughter is different and will need me differently.

All our lives are marked with firsts that can leave us feeling very lost. When I survey back through my life, it feels like it was not long ago that I found myself facing these firsts:

> *First time I've had a mother with cancer*
> *First time I heard an emergency room doctor say my daughter has croup*
> *First time I was let go from a job*
> *First time I bought a car*
> *First time I purchased a house*
> *First time I yelled at a kid whom I was coaching in youth basketball*
> *First time I saw my wife in tears*

First time I saw my wife in tears only to find out that she was exceedingly happy
First time I saw my wife in tears only to find out that it was because of me and she wasn't happy at all
First time I counseled a couple, and their marriage renewed
First time I counseled a couple, and they filed for divorce anyway

Though some of these "firsts" happen in a moment, it may take years to recover from them. A trip to the hardware store for a new set of keys will solve that lost key problem and we can get on with life. Unfortunately, the store has nothing on aisle four that will heal our heartache or remove the hurt from many of the losses we will encounter along life's way. What is lost in many of life's "first time" moments can take years to be recovered, rebuilt and restored.

I've learned that these "firsts" have a way of repeating themselves. I often find myself standing somewhere feeling like *I've been here before*, and yet I'm frozen again, not knowing what to do. I realize once again *I'm lost*. I have handled many of those first-time moments poorly, and second chances seem to be in short supply.

Why do I seem so ill prepared for these moments? Why is it that I'm several minutes into these experiences before I realize *That's not what I meant to say* or *I should've handled that differently*? I start to feel like a janitor, constantly picking up the pieces or sweeping up messes I've made. There are wonderful first times, of course, but *glorious* firsts seem rare. Most of the first times in my life were a bit rocky, if not an outright semi-disaster. And they have left a mark and made me conclude one of two things: *I'll never do that again* or *From now on I'll...*

But what if it doesn't have to be this way? We all have a deeply held hope that somewhere in the world a search and rescue party is searching for us, that we will receive the help we need and that we will experience an outcome like the story of Baby Jessica. We are all longing for a glorious rescue and recovery that leads to a glorious reunion. Recovery and restoration can happen and are available if you know where to go, whom to ask and whom to invite into the hurts caused by those "first times." They *can* be redeemed. Calling in the right help will make all the difference.

HOTTER-COLDER

When I was a young boy, I played the game "Hot or Cold" with my brothers and friends. I would place a rock or an army man in the drawer or under the pillows and then guide my brothers with "hotter" or "colder" clues as they searched about the room for it. The closer they got the *warmer* they were, the further away from the hidden treasure the *colder.* We would play for hours. It was a great rainy day game. Now, as an adult, I am reminded of this game when things in my life have been lost or hidden from me. There are many different voices shouting out instructions: *Hotter! No, colder!* Often I find myself standing in one place, unable to move, not knowing who to listen to.

During much of my lifetime, I have found myself searching for lost things. Just like everyone else, I've lost my share of *personal items*. I have to confess I've made my fair share of trips to the hardware store to buy another tool that I know I have somewhere in the mess of my garage (although the sneaking suspicion that one of my kids has swiped it always lingers in my head as I make my replacement purchase).

But the time spent searching for a set of keys or a screwdriver doesn't come close to the amount of energy and effort I have put in over the years, searching for something more important: *Life*. My heart's search for Life has been a major expedition, a search for something I've heard exists, yet feels like it will forever elude me. I can't tell you how often in my past I felt like I was "warmer, *warmer* and so close," but never quite there. In the truest confession of my heart, I must admit that for years my search for Life felt like the proverbial *almost there, but not quite*. I could swear the treasure I was looking for kept getting moved just when I heard "warmer, warmer, you're boiling hot!"

These frustrating moments lead to questions that spring up from my heart: *What if I'm doing it wrong? What if this isn't the right road? Why isn't this working out better? Where is the missing piece that will pull this all together? Why is this so hard anyway?*

What if there were good answers to all these questions, and the answers *mattered* and made all the *difference*? What if there was a framework or an orientation needed to find them? What if I have been using the wrong equipment to search? Or bad or faulty equipment? What if I've been looking for the wrong things, searching in the wrong places and asking the wrong people for help and direction? What if those who have been guiding me are just as lost as I am?

TRYING TO CHEAT

I've come to realize that of all the things that could be lost in my life *I* am the most misplaced and mishandled. To recover and find my way, I've done what I think most people do. I have often tried to copy other people's journeys. After reading books in which the authors offer their own discoveries, formulas, road maps and directions, I tried to follow in their footsteps. But it hasn't worked for me—not over the long haul anyway.

I can remember being caught unprepared for a few spelling or math tests back in my elementary school days (okay, maybe some junior high days too). For multiple reasons, I concluded that my best option was to find someone who knew the answers, sit close to them (really close) and accomplish success *through* them. The pressure would often get to me during those tests, and I was sometimes more guilty of being sick to my stomach than I was of cheating. Nonetheless, my plan was based on some kind of a *vicarious victory* through the efforts of someone else. One time I was *somewhat* successful in the swiping of answers. Only *somewhat* though, because I came to find out that my partner, from whom I was stealing the answers, didn't know much more than I did. We were both invited to meet with the fourth-grade teacher to explain why we missed so many of the same questions!

I've felt unprepared a lot over the years of my life. I've graduated from elementary school tests to marriage, parenting, jobs, finances, and many other *grown-up* things. Unfortunately, my elementary school strategy seems to have graduated with me into these later stages of life. I started to believe that others had found what had eluded me and were enjoying their lives, while the answers seemed to still be unavailable to me. But if I could copy their papers, adopt their life plans as my own and learn from their successes or mistakes, then I could find the Life I was looking for. I know I am not the only one who searches for Life this way. Sales of self-help books provide the evidence—and my shelves are *full* of self-help books: parenting books, marriage books, addiction recovery books and manuals of how to do life. There is nothing wrong with these books as a general rule; there are many helpful perspectives and ideas contained in their pages. The problem seems to be with our ability to translate these perspectives and ideas into our own lives.

A change began to take place in my search when I recalled what John Eldredge said, *Life is not a bunch of problems to be solved but a great story to be entered into.* My life's orientation was exposed, and clearly it had been way off base. I was busy solving problems and was oblivious to the Great Story that I was in the middle of.

Knowing where we are might be the most fundamental piece of equipment in navigating life. But you get that equipment *on* the journey and not before; some things you cannot learn until you are "on your way."

BEING SEARCHED FOR

My journey has led me to the major presupposition that there *is* One who knows how to put life together. There is One who desires for us to recover from our loss and "lostness" and who longs to help. The proposal I want to make, and the invitation I need to offer, is that the Life we are looking for...the Life that can be found...and the Life we *need* to have recovered is somehow, someway *connected* to God. This Life is so significant, dramatic and stunningly central to our searching that, when found, *it will change everything.*

As I mentioned earlier, I have often moved—fiercely at times—from person to person, situation to situation, book to book and idea to idea, always seeking the treasure that would bring happiness, joy, clarity and love—the Life I longed for. What a discovery it would be to unlock the vault and see the answers to all my life's questions and unsolved mysteries! If I could just know *who I am, where I am* and *what I'm here to receive and offer*. If I had these coordinates in place, my exhaustive search would be over and I could get on to even better things—like *living well*. Not easy living, all comfortable and carefree, but a life *worth* living.

Now, I'm not suggesting that everyone who shares some hints, helps and insights from his or her life's journey has offered nothing of value. Over the last 6,000 years, many have left us critical and significant tools and guidance that we would be wise to take to heart. We would be in trouble if we didn't learn from the explorations and life experiences of others. We need others who have gone ahead of us, been trained on their journey, learned well through the school of hard knocks and arrived at a place where their knowledge, through experience, can help us on our way.

But this is where our steps must be careful ones. We must be wise and discerning of the people and advice we allow to guide and direct us. These choices will have significant repercussions for good or bad throughout our lives. How can we know good help from bad? Sometimes it is only *after the fact* that we are able to evaluate the counsel of others—after their advice has either helped or hurt. I have found that advice given, often says more about the one giving it than the one receiving it. Just the other day, one of my friends was getting marital advice (not really asking for it, mind you) from another friend who is a few years into his third marriage, which isn't going all that well. Be careful of the words *You know what you ought to do is*...If the one sharing is disoriented, you might end up even more lost.

IN NEED OF RESCUE

What I am proposing is that we all must, at some point, give up this *vicarious pursuit*–looking to other's lives to find the pieces that will allow us to manage our own–and *engage in our own stories*. We all need help to find good answers to the questions of *Who am I, Where am I* and *What is going on here?* We all need someone to counsel, guide, comfort, teach and share with us answers to these critical questions. After all, these questions don't get answered just once in a person's lifetime, but dozens, even hundreds, of times. If we are not careful, wise and discerning with the people and influences we employ to help us, we can truly be worse off as a result.

Two great, tragic stories come to mind to illustrate the vital importance of listening to wise counsel and getting the proper orientation. First, it is recorded that the radar watchtower on the island at Pearl Harbor showed the massive Japanese invasion of planes in plenty of time to call men to arms. Also, naval intelligence had intercepted enemy communications, alluding to the coming hostilities. The newly installed radar equipment had been prone to occasional glitches over the previous weeks. So, instead of taking the information and springing into action, operators assumed the radar was faulty or was simply picking up maneuvers of our own planes that had not been reported in the daily logs. Regarding the intelligence, well, you know what happened. It was ignored.

The second great tragedy to come from a faulty orientation is the sinking of the Titanic and the lost lives of many passengers to the frigid waters of the Atlantic. After the Titanic had struck the iceberg, but before it had sunk, SOS and distress calls were sent frantically from the bridge of the great ocean liner. Flares, like rockets, went off into the cold and clear night. A nearby freightliner saw the flares and misread the distress calls of the Titanic and, while only four or five miles away, didn't respond. Through the series of misfortunate events, the ship and the crew aboard the *Californian* missed their heroic opportunity. In the end, the Titanic gave up its cargo and 1,523 people to a watery grave. (Wikipedia: SS Californian)

When I hear these "rest of the stories," I am sad and a little ticked off. How could they? What if someone had told them the day before, *Hey watch out, tomorrow is going to be the biggest day of your life. Something is going to happen that will need you to step in and make the difference.* Could it have prompted them, maybe prepared them, for the moment that was ahead? Often we fall into such a slumber, such a sleep within life's day to day. Another night watch looking at a screen where nothing ever happens. To underestimate a day, much less thousands of them, and the cumulative affect they have on our lives is a grave mistake. We don't know when a large day in life is coming. But, we can bet, *large and significant days are large* because they give us intelligence on who we believe we are, where we think we are and what seems to be going on in that moment. If we miss the signs, we'll miss the opportunity to get help and perhaps the very answers we've been searching for.

THE HAUNTING QUESTIONS FOR US ALL

Who am I?
What is this place?
How did I get here?
What am I to do?

To answer these questions that seem to haunt us all, we need to explore our past and examine the many, many steps we have already taken. Only then can we get to the place of finding answers.

A couple of paragraphs will not resolve these questions or do justice to their weight and significance. For real understanding, there is story after story that must be told and understood, examined, related to and entered into.

These questions aren't new; we've been asking them since our earliest days. As young boys and girls we've asked questions like *Where are we going? Are we there yet? What's this?* and *How come I have to?* Not a lot has changed over the years. The questions grow up with us. Instead of a parent announcing, *To the store, Not yet, It's a casserole and eat it because I said so,* our questions often go unanswered, leaving us unsettled.

I have come to understand that some of the answers to my life's questions are found in the archives of my own personal journey, not someone else's. Do you realize the number of variables in one person's life compared to another? Look at the diversity of our experiences: our families, parents, childhood home addresses and friends. The deeper you go into a person's story, the more specific variables you will discover. It is each individual's experience and his or her conclusions about himself or herself that shape beliefs and ways of seeing the world.

Is it any wonder we get lost? What are the odds of interpreting and understanding life's experiences accurately or well? For starters, look at the family you grew up in...your mother, father and siblings, and your current family...spouse, children, in-laws, extended family. Look how varied your family is from everyone else's you know. My three kids came from the same parents (me and my wife), live at the same address, eat at the same dinner table, and have even had some of the same teachers and coaches. But the similarities between my three girls give way to differences pretty quickly. You and I are unique even though we are on the same planet and may have some things in common. Again, there is no "one-size-fits-all," no recipe that works for everyone. We must give up that notion.

Our uniqueness makes going through the search for Life messy rather than neat and tidy. If you are looking for a simple equation to live from or one principle by which to run your entire life, then you are going to be forever frustrated. You are also going to end up living in a story that is so much smaller than you deserve. A small story is not what you're made for! The good news is that you and I don't have to settle for that small story, that small life. For me to uncover, or better yet *recover,* my story and my role in it, I must know the *Larger Story* in which it is taking place. This Larger Story is the answer to the important question, *Where am I?*

You and I are living in a wonderful and dangerous story in which we matter, our role is crucial and no one can play our part but us. In this grand story, something has been lost. That something is more precious and valuable than we have understood or been led to believe. What has been lost is *us*, not some "thing" but *us;* and we must engage in the story that is our search and rescue, our restoration.

ELEMENTS AND ENVIRONMENTS

Our world has professionals who do search and rescue for a living. Before these search and rescue teams engage in the mission to find and recover lost and missing persons, they spend hours training and practicing so they are prepared for emergency situations. These courageous men and women understand the dangers of the *elements* and *environments* in which they will find themselves. A weather report can give them helpful information about the conditions coming their way. One wrong move or poor decision increases the chance that the search and rescue team members could be added to the number of victims or casualties. A disregard for the elements and environment where they are headed can yield disaster times two. Knowing what they are looking for is essential. Knowing where they are headed and what they are going to be encountering will make all the difference in the world. Gloves, snow shoes and thermal underwear won't do much good for trying to recover a life trapped in a sinking ship off the Gulf Coast. Diving gear is not helpful to a rescue team searching for a life lost in the woods off the Appalachian Trail.

In the same way, knowing and understanding our *whereabouts* (elements and environment) is our first mission and vital to our recovery. Having complete data on the variables of our location is critical. Stories abound of failed explorers, unsuccessful rescuers and unfortunate journeyman who died either ill-equipped, uninformed or both. Let's not be among them; we must understand where we are. Like Dorothy, we're not in Kansas anymore; we need a similar discovery and declaration. We are lost and searching for Life—Life that is of supreme significance and tremendous importance. There is no formula out there that makes everything right. It's not that easy; but we're not alone in our search. Someone glorious, as well as something dangerous, is also on the move and in motion, searching for us.

It is time we got moving. It is time to discover what is really happening around us. It is time for our orientation.

CHAPTER 2

ORIENTATION

Be very careful, then, how you live—not as unwise but as wise, making the most of every opportunity, because the days are evil.

-Ephesians 5:15-16

"You will seek me and find me when you seek me with all your heart. I will be found by you," declares the LORD, "and will bring you back from captivity."

-Jeremiah 29:13-14a

In Him was Life, and the Life was the Light of men. And the Light shines on in the darkness, for the darkness has never overpowered it [put it out or absorbed it or appropriated it, and is unreceptive to it].

-John 1:4-5 (AMP)

A few years ago, someone recommended to me the HBO film series *Band of Brothers*. I've watched it many times since then and continue to be impacted by the story. I find one of the most compelling components to be the interviews with the men from the 101st Airborne Division. These men, now in their eighties and nineties, tell of their experiences and encounters as World War II paratroopers. In spite of all they saw and encountered on the actual battlefield, they all mention again and again the difficulties, and ultimate importance, of their time in Basic Training. Surviving that rigorous orientation was their actual first mission.

One example of how the training paid off occurs in the following story.

With less than 100 men assembled in a battalion, its commander could only afford to send Easy Company to attack and overrun a four-gun, German battery, defended by a fifty-man platoon. In the book Band of Brothers, author Stephen Ambrose describes the scene with this quote from First Sergeant Carwood Lipton: "Here the training paid off. We fought as a team without standout stars. We were like a machine. We didn't have anyone who leaped up and charged a machine-gun. We knocked it out or made it withdraw by maneuver and teamwork or mortar fire. We were smart; there weren't many flashy heroics. We had learned that heroics was the way to get killed without getting the job done, and getting the job done was more important."

The purpose of Basic Training is to teach a new recruit not only to survive as a soldier but also to fight well, with competence and success. For nearly a year, the men of the 101st Airborne Division, Easy Company, trained to be soldiers—this was their orientation. They were deconstructed and rebuilt for the sake of a greater mission. Some never made it through Basic and never got their jump wings. A few made it through the training but, when they had to face the real battle, became casualties or fell apart under the pressures of war.

A proper orientation (gained through Basic Training) is crucial to surviving such an ordeal as World War II. Actually, the idea of a "boot camp for life" sounds attractive to me. Life, at times, is hard enough to endure; to live disoriented, untrained or ill equipped puts my life in jeopardy as well as that of my families and my friends. Though I try hard to hide it, I've felt the need of a little training myself—how to survive, how to fight when necessary, how to guard and protect those most valuable to me as well as those I will encounter who might need my help. I would love for someone to show me just how all this can be done and done well. All the armed forces provide essential Basic Training; each man who goes through it will tell stories of how tough it was as well as how significant and important it was to their survival and fulfillment of their mission. We all need this same kind of training, a similar orientation, to prepare our hearts and minds for the environment we live in and the surroundings we will enter into on our search for our true Life.

I have some good news: there is Someone who offers us this kind of orientation. God wants to train our hearts and minds and prepare us for the Great Mission, which he has created us to fulfill. He invites us to let go of all we thought we knew and enter into training—training that prepares us for the Great Story in which we are already living. Part of our training is getting our bearings and knowing what we're searching for. We may be looking for a better job, for effective ways to raise our kids or for the secret to a better deal on that latest gadget we've seen on TV. But that is physical realm stuff—it isn't what our hearts are longing for. What we're really searching for is far larger than anything this world is offering because we were made for far more than this world. When this life is over, it ain't over. And what we're all searching for is exactly what our Creator is offering.

WHAT WE'RE SEARCHING FOR

What are we searching for? What is this Great Battle about, and what is it for? Simply put, it is Life. A full, rich, fulfilling life. And we search for this Life because we have lost it. You know the story of our heritage; it's all in living color in Genesis 3. Our ancestors ate of the wrong tree. Adam and Eve were tempted, disoriented, confused and tricked. They went cross grain with God. They bought the enemy's story that somehow God was withholding something good from them ("Surely you won't die but rather you will be like Him." Genesis 3:4). They disobeyed God's clear instructions and ate of the tree of the knowledge of good and evil. The results and consequences of that fateful day reverberate to this very day—we feel it every day. So much was lost. We were lost.

The day before that fateful one, Adam and Eve had Life with a capital "L"—abundant, full Life. Paradise was their address, God was their closest friend and constant guide and they were in an intimate, connected relationship with their Creator —it was nothing short of glorious. One moment they had this glorious Life; the next, it was gone. Lost. And ever since that day, we have been searching for and attempting to recover and restore this Life—the Life for which we were created. The Life we had once possessed and that we continue to long for in our deepest hearts. The great invitation on the table, the offer to our hearts, the promise before us, is that we can and will have this Life again.

You see, our story—the story of our creation—starts out as a beautiful and glorious narrative. After each stroke of creation recorded in Genesis 1, God pronounces it good. Then, as God creates His masterpiece–mankind - He announces His handiwork as very good. But tragically it all comes crashing down because Adam and Eve listen to a lie. In Genesis 3, after God hands out the consequences and punishment to all involved (the serpent, Eve and Adam), Adam and Eve are escorted out of the garden.

> And the Lord God said, Behold, the man has become like one of Us [the Father, Son, and Holy Spirit], to know [how to distinguish between] good and evil and blessing and calamity; and now, lest he put forth his hand and take also from the tree of life and eat, and live forever—Therefore the Lord God sent him forth from the Garden of Eden to till the ground from which he was taken. So [God] drove out the man; and He placed at the east of the Garden of Eden the cherubim and a flaming sword which turned every way, to keep and guard the way to the tree of life.
>
> Genesis 3:22-24 (AMP)

Adam and Eve take the bait of the evil one and, because they eat from the wrong tree (the Tree of the Knowledge of Good and Evil), everything gets altered. They changed. Life got lost. We got lost. We are their offspring. As though a great earthquake had taken place, the life we had shifted; it was marred, maimed and broken. Not only for us, but for every part of creation! And the tremors and aftershocks continue.

Our ancestors eat of the wrong tree. Immediately, God comes for them (and us), and the great rescue is under way. Yes, Adam and Eve are banished and cursed, escorted out of the Garden, but it is for their protection... and for our eventual good.

Picture a little boy or girl going to the doctor after he or she is old enough to associate doctors with shots. Mom and Dad escort (or maybe drag is the better word) the child to the doctor's office. The whole time, the little one is yelling, "Please, no, don't take me in there! I want to go home, please, please, please, NO!" Now, imagine Adam and Eve, post apple-bite moment. God, the Father, calls for them, "Adam, Eve? Where are you my dear ones? Don't you know where you are now? It's time to go."

Adam begins pleading to stay, "Please let us back in. Don't do this! We're sorry." Eve begins to cry...maybe for the first time, "We don't want to live on the outside, please let us come back." God refuses: He knows what He must do. He says, "No, we will have to redeem this another way...my way. Come dear ones. It must be done." He doesn't take the Tree of Life out of the garden. He takes Adam and Eve out of the garden, and then He places a sentry, an angel with a flaming sword, to guard and keep watch over the garden and the life-giving tree.

Yet from this, the darkest of all moments, the worst of all days, the moment we fell and were lost, the Hero of our story, God, initiates a massive search, rescue and recovery mission. This rescue effort is no small feat, nor will it be simply done. We're not talking about a simple recovery like gluing a handle back on or covering up a scratch with the right color pen or even pounding out a dent. This rescue work will take time and come at a great cost. Scripture unfolds the recovery blueprint and it shows that we're almost home–but not yet.

ARRANGING FOR LIFE

If we had been in the place of Adam and Eve, what would we have tried to do? I know what I would have done. I would have tried to come up with my own plan for a "do-over." I would have tried to set things right and make it all good again. When I take a good look at my life, and of those trying to do life around me, that seems to be our plan of choice—"arranging" for life.

If I can just control the variables around me, control the people around me, time the traffic lights so they are always green for me, put everyone else in the slow line at the grocery store, make my kids do what I say when I say it, have my wife ready for romance the moment I look her way, then I would have a full and fulfilling life, right? Nothing ever breaks; everyone always likes my ideas; I get what I want, when I want it, where I want it, and in the right proportion and at the perfect temperature. That's what we all want, right?

We've even come up with our own set of rules to govern this self-arranging system:

When the going gets tough, the tough get going.
If it is to be it's up to me.
Do unto others before they do unto you.

The crazy thing is that everyone is running his or her own system, and it results in far more chaos than it does any semblance of harmony. We already broke one life, but surely we can fix it by making a Plan B for ourselves.

When I step back and look at it, I must admit that if I had been in Adam and Eve's shoes, I would have grabbed some cover, as they did, attempting to make things appear better than they really were. Remember that the fruit wasn't the real temptation; it was the role, the position the serpent offered (surely you won't die, but rather you will be like God).

I think it is safe to say that if Adam and Eve knew then what we know now, they would have done things a little differently. We think that, if we had been in that position, we definitely would have made a better choice. But would we have really been any wiser or any more obedient? Maybe it was one of those "first times." The first time a serpent spoke to me, I think I'd be inclined to listen! Perhaps this was the first time humans were offered a self-improvement program. I wish we could say, *Glad we don't keep subscribing to that old trick!* But sadly, that isn't the case. I would have been no different than Adam and Eve in the same situation, because I find myself making the same mistake they did, over and over in my own life. If it were me, I would have apologized and asked God to take me back. When we offend those who love us, if we truly love them and want to set things right, we apologize, ask for forgiveness and hope they take us back. That is a good first step. But trying to make my life work, trying to arrange it all and make it all right is simply a mess I can't fix on my own. After all, who has ever been successful at taking a splinter out of his own eye? It's like we are the little boy who picks up the limp and motionless sparrow he just shot with his BB gun, tosses it in the air telling it "Fly, fly away! Please fly away!" It's not going to happen.

This is where we need help. This is actually the good news. When we stop our striving and arranging and ask for help, we will then begin to find the Life we have lost. Remember Jesus' offer: *Come to me, all you who are weary and burdened, and I will give you rest.* (Matthew 11:28, NIV) God has a plan. He says to my plans and arrangements, *My child, you don't realize what you've done, but I do, and I can and will fix it. It's Life you really want and Life that I made you for. This genuine Life is only found with Me, in Me and from Me. I'll restore it all, I will make it right…trust Me. You can and will fly again.*

We're not the little boy with the BB gun, we're actually the little bird.

LIFE

You can tell a lot about something once you know what it is made for. I've used many things to hammer a nail in my time: rocks, wrenches, the handle of a screwdriver, a baseball bat, and more. Only one thing does the job well—a hammer. That is what it was made for. A blender doesn't make a good hammer; but if you want a smoothie, I know something made just for that!

This brings us to a very important question that needs answering. What were we made for? Now, some of the traditional answers passed along in church include "serve God, do his work, be a tool in the Master's hands, evangelize, fulfill the Great Commission, etc." But none of these are the primary thing we were made for.

We were created for one thing: to be in intimate relationship with our Creator God, the Trinity. (Genesis 1 says "Let us make man in our image…") This is not just any kind of relationship but the key and central relationship we were made for. The relationship through which we will find our true meaning, identity, significance and purpose—our Life. Above all else, centrally and primarily, we were made for intimacy, connectedness and oneness with God. That is where Life—real Life—is found. Jesus' mission on earth showed us how to live in relation to God and how He longs to relate to us. He showed us how to relate to others. He showed us how to find Life. When the Pharisees asked Jesus which of the commandments in the law was the greatest, Jesus replied, "'Love the Lord your God with all your heart and with all your soul and with all your mind.' This is the first and greatest commandment. And the second is like it: 'Love your neighbor as yourself.' All the Law and the Prophets hang on these two commandments." Matthew 22:37-40

Jesus was saying, *This sums up the law; do this and you will have Life.* These things are exactly what the life of Jesus was about: loving God and loving others and, in doing so, He was showing us how to live, how to love God and how to love others. That is the essence of the image we bear and the Life we were created to live. The invitation from our God is to step into what we were created for—a love relationship with Him. As Brent Curtis wrote in his book with John Eldredge, *The Sacred Romance:*

For above all else, the Christian life is a love affair of the heart. It cannot be lived primarily as a set of principles or ethics. It cannot be managed with steps and programs. It cannot be lived exclusively as a moral code leading to righteousness...The truth of the gospel is intended to free us to love God and love others with our whole hearts.

We were made for this: Life and Love. And as you will discover throughout this book, Life and Love are deeply, deeply connected.

Let me ask you some questions. When do you feel most alive? What are the ingredients in your greatest life experiences? Don't they almost always involve others? When I take inventory of my life and look over my memories, the collective evidence shows me that I'm most alive when I am loving others or being loved. From my childhood until now, my life's best moments seem to have one common thread—being with others, enjoying them and being enjoyed by them. It is in those moments—when I am with my wife, children or a good friend and we are experiencing something together, when in the moment a word of thanks is expressed or a validating compliment is shared like, *I'm so glad you're here with me*—I experience Life large and full!

We were created for relationship. That is one of the most significant ways we bear the image of our relational God. And, therefore, we are most alive when we are enjoying what we were created for.

On the other hand, in this broken world, the very thing we were created for is also the very thing that can wound us most deeply. Nothing can hurt us more than the actions or words of another. Sadly, we all carry with us both positive and negative memories when it comes to relating with others. My life has wonderful and glorious moments for sure, but it has hard and awful moments as well. They all involve other people and my relationships with them. For some of us, the scale tips much more toward the awful side. Unless they are healed, redeemed and replaced, the messages and memories of those moments have a larger impact than the wonderful and glorious ones. This can change—and so it must if we are ever to find and live the Life we were meant to have.

LOVE

Now that we have established the connection of capital "L" Life and Love, we can begin to awaken to the fact that these have been lost to us and need to be recovered. Here, I need to explain a bit more on the subject of Love and how I believe it works. I will not do justice to the word or its full experience in a few paragraphs, but I want to give you a short introduction to the kind of Love I mean here.

Everyone on the planet–past, present and future–desires to be noticed, validated, affirmed, encouraged, accepted and significant. Look around and you will see that most, if not all, of our behavior stems from the hope that we will find these things. What is the greatest expression of these things (validation, acceptance, and significance)? The answer is Love.

When, with a good heart and good motives, I tell my wife "I love you," I am saying: I see you and want to be with you. I accept you, and you are significant to me. Wedding vows are a declaration of love and a promise to love. When my wife or kids tell me they love me, when I sense in my heart that I am valued, seen, wanted and enjoyed—that I belong - it makes me feel alive. I feel and experience Life in those moments. First John tells us God is Love, so where is this Love found and how can it bring us Life? We find Life when we find it in the Love of God. That is why we were created. God is speaking with all of His being (since He is Love), over and over again, the words we all long to hear—I love you! You are my beloved! Upon hearing this we feel and experience that for which we were made—relationship. And I can be alive in that moment forever because of the wonderful and glorious impact of His supernatural Love.

Life is what God is going to provide at the end (Revelation 22), just like it was in the beginning (Genesis 1). Among His many incredible purposes for coming to earth, Jesus declared, "I have come that they may have life, and have it to the full." (John 10:10b) Assuming this promise and declaration to be true, then this Life must be what we are most in need of, what we most desire and long for and what we were made for. The God who is Life and Love is what we are searching for—and remarkably, He is searching for us as well.

But, in order to Live and Love well, we need to settle some things in our hearts. Being oriented is very different than being in control. To be oriented is to know with certainty, and from experience, what is true and what is right. Yes, there can still be mystery, but when we don't understand something it only drives us to a deeper, more intimate experience with God. We all have a great deal of experiences, but we're not so good at interpreting them because we're so badly disoriented on two critical fronts.

WHO AND WHERE?

The first front of our disorientation is in the area of identity. Each of us needs to know the true answer to the heart's question *Who Am I?* If you can settle this, obtain your bearings and orientation about who you are, you are half-way home to living and loving well. My usual way of getting an answer to this question has been to ask other people—tell me who you think I am or who you want me to be, and I'll give it a go. When I do this I feel like some kind of panhandler, begging for gifts from other panhandlers who are begging for gifts. The tragic flaw in finding your identity by asking others is that none of us is a healthy source for the answers; we're all panhandlers. There is only one Good Source, one Good Person, who can tell me who I am and who I'm meant to be. That is the One who made me. Now believing what He says about me is another whole set of issues altogether. But I have come to realize that He has a strong opinion on the matter and wants me to know I am more than I can possibly imagine.

The other major question we must answer to become correctly oriented is *Where Am I?* Like many symbiotic relationships, when you get the answer to one of these questions you inherently get the answer to the other. They don't operate apart; they are connected and rely on each other. Get the two answers together, and the perspective of your life and its story will move from black-and-white to color, from a photo album to HD3D.

JASON BOURNE

In 2002, the first film of the Jason Bourne series, *The Bourne Identity*, debuted in theaters. The Bourne Trilogy has been a huge success all over the world and is a great example of being oriented in the area of *Where am I?* but not in the area of identity, *Who am I?* The story is a man's journey to recover and restore both of these orientations in his life.

This man, the lead character, has been employed by the government as a Top-Secret Special Force, a one-man wrecking crew, a highly trained assassin. Early in the first film, we see Bourne "malfunction" and decide he doesn't want to do the job he was trained to do. Though he doesn't know who he is—his identity has been erased and lost to him—he lives with certain clarity that where he lives is dangerous and fragile. He isn't sure who to trust or where the clues will come from to give him his life back; his mission becomes just that—putting the pieces together—so he can be free.

When Bourne steps into a train station, a bank or an embassy, he assumes one thing— someone is searching for him and that someone doesn't have his best interests at heart. Bourne is highly oriented to his surroundings and, though he is trying to answer the question, *Who Am I?* he lives with a deep orientation that the environment he is searching in is by no means tame or friendly...it's hostile.

In many ways, our lives are similar to Jason Bourne's. We would be well served to adopt his awareness and orientation regarding our location. As a confirmation of this, C. S. Lewis wrote in The Weight of Glory:

> *War creates no absolutely new situation: it simply aggravates the permanent human situation so that we can no longer ignore it. Human life has always been lived on the edge of precipice. Human culture has always had to exist under the shadow of something infinitely more important than itself. If men had postponed the search for knowledge and beauty until they were secure, the search would never have begun. We are mistaken when we compare war with "normal life." Life has never been normal.*

THE INVITATION

Everyone likes to be invited. An invitation says, *Come be with us. We want your company. You're welcome.* Nobody likes to be indicted: *You're doing it wrong. You don't know what you're doing. Don't take another step.*

This book is an invitation.

I ask some important questions and invite you to seek the answers, answers that are bound up and tied to the story that is yours. There are no grades, no evaluations or judgments to be placed on your answers or your heart at the end. This is just an invitation to take two steps back and look at the larger landscape so we can take 10 steps forward and be found.

When we are found, we will soon discover we have settled for being so much less than our Rescuer created us to be. Many voices have been telling us lies about ourselves and about God. We have so much to offer a world, which is just as lost as we have been. There is One Opinion that matters most on this journey of life for Life, and He is battling to be seen and heard. He is fighting to deliver a message to your heart that will settle your mind and offer you the courage needed for the days ahead. This is an invitation and not an indictment: the thing which you most long to be you are becoming. Knowing where you are now, knowing where you're headed in the future and understanding the environment where your journey is taking place will make all the difference in the world.

In this journey, we will likely be surprised at what we find or, more accurately, what finds us. There are lost things in us that need to be passionately and intentionally searched for, rescued and recovered, as if our lives depended on it—because they do.

So I invite you to turn the page, see what questions—and hopefully answers—wait around the corner. At the very least, I hope you will discover that there is a larger world, a bigger journey, and a more significant Life than you have imagined waiting out there to be discovered. God has declared that He is searching for you and desperately wants to rescue and recover you. He desires for you to experience Him and the relationship He is offering. And He promises to guide, counsel, teach and comfort you all along the journey. He is the one who says, "I love you. I'm coming for you. You are just what I've always wanted. So trust me, come to me, and I will help you if you will just let me.

> *Come to Me, all you who labor and are heavy-laden and overburdened, and I will cause you to rest. [I will ease and*

relieve and refresh your souls.] Take My yoke upon you and learn of Me, for I am gentle (meek) and humble (lowly) in heart, and you will find rest (relief and ease and refreshment and recreation and blessed quiet) for your souls. For My yoke is wholesome (useful, good—not harsh, hard, sharp, or pressing, but comfortable, gracious, and pleasant), and My burden is light and easy.

Matthew 11:28-30 (AMP)

In other words, *I'm your source of Life; I will get you home.*

This is the grand mission of our all our lives: To be found, to have our Lives and our Love recovered in full, then to live out our days with this orientation.

LET'S GET MOVING

Critical to any mission is what to bring along for the journey. The more important the mission, the more important it is to pack well. A honeymoon or a family vacation has a whole different "what to pack" list than a medic's trip to a third-world country. The Boy Scouts are on to something with their motto: Be prepared.

It's usually the umbrella I forgot to pack, the sunscreen I didn't buy or the tool I've misplaced that is the item I need on a trip. Because I'm without it, I suffer the consequences. What if I'm missing some key and critical items needed for Life? What if the items I'm carrying aren't helpful or have me ill-prepared? The consequences of an unprepared life could be much more catastrophic than those of a poorly planned vacation.

If my life were all about fixing a door or repairing a table, I think I would be a master craftsman by now. But my life isn't that simple and neither are the things that are broken. You know the scene in movies where the city boy or Hollywood girl is stuck on a camping trip? I've been that character numerous times—unprepared, a fish-out-of-water.

For this great journey and mission of life that we are all on, we must "pack" some crucial items to prepare for the moments ahead.

Pack well. Real Life will depend on it.

CHAPTER 3

PACKING UP

You can tell a lot about a man by what he complains about. A man who complains that the coffee is too cold or the beer too warm is a man who thinks he is on a cruise ship. A man who complains that he doesn't have enough ammo is a man who knows he is in a great battle. Which man are you?

Howard Hendricks

...let us throw off everything that hinders and the sin that easily entangles, and let us run with perseverance the race marked out for us.

Hebrews 12:1b

When planning for a journey, we all have different methods of packing our bags. I'm the type that usually collects my desired items over a few days prior to departure by throwing them in the chair in my bedroom. This is my central collection point. I also try to pull as much from my clean laundry piles as possible so I don't have to put them away. I also keep a hang-up toiletry bag stocked with the little soaps and shampoos, toothpaste and a toothbrush, a razor and a few items from the medicine cabinet (that I'm sure have long surpassed their expiration dates, but usually will do in a pinch). Then, on the night before my departure, I drop my collected pile into the suitcase. Done! Packed!

    The problem with my method, though, is that I often over-pack by putting too many of my favorite clothing items in the chair. I don't plan out my outfits. I just throw things I like to wear on the pile until it looks large enough for the number of days I'll be gone. My hope is that what I'm piling up will be appropriate for where I'm going, what I'm doing and who I'm doing it with. On a few occasions this method has failed me, and I find myself in a distant city with something crucial still unfortunately hanging in my closet at home.

The problem is not that I don't have stuff, it's that I don't have the *right stuff*.

A quick glance at the weather forecast before I left home often would have reversed my fortunes. A few of the rain jackets I own were bought in a desperate moment in a hotel lobby or a truck stop. Why do I own five raincoats and 15 pairs of cheap winter gloves? My ignorance of the conditions I faced and the equipment I needed led to *unpreparedness*.

This journey of life we're all on, this searching for Life, will require some important equipment we won't find at the first convenience store we come across. The items we desperately need are only to be found when we ask for and are willing to receive them. What we need, we need to be given: *eyes to see*, *ears to hear* and a *heart that is engaged*. Not the eyes, ears and heart we are born with (which have been badly trained throughout our years), but the ones we can only get through a great, divine upgrade. These are the things that will allow us to live Life on a whole new level, equipped and oriented to live *spiritually*.

When Jesus wanted to really get his listeners' attention, He often started His teachings with phrases like...

> *If you have eyes to see and ears to hear...*
> *I tell you the truth...*
> *Truly, truly I say unto you...*

Now, Jesus was talking to people who could physically see and hear. But His question, or better His invitation, was *Can you see? Look for me*, and *Can you hear? Listen to me*. Jesus is inviting the hearts in the audience to see and hear beyond a physical existence, beyond the physical realm. Christ invites us to have eyes to see and ears to hear the Life that is larger and, most importantly, the Life you and I are really looking for—the one found only in and through the *spiritual* realm. This is the Life for which you and I were truly made and the one that must be recovered.

BELIEVING IS SEEING

If you have children, you have no doubt heard these words, *Dad (or Mom), come quick! You gotta see this!* It is an urgent request often made (usually shouted) around my house. Sometimes the cause for urgency is a fresh piece of art one of my daughters has exhibited in her room for viewing, but most recently it was a king snake sunning on the creek bank in the woods just behind our house, where we often walk and explore.

In the holiday film *The Santa Clause*, comedian/actor Tim Allen plays Scott Calvin, who finds himself in a binding contractual "clause," making him the new Santa. When he arrives at the North Pole amidst the workshop, elves, decorations and the overwhelming sense that he is dreaming, a little elf named Judy takes Calvin and his son, Charlie, to Santa's bedroom. Calvin peers through an open window to a street below and exclaims, "Is that a polar bear directing traffic?" The little elf who escorted them to their room answers with a pleasant matter-of-fact tone, "Why yes, it is." Calvin then responds with a furrowed brow and a tilted head, "I see it, but I don't believe it." At which Judy says, "You're missing the point. Seeing isn't believing—believing is seeing."

The question before us, then, is *What do you see?* The answers we give will tell more about the condition we are in than any x-ray or digital scan. Have you seen *Antiques Roadshow* on PBS? The main story line is usually, *I picked this up at a garage sale* or *I found this in the attic when we were moving Grandma's stuff.* For those who have watched the show and been sucked into its drama, you understand what it's like to be waiting to hear the item's story and its evaluation from one who knows the value and worth. The expert tells the story and then puts a price tag on Grandma's old picture of poker-playing mice or Aunt Ellie's ugly vase. What was often picked up for nickels at a garage sale or stumbled across when cleaning out the attic is reassigned a "real" value because of its *story*. It is the story—who made it, who owned it, what it has been through and what it represents—that establishes its worth.

On this show, evaluating these items and declaring their true value takes someone who knows the story. It takes someone who has the *eyes to see*. Usually *a number* of things prove the antique's new-found worth: the craftsman who created it, the time period in which is was made, the item's function, its degree of preservation and sometimes, its original owner. All of these make up *the story,* or *the journey,* of the piece. It is this collection of facts from a larger story that determine the antique's value. And so it is with us. Knowing and having eyes to see the Larger Story we are in will go a long way in helping us truly understand our worth.

Wouldn't it be good to know the real story that *we* have been in and currently are a part of? Wouldn't you like to have eyes to see and ears to hear the *details* in which we live? Answers come to good questions. Good questions come from those who want to understand more clearly. Clarity is a treasure that all of us would like to possess in greater measure, isn't it? What if we could know and grasp the dimensions of our story, the Author and His intent, our purpose and function, and the weight and scope of our existence... Then live well within that framework? Wouldn't that be wonderful? We are invited to know this framework and to live within it. It's not an invitation to learn the smoke and mirrors technique of some magic trick or the secret of some grand illusion. Rather, this is an invitation *to walk away from* the trick or illusion that has far too long had us under its spell—to *see* what is real and to *know* it as real.

EYES TO SEE

When we introduce our children to the concept of heat from a burning candle or a hot stove, we say with nose-to-nose or eye-to-eye instruction, *Sweetheart, this is hot, HOT. No touchy, no, no touchy. It's HOT. It could burn you! Ouchy, ouchy, no touchy, it's HOT!* We are giving them the truth and the facts. What we tell our kids in that moment is true. But when do they actually believe us? When does it become *more true*? Only when we are headed to the cabinet for the Neosporin® and a Barney bandage. The *experience* with the heat source shows our child that what we said is true, and now they *know*, now they *believe*. The same is true in our relationship with God. Having a brochure on Life and Love is not the same as *experiencing* Life and Love. The largest offer of the Gospel—Life—is one that is *to be experienced*. It's not just a collection of biblical facts and theological principles. Sure, understanding the facts and principles is important, but only in as much as they invite us into *more*—into the experience of a relationship with the One who knows where we came from, what we are worth and what we are made for. Grasping this vision will make all the difference in the world—*if* we have eyes that can see.

All of our days past and all of our days ahead are best understood when we are equipped with eyes that see the Spiritual Realm. I'll write more on this in a later chapter, but for now we must realize that this physical world is not all there is. Having our eyes open to this reality leads to understanding, knowing and *experiencing the truth of who we are, where we are* and *the good that God is up to in our lives*. The Scriptures invite us to see the Spiritual Realm in a way that will change how we live in the physical realm. With a proper orientation to the Two Realms, the spiritual and the physical, we can begin to see with more clarity what they are, how they work and how we are to live within them.

As our eyes are opened to what is really going on all around us, we will get new insight about who we are and where we are as well as about God Himself. Our beliefs about ourselves and God will begin to take on a new shape. Belief is of utmost importance in the Spiritual Realm, and it can be one of the most dangerous things in life.

What you believe *matters*. It matters *a lot*. What you believe has authority in your life and will influence everything: what you see, say, hear and do. Ultimately, *what you believe* dictates *how you will live* and how you will go about your search for Life.

This deeper exploration into the Two Realms (especially the Spiritual Realm) will take us several steps closer to being rescued from a life of naiveté and severe disorientation. Once we acknowledge that the spiritual realm exists, our attention turns to how we live in it and if our eyes are open to see it. The Spiritual Realm is inviting each of us to live in a larger world than we've known. To accept this invitation we will need to not only be well equipped but we will need to have our bearings. Like the little elf said, *Seeing isn't believing. Believing is seeing.*

EARS TO HEAR

Not only is the spiritual realm something to be seen, it is also something to be heard. Jesus started many of his teachings with *Truly, truly I say unto you.* Other translations say *Verily, verily I tell you.* Do you know what these phrases mean? Today's equivalent would be something like *Hey, listen up, give me your ears, this is important!*

Before Verizon made famous the phrase *Can you hear me now?* Jesus was asking the same question. *Can you hear me? Can you hear me now? Are you listening? Come close. I want to tell you something.* In Matthew 11:15, Jesus announces, "He who has ears, let him hear." The Amplified Bible states it like this: "He who has ears to hear, let him be listening and let him consider and perceive and comprehend by hearing."

Hearing is fundamental to life. *Listening* is even more so. They aren't the same. The 2007 film, *August Rush*, provided a wonderful example of this. The underlying message of the film was *music is all around us, but only some people can hear it. Only a few are truly listening.* Our ears pick up all kinds of sounds. Have you ever heard the term *ambient noise*? Ambient noise is sometimes called *background noise*, *white noise*, *reference sound level*s or *room noise levels*. Right now, as I'm writing, if I turn my attention to what I hear, and I listen for the subtleties of sounds, I am surprised to discover sounds I was unaware of until I began deliberately listening for them. I now hear the air-conditioning blowing to cool the room, the computer keys striking with every movement of my fingers, traffic sounds from outside the second-story window of my office/cave and printers humming. *Listening,* not simply hearing, is the key. Listening is the first step toward clarity and understanding. Only after we listen can we assess, discern and respond well to what we hear. *What are you listening to?*

I am amazed at how those who are deaf can skip the step of *hearing* and form skills and abilities that allow them to *listen* and *understand.* But the rest of us, whose ears seem to work perfectly, can still be deaf to the most important things. Just the other day, my youngest daughter, Abbey, was out of sorts. Her whining and complaining was what I initially heard. But since I have come to believe and live within a Larger Story, within Two Realms, I've learned to pause and listen for more in these moments. It's easy to see her behavior and listen to her declarations of the hardships of her 12-year-old life and dismiss them as frivolous. But am I listening to her heart? If I miss the true cry of her heart, the odds are great that I'll miss out on who she really is and what she really needs. So I took time to ask some questions of Abbey. But most of all I took time to really listen. And what did I hear? I discovered that at the heart of her irritability was sadness because she was feeling left out and unwanted. When I listened, I heard her heart, and what it said was not frivolous. It was deeply meaningful and offered me the chance to love her and father her in the way she needed most.

I don't always get it right but, by God's grace, this time I did. These were the whines of a *lonely little girl.* They were the sounds of her heart's sadness and the ache that comes from not being seen and feeling like she didn't belong. I know how to treat this. Sure, I could have sent her to her room for whining or put her to work for inconveniencing me with such an ungrateful display of behavior. But that would have been dealing with symptoms not sources. Instead I made a few phone calls to invite some of her friends over, and her despair turned to joy.

The hearing vs. listening problem goes both ways in the parenting relationship though. My wife and I often find ourselves saying to one or

all three of our kids...
> *Did you not hear me?*
> *What did I say?*
> *What did I tell you?*
> *What did you think I said?*
> *Are you listening to me?*

Although I don't always ask all these questions in the same moment, I have been known to bring a full inquisition to my three girls in certain situations. Usually these conversations come after something I told them to do *was not* done or something I told them not to do *was* done. I am cross-examining them to discover whether or not they were *really* hearing, listening and understanding me.

As our Father, God is inviting us into this same conversational process as we journey with Him.

In order to engage with God in this way, we need to take a moment to explore the question, *Does God still speak?* I love what Dallas Willard says about this in his book, *Hearing God*:

> *In our attempts to understand how God speaks to us and guides us, we must above all hold on to the fact that it is to be sought only as a part of a certain kind of life, a <u>life</u> of loving fellowship with the King and his other subjects in the Kingdom of the Heaven. We must never forget that God's speaking to us is intended to develop into an intelligent, freely cooperative relationship between mature people who love each other (God and us) with the richness of genuine agape (deep and unconditional) love. We must therefore make it our primary goal <u>not just to hear the voice of God</u> but to be mature people in a loving relationship with Him. Only in this way will we hear him rightly. (Emphasis added)*

Like Willard, I believe that God speaks to us. I don't know how anyone can become a believer if He doesn't. In the Gospel of John, chapters 14-

17, Jesus teaches about the coming of the Holy Spirit and His role in our relationship with God from that time forward. To get His point across, Jesus introduces us to the person of the Holy Spirit, describing Him in those chapters as a guide, counselor, comforter and teacher.

The implications are obvious, but let me state them just the same. If He who is coming after Jesus (the Holy Spirit) is now here, then what is Jesus suggesting we're going to need? *A Guide, Counselor, Comforter and Teacher*. Now, I've had some good guides, counselors, comforters and teachers, and I've had some who were not so good. What makes the difference between the good ones and bad ones? It is their ability or inability to communicate, explain, help, encourage, share and speak truth that sets them apart.

Notice that all the roles of the Holy Spirit in the Larger Story of our lives point to and promote relationship. What good guide or teacher wouldn't be relational? When we step into the Kingdom of God from the place where we previously lived (the kingdom of darkness), it is only because we were "invited" by the God of heaven and earth to become part of His family. And with that move, that adoption, comes many privileges—probably the greatest of which is the presence of His guiding, teaching, comforting Spirit.

Many times, people hear from God powerfully in the first moment of invitation that leads to acceptance. But then His voice seems to fade. When was the last time you heard from God? If it has been too long, it is time you start believing that God wants to communicate to you important things for the important journey you are on. It is time we all started listening. It is time to see and hear.

There are many voices speaking to us, wooing us, inviting us and offering things to us. They are putting before us glorious things as well as dangerous things. Advertisements and marketing campaigns abound in our culture. And they're not limited to TV commercials and pages in a magazine or newspaper. *People*—other broken, confused, disoriented and controlling people—have agendas for *our* lives, and they speak into our lives every chance they get. They give advice and counsel; they make demands and threats. We find it so very easy to follow these voices, to listen and even believe the lies they tell us. What if we would realize that their "counsel" has more to say about them than it does about us? That their words are simply how *they* see and how *they* hear and they are attempting to impose those on us. What if there are forces at work in their lives, forces both for and against them, and we have simply walked into a moment when darkness was winning the tug of war in their hearts? The Spiritual Realm encompasses a greater throng of participants than we realize, both of this world and beyond it.

How will we know what to choose, who to listen to and what our next step should be? There are forces out there searching to find us, and not all of these forces are for us, not all are offering the abundant Life. If we're not careful, very careful, what we don't see or hear can and will hurt us.

A HEART ENGAGED

"You will seek me and find me when you seek me with all your heart. I will be found by you," declares the LORD, "and will bring you back from captivity."

Jeremiah 29:13-14a

The heart plays a central role in our journey toward Life. I will address this crucial element in our stories more fully in chapter eight, but I want to introduce the importance of the heart here. There is no Life without **heart**. In the physical sense, it is the heart that keeps us all moving. Pumping at an average of 72 times a minute, the heart is crucial to sustaining life. Though the physical heart is a remarkable thing, it does not compare to the importance of the *heart* of a man or woman in a larger and more significant context—a spiritual one. God urges us through His Word, to be fully aware of the importance of our hearts:

> Keep and guard your heart with all vigilance and above all that you guard, for out of it flow the springs of life.
>
> Proverbs 4:23 (AMP, emphasis added)

I like the way the New American Standard Bible unpacks this same verse: *Watch over your heart with all diligence, for from it flow the springs of life.*

Additional verses give us insight into the central role of our hearts:

> I will give you a new heart and put a new spirit in you; I will remove from you your heart of stone and give you a heart of flesh.
> Ezekiel 36:26 (emphasis added)

> "The word is near you; it is in your mouth and in your heart," that is, the word of faith we are proclaiming: That if you confess with your mouth, "Jesus is Lord," and believe in your heart that God raised him from the dead, you will be saved. For it is with your heart that you believe and are justified, and it is with your mouth that you confess and are saved.
> Romans 10:8-10 (emphasis added)

Speaking of hearts reminds me of the Tin Man in L. Frank Baum's classic children's story, *The Wonderful Wizard of Oz*. Looking at it from a deeper level, this classic paints a beautiful picture of our lives. Dorothy must take a journey to learn some significant things, qualities, that up until this point have eluded her. She desperately needs to find them or, maybe more to the point, let them find her. She will need three companions for this mission of recovery and getting home: *Wisdom* (the *Scarecrow* whom she *frees* from the corn field post), *Heart* (the *Tin Man* whom she *restores* with the help of an oil can) and *Courage* (the *Cowardly Lion* to whom she *imparts* her own courage). And you thought the story was about flying monkeys, witches and munchkins!

John Eldredge, in his book *Waking the Dead*, writes about the Tin Man's story from *The Wonderful Wizard of Oz*. We enter the story soon after the Scarecrow and Dorothy come upon the Tin Man, who is rusted and without a heart. After they oil him up and get him moving again, they resume their place on the yellow brick road, walking with their new companion. He tells them the story of how he became the Tin Man, his love for a munchkin maiden and his encounters with the Wicked Witch of the East. He tells how he lost a leg when chopping wood to make enough money to ask his true love for her munchkin hand in marriage, how the Wicked Witch had enchanted his axe, causing it to slip and injure him and how he sought out the tinsmith for help. This went on, one limb at a time, until a fateful day when he encountered the final blow. Here is the end of his story…

> "I thought I had beaten the Wicked Witch then, and I worked harder than ever; but I little knew how cruel my enemy could be. She thought of a new way to kill my love for the beautiful Munchkin maiden, and made my axe slip again, so that it cut right through my body, splitting me into two halves. Once more the tinsmith came to my help and made me a body of tin, fastening my tin arms and legs and head to it, by means of joints, so that I could move around as well as ever. But, alas! I had now no heart, so that I lost all my love for the Munchkin girl, and did not care whether I married her or not. I suppose she is still living with the old woman, waiting for me to come after her.
>
> "My body shone so brightly in the sun that I felt very proud of it and it did not matter now if my axe slipped, for it could not cut me. There was only one danger–that my joints would rust; but I kept an oil-can in my cottage and took care to oil myself whenever I needed it. However, there came a day when I forgot to do this, and, being caught in a rainstorm, before I thought of the danger, my joints had rusted, and I was left to stand in the woods until you came to help me. It was a terrible thing to undergo, but during the year I stood there I had time to think that the greatest loss I had known was the loss of my heart. While I was in love I was the happiest man on earth; but no one can

love who has not a heart, and so I am resolved to ask Oz to give me one. If he does, I will go back to the Munchkin maiden and marry her."

Both Dorothy and the Scarecrow had been greatly interested in the story of the Tin Woodman, and now they knew why he was so anxious to get a new heart.
"All the same," said the Scarecrow, "I shall ask for brains instead of a heart; for a fool would not know what to do with a heart if he had one."

"I shall take the heart," returned the Tin Woodman; "for brains do not make one happy, and happiness is the best thing in the world."

Like Dorothy and her companions on their way to Oz, our search for Life will demand much of us. Most worthwhile quests do. Like the Tin Man, we all have a story to tell; many of the answers to our Life's questions are found in the chronicles of our personal stories. *Where am I? What happened to me, and how did I get here?* These are weighty and significant questions to ask. How do we respond when someone poses the question *So, what happened to you?* Do we know our own stories? Coming to understand our story will be a core ingredient that helps shape the perspective and orientation to set us on the right path and carry us toward the Life we most want and so desperately need. So...*what's your story? What happened to your heart?*

SURPRISES

We've all been surprised at some point in our lives. My wife, Robin, pulled the best one for me when she orchestrated a surprise 40th birthday party. She made all the arrangements...parking our friends' cars a few blocks away, having Grandma and Grandpa scoop up our three girls and planning the strategic "surprise" date two days before my actual birthday. The results of her planning set me up for the surprise of my life. The craziest thing was that all my friends knew for weeks...the invitations went out, RSVPs came back a month ahead of time...and I still had no idea. As I drove around our neighborhood that night and noticed an unusually large bunch of parked cars around, I exclaimed *Wow, somebody is having a party!* I had no idea I was! When I invited the grandparents in for coffee and they refused, I thought *Huh. Hope they're feeling all right.* I stepped in the door, went around the corner, walked into the kitchen and bam—the cheer of *Surprise!* I couldn't believe it. I was overwhelmed, and the night was one of the greatest of my life. Up until that moment, I was oblivious and didn't see it coming at all. What a *wonderful* surprise.

Unfortunately, not all surprises are wonderful. Being surprised on your birthday by family and friends has a very different feel than receiving a notice from your bank saying you are overdrawn—*surprise*! All of us have walked into a day and been *surprised* by news that left us dazed and confused. A secret comes to light, unveiled like a blow to the stomach, and it leaves us gasping for air. A wife says to her husband, *The affair has gone on for some time now...two years...I'm sorry, I'm leaving, I didn't mean to hurt you and the children.* What a devastating surprise. In a moment, life is utterly changed. A husband looks into this unwelcome surprise package and immediately begins believing in his heart the weighty accusations and substantial self-degrading lies it brings: *What an idiot I am. I should've known. How did I miss this? What did I do wrong? I am so worthless.*

Abrupt hairpin turns in our lives can put us in the ditch for a time. Shock has a way, like nothing else, of helping us wake up to the reality of our lives. But when we believe that the bulk of these moments are simply scenes in the physical realm, it's like believing a picture is better than the actual place. Pictures are great, but there is always more to a place than what can be captured in an image. And likewise, there is more to these moments than what we see with our physical eyes. If you miss the connection of the Two Realms, their great intersection, you will misunderstand the life and the drama that is unfolding all around you.

The affect and accumulation of these hard and painful moments will often lead a person to consume large helpings of shame, guilt, fear, anger and resentment. These dark attitudes and feelings plant seeds in our lives that grow to choke us and make us lose our way. These "weeds" impede our freedom, producing anger, fear, guilt, shame and a desperate need for self-protection at all costs. No wonder we are so determined to control our own lives, despite the mess we're making of them. Who wants to be hurt, disappointed, let down and ignored?

In turn the determination to control all aspects of our lives affects our relationships, spreading our own dark struggles to others like a virus. A sure way to spot a lost and wandering soul is to see the extent to which someone tries to control the other people in his or her life. How sad and unfulfilling it is to believe we are on our own to *make* our lives work and that we must also make others work for our happiness.

My point here is that there are *reasons* we evolve to such levels of lostness and choose to live like this. The difficult surprises of our story have taught us that we need to do all we can to arrange for a certain kind of life so we won't get hurt again. These moments, and the deep emotions they bring, lead us to make declarations in our hearts that are demonstrated and carried out in our choices, actions and behaviors. Our wounded hearts develop deeply held beliefs that become firmly rooted in who we are, and we must do the hard work of untangling and straightening out this mess in our hearts. It is only by allowing the Holy Spirit to do the spiritual work of cleansing our hearts that we can have hope of finding the better way.

FURTHER UP AND FURTHER IN

The search, rescue and recovery of a life is costly and painful, but a venture worth every step. Anything of true value and worth always is.

The alternative is to continue in our costly and painful old ways. The call to self-sufficiency we've all inherited, the declarations of *If at first you don't succeed, try, try again* or *If you set your mind to it, you can do anything* make for great commencement speeches, but they aren't very helpful in the search for true, full Life. They are the ingredients we pull off the shelves of a wounded belief system that always over-promises and yet never fully delivers.

So we must pack light and begin our search. With eyes to see, ears to hear and a heart engaged, we set out to discover a new way of living, a new way of Life. *Packing light doesn't mean the mission is light.* Just the opposite. This is a long journey, one we have already started and one that will continue for years to come. We are all pilgrims and pioneers, not settlers or squatters. C. S. Lewis said it well when he wrote in *Mere Christianity*, "If I find in myself a desire which no experience in this world can satisfy, the most probable explanation is that I was made for another world."

Here is one of the greatest surprises we will find on our journey: this world is not all there is, we live in the intersection of Two Realms—the physical and the spiritual. I must confess that for the longest time I was unaware of this reality. I believed the Spiritual Realm was for the afterlife and was in a galaxy far, far away. If you had made me vote on which realm was more prominent, I would have easily cast my vote for the physical. It's here and now, and you can see it, hear it, touch it and feel it. This adds up to all the ingredients needed to live in a very small, limited story. When I look back at the dominance of this belief in my life, I realize it actually kept me far away from Life, *true Life*. And I think this is what most of us experience regarding the Two Realms in which we live. We seldom see what is really going on, and when we finally do, *Surprise!*

The physical world is not our home. As reflected in so many stories we love, we are on a journey that will *take* us home. Ironically, what will go with us on the journey are the very things that will be needed once we arrive: *Our Eyes, Our Ears* and *Our Hearts*.

Like any orientation, we have to start at the beginning. The beginning is critical. But that's all it is—the beginning. With that first step, you are at the beginning of awareness, the beginning of becoming equipped, the beginning of experiencing Life that is far better than any you've experienced *before*. Remember that we live a life of firsts.

Hopefully now, for the first time, your eyes are opened to a glimpse of a new reality. Hopefully you know more now than you did when you started on page one. Hopefully you see, hear and are engaged differently than when you first started.

Now it's time to step further up and further into the largeness of the story that has been our lives all along, whether we knew it or not. We are going to need to see, hear and engage our hearts as we seek to understand our role in the Larger Story of life and in its Two Realms. We must learn to recognize the Life that we are searching for as well as the ones who are searching for us. Darkness is now giving way to a dim light. We're packed up with what is crucial to our journey, and it's time to stand over the map and discover more of *where we really are* and *who we really are*.

PART II

WHERE ARE WE?

CHAPTER 4 GETTING OUR BEARINGS
CHAPTER 5 TWO REALMS AND THE REALM THAT MATTERS MOST
CHAPTER 6 TWO KINGDOMS
CHAPTER 7 THE ECONOMY OF KINGDOM

Where am I?

This is *the* great question often asked, or sometimes simply thought, just before the painful declarative answer—*I'm lost*. Asking the question *Where am I?* is both crucial and fundamental. If I never come to the point of asking it, then I am likely to stay in a stubborn mode of self-reliance and self-sufficiency. Asking this one question is the first step in asking for and finding help.

For so long, I believed that asking this question was a declaration of personal failure, not an invitation to adventure. I also believed the majority of people around me *knew* where they were in life. Tragically, I've come to discover that this is quite often not the case. To assume that I know and comprehend all the variables at play in my own life, much less in the lives of others, would be rather big-headed and narcissistic of me. And yet that is how I lived much of the time.

A GPS unit can tell you your location, but you have to look up and look around in order to take in the reality of your environment. Despite your best efforts to be aware of your surroundings, it would be unwise to assume your eyes can take in everything around you at any given moment.

The reality is that most of us are living with some degree of blindness and we don't even realize it. Only a small portion of people are rightly-oriented so they can truly see, hear and understand. Most of us, including me at times, find ourselves living in a story like Truman in the film, *The Truman Show*. There is far more going on in his story than he realizes, and he will soon find out what the "more" is. And if you and I are willing to have our eyes opened, we too will discover the "more" of our lives and all that surrounds us.

The variables, circumstances and landscapes in which we live are constantly shifting, though we may not even take a step. People come into our lives, and people go. One day stacks up like so many others, and then *pow*, life knocks us off our feet. Your mother is diagnosed with Alzheimer's, your brother and sister-in-law have been in an accident, your teenager is experimenting with drugs or the embarrassing little secret you've been hiding suddenly isn't a secret anymore.

So often in those moments, forces creep in and we're transported to a vulnerable and highly susceptible place. The predators of life: shame, guilt, fear, regret and depression (just to name a few) circle the perimeter of our lives, just waiting to pounce when these opportunities present themselves. Most people never hear these predators growl, see them lurking or have any clue that they're around. The elements around us shift and change like a storm coming over us without warning or time to prepare.

Asking the question, *Where am I?* establishes our need for help. It also serves as an invitation for a guide to search either with us or for us, to help us find a way through and out of harm's way until the next time. Oh yes, there will be a *next time*. During our lives we will not need only one rescue but several. As hard as I may try, I cannot control my life's circumstances, nor can I make this story easy, safe or comfortable. I am not the author nor am I life's creator. If I believe the story is all about me, then I'm living in much too small of a story and I will miss most of Life. It's not that I am not important to the story; I am vital to it. My story is part of a much larger one, larger than I have been led to believe. When I first learned life wasn't about me or up to me, all the coordinates and bearings I was using for my life became obsolete—like the computer languages of Cobol and Fortran and eight-track or cassette tapes. All that I have known has become useless. Suddenly I am left asking another question, *If these ways of arranging for life aren't helpful or useful to finding my place and navigating my way home, then what is?*

Now where am I in this Larger Story of Life?

KNOWING YOUR SURROUNDINGS

When I can't find my cell phone, I think…*maybe I left it on the charger in the car.* If it is raining, I may throw on a coat in order to hustle out to the driveway and get it. If it is raining *hard*, I might wait until later. If it is raining hard and it is *urgent* that I have my phone, I will open an umbrella and proceed with the search and recovery. Considering the elements is important to being prepared for your mission, however small or large that current mission is. Who hasn't left the car windows down only to have the forecasted rain make a mess of the interior? Or set out for a family fun-filled picnic on a summer day without SPF 30? When we don't consider the elements that we live in, we find ourselves cold or wet, sweaty or sunburned…or worse.

A few years ago while at a North Carolina beach as a family, my father-in-law and I were at the shore with my three girls, playing, splashing and looking for shells. My middle daughter, Hannah, was in the water just a couple dozen feet away. She was nine at the time and a good swimmer, but she was no match for the strength of the ocean waves that day. The wave that crashed over her was not particularly violent or large. It was just big enough to keep her feet from bouncing off the bottom and gaining a footing. The backwash of the previous wave was strong enough to pull her a few more inches out to sea. If she hadn't screamed for help—or had been unable to—I hate to think about what might have happened.

It all occurred in about four seconds. My father-in-law heard her yell and so did another man who stood watching on the beach. The speed in which I closed the 20 yards between Hannah and myself is a personal record of mine that still stands to this day. We were all sprinting toward her and, praise God, got hold of her just before the next ocean waves could take another turn and take her out and under. After spending the rest of the afternoon literally sick, I established a new rule in the Thompson family that day: We will always wear life jackets at the beach—even if we're just playing in the shallows.

At times we take into account the elements and environments in which we live—but not nearly often enough. Like on that day with Hannah, we are apt to do so only after we've learned a traumatic lesson. We often only learn to be wisely cautious through painful and costly, yet beneficial, mistakes.

In searching for the answers to the questions that matter most in life, *Who am I? Why am I here? What does this mean?,* we all hope the answers will come eventually. We hope the answers will unlock our lives and bring about the confidence and competence we desire.

I take inventory of my life only to find the great absence of a settled identity and an uncertainty of my life's purpose. It feels as if I am under some kind of spell. Some influence has a pull on me, and its power leaves me feeling ignorant about what is going on. There's a nagging sense of incompetence, accusing me of being lost and not knowing my way. As a result, like my daughter in the ocean that day, I am pulled under and taken out, time and time again. I scramble to excuse my mistakes by claiming that I didn't understand, misunderstood what I was supposed to do or received poor instructions from someone else. In reality, most of my mistakes in life come from my unwillingness to admit my own ignorance, incompetence or lostness. All this and more seems to describe the effects of this spell, this influence over me and my life, as I journey and search for Life.

And I don't believe I'm alone.

When I look at Jesus' life, teaching and ministry, I discover that He so often worked to clear things up, impart understanding, forecast what lay ahead and invite people to a new way to live. It was an invitation to live the way *He lived.* Jesus went out of His way to help people understand that there is a life that is good *and* available. He knew people were, and still are, looking for orientation and answers, and that is exactly what He was, and still is, offering.

Early in the 2005 movie, *Batman Begins*, the young Bruce Wayne (Christian Bale) is in training under a master martial arts teacher, Ducard, played by Liam Neeson. Their training sessions are heated and intense. Ducard is offering directions and counsel to Wayne as they are engaged in philosophy and theories, sparring and fighting. In one scene where they are training with swords, trading blows and clashing steel on a frozen lake, Ducard says to his young apprentice, "Always mind your surroundings." As they battle on, Wayne finds himself in the dominant position and demands his teacher to yield. Ducard replies, "You have sacrificed sure footing for a killing stroke," at which point he smashes his sword into the ice, breaking it at the feet of his overconfident pupil, sending the young Wayne into the freezing waters for a hard lesson learned.

This scenario reveals the "lostness" of the young Wayne; the reality was not what he thought it to be. This is a theme repeated often in the great stories. The Pevensie children, who wander through the wardrobe and into Narnia in C. S. Lewis' *Chronicles of Narnia,* cannot believe where they have arrived or the incredible story they are caught up in. Thomas Anderson must be transformed into Neo and be reoriented to reality before he can fulfill the role he is to play in the story that is *The Matrix*. The disciples often misunderstood the teachings of Christ and were guilty of saying the wrong things at the wrong times.

I have misunderstood, misinterpreted and mishandled so many things in my life that the sense of being lost has been the norm for me rather than the exception. *But things are changing.* I'm finding a new way to live, or rather I'm starting to believe a new way to live is finding me. As in all the great stories, things change. There is a progression and a journey the characters find themselves caught up in. They start to become aware of the environment around them and, when they do, it moves them to higher ground. It brings them to a larger perspective and a better understanding of their story. Only then and there can they see more clearly the Larger Story as well as their role to play. In turn, they are able to navigate their next steps more strategically.

CHAPTER 4

GETTING OUR BEARINGS

What kind of deal is it to get everything you want but lose yourself?
What could you ever trade your soul for?

Matthew 16:26 (MSG)

The place for which He (the Creator) designs them (us the created) in His scheme of things is the place they are made for. When they reach it...their nature is fulfilled and their happiness attained: a broken bone in the universe has been set, the anguish is over. When we want to be something other than the thing God wants us to be, we must be wanting what in fact, will not make us happy.

C. S. Lewis, The Problem of Pain

In the 1984 film, *The Karate Kid,* Ralph Macchio plays Daniel, a New Jersey boy who is transplanted to Southern California. Early in the film, he learns the hard way that he doesn't fit in. When the local bullies attack him, his rescue comes in the unlikely form of his apartment's maintenance man, Mr. Miyagi. With an impressive display of martial arts skills, the elderly Asian man soon reveals that he isn't what he seems. Soon after, Miyagi takes on Daniel as his karate student. Daniel is excited to think of the day when he will fight like Miyagi. But with his first lesson, instead of karate instruction, Miyagi puts Daniel to work on a list of chores like waxing cars, sanding the porch floors, painting a fence and eventually painting the whole house. For each chore, Miyagi gives Daniel specific instructions on how to accomplish the task. *Wax on with one hand, wax off with the other; move the brush up and down; and always breathe in through the nose and out through the mouth.* Frustrated with what seems to him to be a huge waste of time, Daniel follows the old man's instructions, supposing the chores are payment for his training. In a pivotal scene, Daniel's frustration with Miyagi finally explodes:

> **Daniel** (to Mr. Miyagi): You're supposed to teach, and I'm supposed to learn. Four days I've been busting my #@*%*, I haven't learned a thing.
> **Miyagi:** You learn plenty.
> **Daniel:** (sarcastically) I've learned to sand your decks. I've waxed your car, I paint your house, paint your fence.
> **Miyagi:** *Not everything is as seems.*
> **Daniel:** Oh, Bull#@*%*, man. I'm going home. (Daniel throws up his hands, turns and begins to walk away.)
> **Miyagi:** Daniel-san…Daniel-san!
> **Daniel:** (Daniel stops walking) What?
> **Miyagi:** Come here. (Daniel returns. They are face to face.) Show me sand the floor.
> **Daniel:** Sand the floor? (Daniel starts to go to his knees to sand floor)
> **Miyagi:** Stand up. Show me sand the floor.
> **Daniel:** Sand the floor? (Daniel shows sand the floor while bending down as if to sand the floor again with hands in circular motions and with a puzzled look on his face)
> **Miyagi:** Get up. (Daniel stands up and shrugs in frustration and confusion.)
> **Miyagi:** Sand the floor. Big circle. Sand the floor. Sand the floor. (Daniel does the floor sanding motions in the air.)
> **Miyagi:** Now show me wax on, wax off.
> **Daniel:** Wax on, wax off?
> **Miyagi:** Wax on, wax off!
> **Daniel:** Wax on…
> **Miyagi:**…wax off. Concentrate. Look in my eyes. Lock your hand, thumb inside. Wax on…wax off. Wax on…wax off. Show me paint the fence. Up, down. Up. Down. Up. Down. Other side.

> Look eye. Always look eye! (Daniel copies what Miyagi is showing him, still puzzled.)
> **Miyagi:** Show me paint the house. Side, side. Lock wrist. Side, side. Side, side. (Miyagi then throws a series of slow punches and kicks. Daniel blocks each advance with the techniques he has been learning the past days in his chores. Miyagi stands face to face with Daniel and throws a barrage of punches and kicks. Daniel blocks them all with his new found techniques. Miyagi bows to Daniel. A bewildered and wide-eyed Daniel bows back and stands there dazed, but slowly beginning to comprehend the true heart of his teacher.)
> **Miyagi:** (looking Daniel in the eye) ***Come back tomorrow.***

This is one of my favorite scenes in all the stories and films that move my heart. Why? Because it's my story, and I believe it just might be *all of* our stories. As I shared before, I have misunderstood so much of what is truly taking place in my life. All too often, just like Daniel, I have failed to see the reality of my life, the bigger picture, *the more than meets the eye* that is going on all around me.

Just think if we could gain a true orientation and a real awareness of how God is working around us, in us and with us every day. In doing so, it would transform our lost wanderings into a purposeful journey toward abundant life.

Jesus' life, His teachings and ministry often centered on exactly that—detangling the skewed perceptions and perspectives; helping people see more clearly where they are, who they are and how God's Kingdom works. Jesus often said to anyone willing to have ears to hear, *Listen up! You've got most of life wrong. Let me tell you about the condition you are really in, the place where you really live and what God is really like. The Father wants you to know His deep love for you. You can do more than just survive. Let me help you see. Let me help you hear. Let me help you discover life at its fullest.*

RECOVERED, REDEEMED, RESTORED

I was talking recently with a friend who was struggling with difficult circumstances. He is so close to his own story and its drama that he doesn't see the situation clearly; but the truth is painfully obvious to his friends who are observing it from the outside. How could he not see what everyone else seems to know? We are all driven to frustration when we encounter this kind of blind spot in the lives of others. When it's my own life that is the source of frustration and *I'm* the one not seeing clearly, *I'm* the one in the dark, and *I'm* the one causing the problem or the pain, that's when the feelings of embarrassment, guilt and shame win the day. In so many of those revealing moments, I wish I had known. Haven't we all experienced 20/20 hindsight? Haven't we all, with a hint of regret, wished we knew *then* what we know *now*?

We're not alone. Throughout history, people have been shortsighted and prone to missing the point and unable to see what was unfolding around them. This was certainly true in Jesus' day. He was misunderstood, misplaced and mishandled by many. His rescue mission took Him into a hostile environment. He knew all along that the stakes were unimaginably high and that the cost to Him would be everything. Sadly, even those closest to Him did not or *could not* grasp the magnitude of God's plan unfolding in front of them. *It's as if they were under a spell*. Jesus labored to open their eyes, but it was only in hindsight that His friends saw clearly, and His efforts took root in their souls.

In Luke 19:10, Jesus says "[I] came to *seek* and *save* what was lost." His mission was to *recover, redeem* and *restore* His broken creation—starting with that which is most precious to the Father's heart, you and me. He came to **recover** what was lost in Eden (the intimate relationship between God and people), to **redeem** all of creation from the clutches of the enemy and to **restore** full, abundant life to all who would receive it. If you miss this, you will miss out on understanding the depth of God's love in the same way that Jesus' closest friends did centuries ago. Thankfully, at last, that little band of believers came to fully understand the reality of Jesus' message. Armed with the truth and their own changed lives, they were empowered to change the world. When they began to live recovered, redeemed and restored—and to proclaim that Jesus had come to recover, redeem and restore a world in ruin—everything changed. That same message can, and will, transform *you* and *me*.

This same Jesus, who declared and embodied this revolutionary message, is also the God of the universe who has made *all* things with rhyme, reason and purpose (Colossians 1). The Bible is so much more than a collection of truths and facts about God. The Bible is the story of God's calculated movements throughout history. He has a plan, thank goodness. And this Great God repeatedly delivers one subtle yet life-altering message through His actions and His Words: **Things are not always what they seem.** There are forces at work, circumstances unfolding and unseen characters, all acting throughout the dramatic moments of our yesterdays, todays and tomorrows. We cannot hope to play our own roles well in this epic drama if we do not have eyes to see and ears to hear the greater story, the Larger Story, that is happening all around us.

We must take hold of the Larger Story of which we are a part, even if it feels like we are hugging a mountain or attempting to saddle a tornado. Trust me. It will feel like a monumental task, an overwhelming undertaking. But if we do, when we do, we can begin to understand the significance and direction of our personal stories. This orientation alone will set us apart from most of the people wandering the planet. If we misjudge or misunderstand the Larger Story we're living in, our hearts will stay on a very twisted path and lead to a very twisted life. When our lives are oriented around a *false picture* of the Larger Story, we will be plagued with confusion, frustration and discouragement. Far too many of us suffer from this painful and chronic condition—the great loss of Life. And we end up living a life that is tolerable at times, struggling often, waiting, wanting, beaten down and, for some, not at all worth the fight.

Now, just to be clear, I'm not talking about the *he stopped breathing* loss of life. The loss I'm discussing here is worse. This is the loss of Life that leaves us lost *in* life. Oh, we're still breathing. We may even have a healthy heart rate, low cholesterol, clear lungs, perfect vision and an acute sense of hearing. But we are not *alive*. True, we might be in great physical shape. But make no mistake, we are only surviving. There is a huge difference between *surviving* and being fully *alive*. "Survive" is what you do until you are rescued. "Alive" is what you *are* once you have been found and restored. Misunderstanding and mishandling our lives will, with certainty, result in a collection of wounds; and these wounds, if left untreated over time, will cause us to resign ourselves to living with the pain. It is perhaps the saddest and yet most common compromise of all—exchanging *living* for just *surviving*.

LIVING WITH THE PAIN

A few years ago, I suddenly realized that my age was catching up to me. There were some mornings I would wake up and my body would just hurt. I hadn't been chopping down any trees the day before, nor had I done anything that would remotely be called strenuous. Getting injured in my sleep was one of the first clues that told me, *Hey M.T., You're getting old.* The mileage on my body from 20 years of a basketball addiction had caught up to me. High school, college and some professional hoops—the years of hardwood, weight rooms, elbows and running miles in-between two baselines in a gym—it had all finally come to collect its payment.

Many of you over-40-somethings (if you were able to hold it off that long) have been to an orthopedist. The waiting rooms hold a wide variety of people, 40-somethings to 80-somethings. The forty-ish crowd (that would be me) is checking in with pain in their knees, shoulders, elbows or feet, and their appointments with the orthopedic doctor all go pretty much the same. The doctor tugs or pokes on the painful areas, making sure they're telling the truth about the extent of the pain by coercing a confession to the question, *Does it hurt here?* If they whine and scream enough, then come the x-rays or MRIs, showing there is no cartilage left where their should be, the ligaments are torn or some other damage has been done. After all that to-do, the doctor's professional advice is finally delivered, *Yep, you're pretty banged up. When the pain becomes unbearable, come and see me, and we can talk about surgery.* Translation: *Live with the pain.*

When we find that the years of running from our fears, the lifting of heavy walls to cover up our weaknesses and the digging of ditches to hide our wounds have finally caught up with us, the professional advice from the Great Healer is altogether different. Jesus calls, *"Come to me, all you who are weary and burdened and I will give you rest."* (Matthew 11:28) Oh what we could all do with a little rest.

Again, don't make the mistake of thinking the Savior is just offering a vacation from busyness. He is offering answers to our questions, answers that put us to rest in the confidence only He can give—especially when answering *who we are, where we are* and *the good that God is up to in our lives.* Answers to those questions will bring *rest to* my heart and yours. The Hero of our story stands ready. He longs to rescue each one of us from the darkness and restore us to our place in the Grand Tale. Are you ready to discover who you truly are? Are you ready to discover the Life that awaits anyone with the curiosity and courage to take the first step? Then *cry out for help.* Rescue is so much closer than you can imagine.

MAPQUEST

The call to a journey toward abundant Life brings hope. But it also brings questions—some of the most important questions we'll ever ask. Most of us have at one time or another gone to a website like *MapQuest* to get directions. Bring up the site, and the first information it asks for is a *starting location.* In other words, *where are you right now?* If you aren't sure where you are starting, the site provides a prompt, *enter as much as you know.* This is where many of us find ourselves in trouble... not only when using *MapQuest* but, more significantly, in life. When we have a serious lack of critical information, we're not sure where we are...we're not sure where we're going...we're in trouble. *MapQuest* isn't helpful when we don't know where we're going, and it certainly is not going to help us with the larger things in life.

> *I see where my finances are, and I know where I want them to be, but how do I get there?*
>
> *I have an idea where my marriage is, and I know, or think I know, what my wife needs so that we can move forward, but how can I get there?*
>
> *My kids aren't where I thought they'd be...I've read all the books and have a map and directions for them, but they just don't seem to cooperate and want to follow. How do I get them on track?*

You've probably heard the old saying, *If you don't know where you're going, then any old road will get you there.* If I don't know where I am or how I got there, or if I'm uncertain of where I'm going, then I'm more than just a little confused. I'm in ***big*** trouble.

To recap, the bad news is we're lost...but there is some good news. Actually, it's better than that, there's some *really* good news—the best news of all. God cares *a lot* about lost things. Jesus tells many stories of things lost and then found—sheep, coins and sons (Luke 15). In Luke 19:10 Jesus declares, "For the Son of Man came to seek and save what was lost." I don't know about you, but that stirs my heart. That brings me hope, the kind of hope that keeps me hanging on and gives me courage to step into another day. Napoleon Hill wrote,

> *What we do not see, what most of us never suspect of existing, is the silent but irresistible power which comes to the rescue of those who fight on in the face of discouragement.*

That's me! Fighting on, whacking away in the dark and looking, hoping, for direction. To know and believe there is One who is out there with me on His mind, One who can change my life and set things straight… Someone who wants to find me even more than I want to find Him—that is really good news. *Help, help me please! Here I am! Right here!*

HOW DID WE GET HERE?

In the third chapter of Genesis, Adam and Eve make a tragic move that affects everybody's story—their story, our story and the story that has shaped all of history. They try to find life without God and, in doing so, a great deal is *lost*. The fatal bite is taken, and the first children flee to the shadows. God comes into the garden for the first ever game of hide and seek. *Adam, where are you?* calls the Father. God isn't asking this because He doesn't know. God's question to Adam is for Adam, *Do you know where you are?* The question brings with it the sobering reality that *everything* has changed. The intimacy between Creator and His creation has been fractured. Life has been lost, and the life lines are broken. Death has arrived, and their time in the garden (and in the unbroken presence of God) has come to an end. So, like our first father Adam, we too find ourselves lost and ashamed.

God asked, *Where are you?* And Adam and Eve, to their credit, responded with the bare truth. *We don't know where we are. But what we do know is that we are naked, ashamed, and we needed to hide.* Well, that about sums it up. What an answer! They felt the shift. They declared their separation and, to think, just a few verses earlier the scriptures declared…*they were naked and not ashamed* (Genesis 2:25). They traded unashamed (freedom) for shame (bondage). That was the ultimate in bad trades. They knew things had changed. Something significant had happened, and they knew it. They even tried to counter it, adjust for it, cover it up with leaves and somehow brace themselves for life *after*. They all too quickly found themselves in a *condition* they had never experienced—*being lost*. And they were overwhelmed by an *emotion* they had never felt—*shame*.

I find it very sad, and a bit ironic, that very little has changed. Sure, we've advanced. Adam and Eve didn't have cell phones. They were without 500 channels of HD-TV. They couldn't Google anything or hit the interstate with Cain and Abel in the family SUV. And yet, what happened to Adam and Eve has happened to all of us. What Adam and Eve did, we all have done. We *all* hide—*lost and ashamed*. Painfully, like them, we attempt to make a life apart from God by covering up our mistakes with elaborate fig leaves. It didn't work then, and it doesn't work now.

This is our point of origin—the starting point for our journey. We begin under an overcast sky at the trailhead called Lost and Ashamed, and the forecast is bad. Many don't want to start here. They try to avoid it, ignore it and even run from it. But until we start here, until we are honest with our beginning position on the map, we can't, and won't, move forward. *Running away* is what Adam and Eve did. *Running to God* is what we need to do. Lost and Ashamed Lane is the address we need to type into the first box on our life's *MapQuest* page. Knowing our starting point, *our starting condition,* is the first significant step in our journey toward our ultimate destiny—to be rescued, redeemed and restored. When we type in our place of origin, God will type in the point of our destination.

PULLING THE TRIGGER

Anything needing to be rescued, redeemed and restored must have had, by definition, a glorious beginning. It was something glorious first, before the clouds rolled in, before the elements took their toll—and so it is with us. Only three people who walked this planet ever experienced creation's glory *before sin* and its brokenness and groaning *after sin*: Adam, Eve and Jesus. The first two brought brokenness through their rebellion. The results were devastation upon themselves and a ruining of their image and glory. Jesus, on the other hand, came to set things straight (Romans 5:12-21), to make all things right, and to bring us out of our awful plight before and into our glorious after…*our restoration!*

C. S. Lewis wrote in *The Weight of Glory*,

> *Apparently… our lifelong nostalgia, our longing to be reunited with something in the universe from which we now feel cut off, to be on the inside of some door which we have always seen from the outside, is no more neurotic fancy, but the truest index of our real situation. And to be at last summoned inside would be both glory and honor beyond all our merits and also the healing of that old ache.*

Lewis felt the longing, and, like him, I find that this longing and desire give me away. It is the declaration of my heart—*I'm lost and I need help.* My worst days, when I find I must give up the fig leaf and striving to find life on my own, are also my best days. Those are the days I admit where I am, and I finally pull the trigger. I finally shoot off the signal flare from my heart into that dark sky and cry out, *I'm here! Please, come and get me.*

Hold on. Our rescue, our redemption and our restoration are coming.

TAKEN OUT OF CONTEXT

I am amazed how often I offend others while driving, standing in line, entering and exiting. It seems to me that much of the time, what I've said or done wasn't what I meant, and what I meant wasn't what I said or did. Things often seem to be taken *out of context*. For far too long, my probability for interpreting things wrongly was much larger than my likelihood for interpreting things rightly. This seems to be the case with newspapers and broadcast media as well. It seems as though they misinterpret on purpose. How many times have we heard a celebrity start an interview with the statement, *First, let me clear one thing up*, or *Let me first set one thing straight*?

What people say or do, the events that unfold around us every day—when taken out of context—sound and appear to be one thing, when in reality they are something very different. These misunderstandings or misinterpretations, when believed and promoted, will affect our relationships. They affect our relationship with God and our relationships with others. And relationships are what we were created for, and where we find Life.

As a happy newlywed couple, Robin and I lived in a small apartment and learned every day. *Learning* is the nice way to put it. One of my first hard lessons as a new husband came in the laboratory of the kitchen. In those early weeks of marriage, I had been loading and emptying the dishwasher. I saw my Dad do it often enough in my family, and I also had plenty of experience with roaches and ants infesting unwashed dishes while living with roommates during and after college. I thought doing the dishes was a great way to help and for me to say *I love you* to my wife. Unfortunately, these were not the messages being received by my wife's heart. The misunderstanding came to light one day while I was sitting on the couch in the living room, just a few feet away from the kitchen, and heard my wife crying. Like any good, new husband-in-training, I got up and asked, "What's wrong, honey?" Her answer floored me: "You don't think I'm a good wife."

> *What?*
>> *You don't think I'm a good wife!*
>
> *When did I say or think that?*
>> *You're always doing the dishes; you don't think I'm capable of keeping things clean. You don't think I'm a good wife.*
>
> *What!? How in the world did we get here?*

I thought I was helping, she was hurting…wait a minute…*where* are we?

Insight into this question and the ability to answer it well requires both *seeing* and *hearing*. Having eyes to see *and* ears to hear leads to a more accurate assessment of your surroundings, of what is going on around you as well as within you, at any given moment.

Understanding all that is going on in any given moment takes skill, and few people have the skill at the moment when they need it most. Way too often in my life, accurate perspective and understanding come several days after the fact, if they ever come at all. I find these belated clues often will shed new light on arguments, hurt feelings, or misunderstood words that landed on my wife like a meteor falling from the sky. How seldom I take into account my motives in the moment. How rarely I attempt to uncover what I am thinking, why or where those feelings and reactions are coming from *before* I let the words fly. Remember, there is always more going on in a moment than meets the eye.

SILLY NEWLYWEDS

Let's go back to my newlywed husband training. What I bumped into that day was historical. It had been there a long time, and it was crafted in me and my wife long before we walked the aisle. Robin's mom had handled the dishes and the dishwasher in her family growing up. Robin looked forward to caring for me and our home as an expression of her love for me. My dad often loaded and unloaded the dishwasher. I saw him modeling a great way to help and lend a hand. I learned, *When I get married, I know one thing I can do to contribute to the household chores.* You might be thinking, *Silly newlyweds*.

But sadly, these silly little interactions in a marriage, compounded daily, with interest accruing weekly, can get two people moving in opposite directions. The accumulative effect of these marital mishaps, when logged on one ledger, would rival the federal deficit. As a counselor, I've seen it hundreds of times. Two adults sit across the table from me, and they get going with personal audits of their spouse's behavior, choices, statements (or lack thereof), and it's time for somebody to pay. After several years of this type of record keeping and accounting, the not-so-newlywed couple truly can't tell you where they are much less how they got there. What one, if not both, *can* tell you is this, *I'm not happy and I want out*. It's another bankrupt marriage.

Having a better ability to see and hear because we accept a greater orientation and larger perspective won't eliminate all the relational riffs caused by miscommunication or unmet expectations, but it will be an effective antibiotic for most. Things that blindside us make for long and painful recoveries; having eyes to see where the danger is coming from gives us at least a fighting chance (if we know how to fight). Living with clarity and understanding is not as much an achievement as it is *surrender*. It's the ability to come out of hiding with my hands up, dropping my preconceived ideas about arranging for life and abandoning self-protection and self-preservation as the means to the end.

When I got married, it was an invitation to surrender and to make a transition from one life to another. It is a transition that will take a lifetime to fully know. I know when it started: June 9, 1990. I also know where I desire for it to end: *Till death do us part*. All the steps in between are what I'm unsure of, and yet I know they must be taken. It's in those steps—the ones taken well and the ones not so well taken—that I have the opportunity to mature and learn to love. Learning what doesn't work and what isn't good is just as valuable as learning what does and is. Knowing I'm a work in progress and surrendering to that reality are the first steps to be taken as a *free man*. As the old saying goes, *It's not so much what you see that gets you in trouble as what you don't see*.

WAS BLIND BUT NOW I SEE

In the Gospel of John, chapter 14, Jesus is preparing to leave the planet and finish the first installment of God's great rescue mission for what was lost. He is about to go to the cross. The chapter opens with Jesus' comforting and encouraging words, "Do not let your hearts be troubled. Trust in God; trust also in me." At the end of chapter 14, Jesus says, "I've got to go but don't worry, it's going to be alright, I'm going to get some things ready for you in the realm that matters most. There is still some work to be done. I am coming back though! But I need to do this so that what you saw me do, <u>you</u> will be able to do."

During this announcement, that no doubt was terribly confusing for the disciples, the apostle Phillip makes a request: "Lord, show us the Father and that will be enough for us." (John 14:8) To this, Jesus replied: "Don't you know me, Phillip, even after I have been among you such a long time?" He follows that with the biggest line of the press conference: "Anyone who has seen me has seen the Father."

What if we could see the whole world and Larger Story as Jesus described it? What if we could know our place in it? How the world really works? Its dimensions and the reality of its objectives (life vs. death)? What if we could know all this *and* possess the wisdom and ability to go beyond mere survival and really *thrive?* I don't believe that in this life our ability to see fully will be accomplished, that *all* the "blinders" will be removed.. We cannot achieve any clarity on our own, but the degree of clarity we *can* have in this life comes from the Father through *training, initiation* and *validation* that He alone can provide. And I believe this clarity is supposed to be the norm, rather than the rare exception.

That is why we need the Holy Spirit (as described in John 14-17) to guide, teach, comfort and counsel us. There is a way to "see" that only God offers—a vision with origins deeper than a physical *20/20*. Because we are spiritual (eternal) beings on a physical journey, we will need *spiritual eyes* in order to make the journey well. We must find our true ability to see so we can see with the *eyes of the heart*. It is through these eyes that we will be able to see more fully all that we are, all that is around us, and more of the One who loves us most and offers us Life. C.S. Lewis once wrote, *I believe in Christianity as I believe that the sun has risen. Not only because I see it, but also because by it I see everything else.*

Jesus often accompanied an important teaching about the Kingdom with the statement, "For those who have eyes to see let him see, or ears to hear, let him hear…" Now this begs the question: *Are the people in the audience missing eyes and ears?* You know as I do, those folks are equipped. The real question is *are they engaged*? Jesus is inviting them to engage their eyes to see and their ears to hear *in a certain way* and from a certain orientation so they can come to correct conclusions and significant understandings. Such engagement will change their life forever.

SEEING WELL

I got glasses at 45, and after my last eye exam my ophthalmologist turned to me and said, "Welcome to middle age!" My wife and I proceeded to spend an hour at the frame counter, choosing from the hundreds of frames; we settled on some cool Nautica frames to hold my progressive lenses. "Progressive" is the new expression for bifocals. Instead of the delineating line I saw in my grandparents' glasses, these lenses "progress" without any evidence—allowing me to see the letters I'm typing and, at the same time, look up at my wife across the table without seeing her as if I just finished swimming forty laps without goggles in a highly chlorinated pool. I'm able to see what I need to see at both distances. One of my objectives for this book is to invite you to see clearly both the physical *and* spiritual objects that need attention. And then, invite you to interpret them correctly so you might respond and engage your heart in that moment.

In the brilliant film, *The Matrix,* the main character Neo, aka Thomas Anderson, knows there is something more in the world and to the world. After he takes the red pill during his meeting with Morpheus (the one who knows the truth and is offering it), Neo is born again into the reality in which he has already, unknowingly, been living. He is transformed and will be *further* transformed. The scene in which Neo takes the step of faith and moves toward the truth is a turning point that sets fantastic things into motion. Once freed from the Matrix, Neo must go through an adapting period; it is here he receives alterations, a reorientation as well as a recovery, to be able to live in the light of what is really real. The initial scene, just after Neo's being born again, opens with him on a recovery table resting, healing and adapting. As he opens his eyes, he senses something tingling through his body. He focuses his eyes and sees his body pierced with dozens of acupuncture-like needles, wired to a strange device, and he overhears his rescuers working on him and around him.

> **Dozer:** He needs a lot of work.
> **Morpheus:** I know. (Dozer and Morpheus are standing over and operating on Neo.)
> **Neo:** (Neo wakes up and asks groggily.) What are you doing?
> **Morpheus:** Your muscles have atrophied. We're rebuilding them. (Fluorescent light sticks burn unnaturally bright.)
> **Neo:** Why do my eyes hurt?
> **Morpheus:** You've never used them before. (Morpheus takes his sunglasses off and puts them on Neo. Neo lays back.)
> **Morpheus:** Rest, Neo. The answers are coming.

The answers are coming...I love that! The *seeing* that Morpheus is speaking of is not simply seeing 20/20 with our physical eyes. There are millions of us who can see landscapes, buildings, ball games or our children playing. That vision is not what Morpheus, nor I, am alluding to.

While on earth, Jesus healed blind people of their physical condition so that they might have *real* sight, *spiritual sight*. He wanted them to see that He was God and take Him up on the offer to be truly healed—healed all the way to their core. This is healing and transformation at the level of the heart.

Again and again we are invited to see the elements and environments around us. Even more than that, we are invited to see the elements and environments *within us*, both in our story and the Larger Story, which our story is encompassed within. The scriptures warn us that if we miss these things then we will miss Life.

It is in being born again of the spiritual kind that a person begins the journey of real Life (John 3). This not only lets us see what we can't do for ourselves, but even more so, it allows us to see the search and rescue team (The Holy Trinity) in the forest, standing right next to us. In becoming spiritually awakened and spiritually aware, we are both oriented *and* equipped to discover and recover the most important thing...Life. This is what we desperately desire and what we were made to have and know. Friends, it is *Life* that has been lost and it is *Life* that will be rescued, recovered and restored. When we look and listen more deeply into the Two Realms in which we live, we will truly find Life and more of it.

CHAPTER 5

TWO REALMS AND THE REALM THAT MATTERS MOST

Unfortunately, no one can be told what the Matrix is.
You have to see it for yourself.

Morpheus, *The Matrix*

God did not create Adam as a spirit and place it inside a body.
Rather, He first created a body, and then breathed into it a spirit.

Randy Alcorn, *Heaven*

M any great stories attempt to bridge the gap between two realms. Some of these stories use time travel to bridge the gaps. The hero launches either into the past to set things right or into the future in order to prevent something catastrophic from happening. There are still other stories in which the two realms are bridged when the characters step from one realm into *the other*. When we take a deeper look at these stories of other worlds, we will find some essential ingredients for our own orientation and search for Life.

The Chronicles of Narnia, *The Wonderful Wizard of Oz*, and *The Matrix* are fiction, yet they give us glimpses of where *we* really are and offer clues that will take us in the right direction. *The Chronicles of Narnia,* over the course of several books, follows the adventures of seemingly normal English children, who find themselves transported into a Grand Story in a world quite unlike their own. A game of hide-and-seek on a rainy day transports four siblings into a wintry world that must be freed from an evil witch.

In one adventure, the children are magically pulled from their train ride back into the land they once had freed from captivity. Once again they are needed. Each time, the inhabitants of Narnia seem to have been waiting for the visitors to enter, believing these simple children are the ones who have been chosen to bring them help and rescue them from the oppressive evil that stalks their land.

In the classic story, *The Wonderful Wizard of Oz*, we are swept up (quite literally) into the drama of a young girl who will learn, through a strange and wonderful journey, that there is no place like home. Lastly, with a modern twist on these *other realm* adventures, is *The Matrix*. Thomas Anderson is made to see and hear all that is really going on around him when he is awakened to the stark reality of his true existence. He goes through such a conversion that his core identity is altered. Thomas Anderson is and becomes Neo. He is reborn, renamed and then reoriented into his true self and into a much larger story—a story he somehow knew existed all along, but one he wasn't sure how to enter.

These stories are our stories.

A SIXTH SENSE

When I was six years old, my family lived in Southern California. It was a great place to be a young boy. We would often take family members who visited us to the different attractions and sites. My absolute favorite was Disneyland. To a six-year-old, Disneyland is a continent. The walks from Tomorrowland to Fantasyland to Frontierland seemed to take hours, but, oh, they were worth it. What an incredible place. We had a map of the park that, when fully unfolded, took both my brother and I to hold it up. Days before we would arrive at the Disneyland park, we would get out the map and put it on the living room floor, plotting and planning for the day that we would step into a larger world and the adventure that awaited us.

Young hearts often have an ability to live in an expanded universe.

Adults will call it pretend or imagination. But if you ask any boy or girl what they've been up to on a given afternoon, they will tell you as if they were delivering the six o'clock news, *I went to Mars, had to fight some bad guys and just got back,* or *I rescued an injured horse and nursed him back to health.* A young heart of four or five, 10 or 11, *knows* there is more to the world than meets the eye and it affects that tender heart deeply. Children are able to dream and imagine freely in an un-*adult*-erated way.

Often children also have a sixth sense that allows them to feel when things are in place and when they aren't, even when adults might think they are effectively hiding the truth. Many a separated or divorcing parent will declare, *The kids seem to be holding up really well. I'm amazed at how resilient they are and how well they seem to be adjusting.* BULLETIN JUST IN: *They are not doing well. Now you're the one pretending.* Children grasp, see and understand so much more than we give them credit for, and they are affected by the choices of others in deep ways. That's how so many of us learned how to hide behind a fig leaf. We were taught.

Many children feel more deeply and want far more out of life than most adults do. Why do we allow ourselves to leave this youthful place of deep heart and desire and get so lost in logic, reason, pessimism and doubt? A good friend of mine announced to me recently, "I'm a skeptic; that's just the way I am." A more honest statement might be, *I've learned to be skeptical.* I believe the tender hearts of our childhood get lost because of the pain we all suffer as we journey into adulthood. When you look at a life and its history, there is a collection of sad, difficult, hurtful stories each individual heart has endured. People leave us. Families break up. We are rejected, we fail, and expectations go unmet. Terrible things are said and done to us and eventually by us. It all contributes to the great lostness—an accumulating road weariness that takes our youthful hopes and replaces them with the scratches and dents of life.

Unfortunately, our sixth sense of seeing and hearing with our hearts fades and we "grow up." And yet Jesus said, "I tell you the truth, unless you change and become like little children, you will never enter the kingdom of heaven. Therefore, whoever humbles himself like this child is the greatest in the Kingdom of Heaven." (Matthew 18:3-4)

If we are ever going to recover and find *Life*—or find it again—we must return to that Larger Story we believed in once upon a time. There *is* a far more glorious and far more dangerous story all around us. We must regain our childlike hearts if we are to see, hear and engage in it once again.

CRASHING IN

Life is big, and being alive consists of much more than just breathing and eating. Finding and having a relationship with God is the crucial element *in Life* and *being alive*. C. S. Lewis once wrote, "God is the **fuel** that the human machine was designed to run on" (emphasis added). We will not run on anything else. Like so many things in life, the ability—the skill—of seeing and hearing from our hearts doesn't come naturally. We need training. Remember what I said about "first times"? They often don't go well, and yet that is how we learn and how we are trained up. Unfortunately, we all struggle with the deep feeling that failure is *fatal*. And so we distance ourselves from what didn't go so well, or we don't even try in the first place so we can avoid the possibility of failure. We do all we can to arrange for less hurt, believing that a good life is a life without failure. But as the saying goes, *Nothing ventured, nothing gained.* Arranging our own lives in this way will never bring the returns we long for because nothing was invested in the first place. The good news is that God is ready, able and *longing* to be involved and engaged with growing us. He longs to train us up into the people we desire to be and into so much more than what we are right now. What if we could participate in this glorious training and discover along the way the benefit of real, true Life? Could we? Would we?

As we jump into our training, we need a greater understanding of what we're getting ourselves into. Or more accurately, *what we are already into* but haven't yet been awakened to. Training has been taking place. The question is...who are your coaches and teachers really?

Where we find ourselves is no less than the midst of a major intersection. It is the intersection of Two Realms that collide. They overlay in and on each other gloriously, intentionally, quietly and loudly all at the same time. Again and again the greater realm, the Larger Story, is crashing in and on the smaller one. There is an ongoing collision that we are not often aware of. Having your eyes and ears opened to truly seeing and hearing the Two Realms we live in will make all the difference in our search for Life.

The Life being offered to us in and through the Bible must be the life we most desperately want and need—and it is ***big***. From Genesis through Revelation, God reveals all its dimensions. To comprehend it fully is impossible for you and me at this time. We are, however, given glimpses again and again, tiny tastes like grocery store samples, of the goodness in store for us at end of our journey. This Life is so big that all we can really do is dig our fingers in and hold tight to the real estate right in front of us. We can only experience one step at a time, but we can look ahead and know there is much more to come. As we hold tight to each piece of this new Life, we are invited to look around, process, ponder and enjoy it. This is part of the training. Then, when the experience is over, we are called to move on, to grasp yet another part of this new Life in the Larger Story and continue our education by God.

If we don't get up and move, it is okay—because the Story does. We can try to stay put, keep all the variables of a moment under our control and in our grasp, but it cannot be done. Our journey *in Life* and *for Life* is much too big for that and demands more of us than most of us have ever offered. As I mentioned earlier, there are so many firsts. How can we possibly control them or even prepare for all of them? What we *can* do is engage with a well-trained eye and keen sense of hearing and a shrewd, expectant and hopeful heart.

Engaging and living in the awareness and understanding of the great intersection of the Two Realms will serve us well in our search and in God's search for us.

SOONER OR LATER

Over the centuries, "discoveries" have been made. We even have a TV channel dedicated to them, *The Discovery Channel.* The concept doesn't have anything to do with us creating, but rather observing. All the great explorers, scientists, philosophers and theologians discovered what was already existing. When large discoveries are made, the results are changed lives. Whether it is a vaccine or a new passageway, whether intentional or accidental, all of our lives are impacted by discoveries. What becomes new to us might actually be ancient or have been available for quite some time. Sooner or later, we all will "discover" that we live in Two Realms. Why not sooner? It will change your life and make all the difference.

The Two Realms, *spiritual* and *physical,* are not separate as we might believe. They are not two separate places of geography like Los Angeles and New York, and they don't exist as simply one within the other. They are woven or meshed together; there is a deep and unbreakable connection between the two.

At the end of *The Last Battle*, the last book in *The Chronicles of Narnia,* C. S. Lewis attempts to provide a tangible description to this connection between the Two Realms. Much has taken place in the six previous stories Lewis created, and the journey is finally coming to its end. However, those on the journey are uncertain how or when the end will come:

> *It was the Unicorn who summed up what everyone was feeling. He stamped his right forehoof on the ground and neighed, and then cried: I have come home at last! This is my real country! I belong here. This is the land I have been looking for all my life, though I never knew it 'til now. The reason why*

we loved the old Narnia is that it sometimes looked a little like this. Bre-hee-hee! Come further up, come further in!

He shook his mane and sprang forward into a great gallop. ...Everyone else began to run, and they found to their astonishment, that they could keep up with him...The air flew in their faces as if they were driving fast in a car without a windscreen. The country flew past as if they were seeing it from the windows of an express train. Faster and faster they raced, but no one got hot or tired or out of breath. (emphasis added)

There are times when the Spiritual Realm shows itself and reveals its presence. As I alluded to earlier, these times can be more of a *crashing* in than a gentle unveiling. But much of the time the Spiritual Realm is subtle, a ceaseless and quite often overlooked presence in our lives. And yet it is critical to see, hear and live well within the reality of the Spiritual Realm because it actually *governs* the physical realm. Let's explore three places in the scriptures that speak of the presence, influence and governance of the spiritual over the physical:

Then God said, "Let us make man in our image, in our likeness, and let them rule..." So God created man in his own image, in the image of God he created him; male and female he created them. ...God saw all that he had made and it was very good. ...The Lord God formed the man from the dust of the ground and breathed into his nostrils the breath of life, and the man became a living being.

Genesis 1:26 and 2:7

In the beginning was the Word, and the Word was with God, and the Word was God. He was with God in the beginning. Through him (Jesus-The Word) all things were made; without him nothing was made. ...He was in the world, and though the world was made through him, the world did not recognize him. He came to which was his own, but his own did not receive him. Yet to all who received him, to those who believed in his name, he gave the right to become children of God—children born not of natural descent (physical), nor human decision or a husband's will, but born of God.

John 1:1-3, 10-13 (emphasis added)

He (Christ) is the image of the invisible God, the firstborn over all creation. For by him all things were created: things in heaven and on earth, visible and invisible, whether thrones or powers or rulers or authorities; all things were created by him and for him. He is before all things, and in him all things hold together.

Colossians 1:15-17

The Spiritual Realm is constantly present, forever at work, active and affecting life. This *is* the Larger Story of which each individual's personal story is a part. Yet, for far too many people, the Realm that matters most goes unnoticed. You've heard the expression, *He can't see the forest for the trees.* It takes a new depth of perception to see things as they are in the Spiritual Realm, and it takes training in order to stay oriented to see the world this way. We have to *want to see* this other world all around us. And, in order to see, we have to believe it exists.

PIVOTAL PLAYS

The Spiritual Realm's presence within the physical realm is in some ways like a pivotal play during the big game—that one shot, that one play, seems weightier than all the rest. In reality, it is just one play. But because of where it is in the game and all that has taken place up to that point, it simply means more. These moments take on a sense of destiny in our hearts and minds and seem to echo long after the actual moment has passed. It is in these collision moments, and often just afterwards, that—in hindsight—the Spiritual Realm not only makes its presence known but most often leaves its mark.

For example, creation itself (the actual days of creation in the first chapter of Genesis) is the first time that the Spiritual Realm makes its mark on our physical world. The Trinity intentionally crafts, creates and speaks into existence our physical realm and all its characteristics: water and sky, land with mountains and plains, vegetation and animals. And creation was all declared *"good"* by the triune Artists who made it.

Can you imagine the physics and chemistry of those moments of creation? How were the molecules arranged to make an elephant, hummingbird or the atmosphere? Or men and women for that matter? We are still discovering what happened at this great and glorious inaugural crashing in. Our current direction in life is still connected to this history, this origin of a first movement called creation. As John Eldredge writes in his book *Epic*, "If you learned about Eden in Sunday school with flannel graphs…you've missed something."

Creation, though it is the first and ever so large *initial* moment, is not the only example, nor is it even the most eventful occasion where the Spiritual Realm invaded space and time as we know it. Yes, it certainly got the ball rolling. Later, the Author of the story actually steps into our physical realm—in the flesh—to play the most significant role ever… *Himself.* The Creator actually steps into the creation as a created being. That invading moment changed everything—not only for everything that followed, but also, amazingly, for everything that proceeded.

The awesome and incredible truth for us is that *we* can experience these moments as well, times that both change our futures and redeem our pasts.

Many of these invasions and encounters are vividly recorded within the earthly story where we live. These events are offered to us in Scripture that we might find our bearings as we live within these Two Realms and that we might understand the elements and environments surrounding us. Spiritually invading events, though some of them took place long ago, still speak to the order of things and forecast things to come.

Here is a review of just a few of these headline-making invasions, encounters and crashes:

> ***The Creation*** (Genesis 1): Humanity is created in God's glorious image to be His friends and to know intimacy and connectedness with Him. I love what Eldredge says, "We were created to be God's intimate allies and lovers."
>
> ***The Fall*** (Genesis 3): We fall, farther than we'll ever really know. And our spiritual fall reverberates far into the physical world. Death enters the story.
>
> ***The Flood*** (Genesis 6): God declares that the thoughts and attitudes of humanity's heart are always evil. He starts over, quite literally washing the earth clean.
>
> ***The Ten Commandments*** (Exodus 19 and 20): God speaks face to face with Moses on Mt. Sinai and gives him the law, which will serve as the statutes for Life and ultimately point us back to our desperate need for Him.
>
> ***The Ark of the Covenant, the Tabernacle, and the Holy of Holies*** (Exodus 25, 26 and 27): God comes to dwell *among* His people, foreshadowing a greater day when His presence will dwell *within* them.
>
> ***The Battles of Israel*** (Most of the Old Testament books involving the kings and the prophets): God fights for His people and goes to battle to establish them while revealing Himself, through them, to other nations.
>
> ***The Prophets*** (Isaiah, Jeremiah, Ezekiel): God reveals His heart

for His people through a faithful few and declares that He is still moving on behalf of His people.

The Life of Christ (Matthew, Mark, Luke, and John): The Gospels, or the Good News, all bear witness to the ultimate invasion of the Spiritual Realm—"Emmanuel, God with us and among us! The Messiah is here!" The Creator of heaven and earth has entered the creation and is in our midst. He is in the physical realm!

Christ's Crucifixion, Resurrection and Ascension (the Gospels): What an event! What a universe-shaking moment as the Two Realms align and usher in the next chapter in our story. How glorious the spiritual work, performed on a physical stage on our behalf, that brought us life and freedom! Here we witness the final stages of God's great rescue and recovery mission!

Pentecost and the Permanence of the Holy Spirit's Presence (forecast by Jesus in the Gospel of John, chapters 14-17, arriving in Acts 2): The Spirit of God has now come to live inside us, walk with us and equip us for life and freedom. Are you kidding me? We are now truly established as the sons and daughters of God!

The Early Church (the whole book of Acts): This is the beginning of this movement called Christianity—a collection and assembly of Christ-followers living under the New Covenant established between God and us, and the launching of God's people living spiritually focused in a turbulent world.

The Second Coming (Revelation): This event marks the end of the Great War for the hearts of men and women. The final battle to end all battles takes place when Jesus comes back on a white horse, His robe dipped in blood and leading angel armies (Revelation 19), to bring the final chapter of our story here to a close and to open the beginning of the next story, the one that will never end.

These are just a few examples of the collision of the Spiritual Realm into the physical realm. The whole Bible is God's story regarding His presence, plan, movement, intentions and provision for the Life He lives and which He has invited us into. It tells how we broke our relationship with Him and recounts the great recovery of that which we were made for: intimacy, oneness and connectedness with Him!

HISTORICAL EVENTS

Do you see it? Do you hear it? Do you feel the Spiritual Realm connecting and crashing in? It has not only been here in the past, it is here now! What a Large Story God is unfolding, and this list of Spiritual Realm invasions is in no way exhaustive. I've only scratched the surface of all God has done up to this point. We would be silly to think that scriptures could or would contain all the invasions there have ever been of the Spiritual Realm into our everyday world. These collisions produce historical events, which were written down and preserved in the scriptures to reveal God's heart to us. But we can't stop there and simply place these events in the simple category of "the past." No, they are still very much present, affecting and infecting the life we are now being invited to live.

The people in biblical times were far more like us than not. People went to work. Kids played, argued and fought. Groceries were needed, markets existed, and everybody seemed to share that age-old feeling of never having quite enough. Times were good for some and rough for most. Yes, God gets ahold of their hearts, and exceptional things happen. They even become better men and women for the experience, but their stories are offered to us *as an invitation into that same exceptional story.* What happened to those people "back then" is spread before us as an *example* of what Life with God, from God and in God looks like. Why? If we don't see it, hear it and know it when it is right in front of us, we will misunderstand, mishandle or misinterpret our own lives. If we miss the message of these personal-level, real-life experiences with the major intersections of the Two Realms, then we will continue to live lost. That is the way I lived most of my Christian life until I finally woke up to this message. Now, thank God, my spiritual coma is over and my great adventure has begun.

GIVING WAY

When the Spiritual Realm makes its presence known, the result is *change*. When the Spiritual Realm takes hold of a person's heart, the change is so eventful and significant it might become permanent. Even *irreversible*. Those preceding us who discovered the Spiritual Realm wrote about their encounters to help and encourage others along their journeys. These forerunners to us—common folk in their day—have a universal declaration, **It's true**. *Look for it! Listen for it! I'm another life forever altered and changed by the One who cared enough to search for me and find me, rescue me and restore me. Keep awake. Be alert. Do you see it, do you hear it? Don't give up. He is coming!*

Only when we leave behind living exclusively in the lesser physical realm and step *further up and further in* to the greater Spiritual Realm will our search for Life be satisfied. It's here that it will also intensify. Jesus said, as recorded in Matthew 6:19-21: "Do not store up for yourselves treasures on earth where moth and rust destroy and thieves break in and steal. But store up for yourselves treasures in heaven, where moth and rust do not destroy, and where thieves do not break in and steal. For where your treasure is, there your heart will be also."

There seems to be a "safer deposit box" in life, which is not a physical one but rather a spiritual one. Scripture stresses this perspective and orientation again and again:

In Matthew 16:24-28 Jesus speaks about the Spiritual Realm and its significance to the journey we're on: *What good is it if a man gains the whole world* (physical realm), *yet forfeits his soul* (Spiritual Realm)?

The Apostle Paul writes to the church (Colossians 3:3-1):
Since, then, you have been raised with Christ, set your hearts on things above (Spiritual Realm), *where Christ is seated at the right hand of God. Set your minds on things above, not on earthly things* (Physical Realm). *For you died, and your life is now hidden with Christ in God.*

Ephesians 6:10-18 invites us to the battle taking place all around us: *For our struggle is not against flesh and blood* (Physical Realm), *but against the rulers, against the authorities, against the powers of this dark world and against the <u>spiritual forces</u> of evil in the <u>heavenly realms</u>* (Spiritual Realm). (emphasis added)

Now, for certain, the Bible also talks about physical realm issues: marriage, parenting, friendship, money, work, love, kindness, leading, helping, serving and many others. However, it always speaks to these issues from a Spiritual Realm perspective.

Here is how the interconnected but ongoing, fluent and moving relationship between the Two Realms works. The greater is the *Spiritual Realm,* and that realm shows us how to interpret, understand and live in the lesser realm, the *physical realm.* What a huge impact the greater has when engaged, heard, seen—and applied—to the lesser.

I have to confess, for most of my life I looked at the Spiritual Realm as somewhere far, far away. It was around the bend of the next galaxy, somewhere just beyond the rainbow or at some safe distance from what we could humanly measure. It seemed invisible and therefore out of touch and out of reach. The scriptures, though, don't speak of the

Spiritual Realm as somewhere else, far beyond the horizon, way up in the sky, over the rainbow or in galaxies far, far away. They teach that it is here with us, right in front of us, and even within you and me (Luke 17:21). The Bible offers again and again a topographical map of this most important realm with aerial views, crucial coordinates and helpful directions—inviting us to see, hear and live...*well*. Scripture invites us to see from a new and specific perspective and then be equipped to live and walk in light of that perspective. This frame of reference doesn't replace one realm with the other, but actually meshes the two realms.

God offers us lenses formulated, crafted and created from Spiritual Realm glass. It's a bit like the old 3D glasses. Have you ever seen a film made in 3D without these special glasses? It's not all that enjoyable. Sure, you can make out what is going on, but the picture is not clear. Seeing with Spiritual Realm eyes not only makes the world around you clearer, but your whole life takes shape and has depth—it *comes at you in 3D.* You suddenly feel a part of the story because you are. Our sight doesn't stop there. It can and will evolve to a more sophisticated perspective that might be likened to the night vision used by the U. S. Army Special Forces. It brings into clarity what was fuzzy or hazy and brings into light those things which would prefer to remain in the dark.

THE LESSER REALM

For though we live in the world, we do not wage war as the world does.
2 Corinthians 10:3

Do not love the world or anything in the world.
1 John 2:15a

The Bible speaks often of the subjects and themes of life in the physical realm. These issues are ones that we want and need to handle correctly. I'll bet you've done what I've done with the Bible. When I've had a problem in a specific physical realm area, such as marriage or parenting, I turn to the concordance at the back of the Bible to get help. I look for a word that will lead me to the page and verse that's supposed to help me solve a problem. *Now where are those verses on husbands and wives? ...children?... finances?*

The scriptures are a great resource for the day-to-day problems we face in our lives. Within them is much wisdom for practical issues pertaining to money, marriage, relationships, conflict, parenting, work, communication, forgiveness and friendship, to name just a few.

> ***Money*** (Hebrews 13:5): *Keep your lives free from the love of money and be content with what you have, because God has said, "Never will I leave you; never will I forsake you."*
>
> ***Marriage*** (Ephesians 5:25-27): *Husbands, love your wives, just as Christ loved the church and gave himself up for her to make her holy, cleansing her by the washing with water through the word, and to present her to himself as a radiant church, without stain or wrinkle or any other blemish, but holy and blameless.*
>
> ***Conflict*** (Ephesians 4:1-3 NASV): *...walk in a manner worthy of the calling with which you have been called, with all humility and gentleness, with patience, showing tolerance for one another in love, being diligent to preserve the unity of the Spirit in the bond of peace.*
>
> ***Work*** (Colossians 3:17): *And whatever you do, whether in word or deed, do it all in the name of the Lord Jesus, giving thanks to God the Father through him.*
>
> ***Forgiveness*** (Mark 11:25): *And when you stand praying, if you hold anything against anyone, forgive him, so that your Father in heaven may forgive you your sins.*

These passages are only a sample of the Bible's wisdom for life in the physical realm. If we miss the realities and forces present in the Spiritual Realm (the realm that is *responsible* for and influential on life of the physical realm), the stories of the people in the Bible won't make sense or will be misunderstood and misplaced. This only adds to our propensity to be lost. When we live lost, we will also misinterpret the hearts and lives of others—projecting our experiences on them, rather than allowing their experiences to inform and wisely guide us. As a recovering lost person, I can tell you from experience that *lost people give bad directions.* I know, not only because of the directions I've been given at times in my life, but mostly by the wrong directions I was giving others. I am more than grateful that this is becoming less and less true as God gives me more and more orientation.

BUCKETS AND WELLS

The "for Dummies" series of books is popular and prevalent: *Computers for Dummies, Stocks for Dummies, Spanish for Dummies, Cooking for Dummies, and on and on.* At times I've treated the Bible as if it were *Life for Dummies.* So often I have turned to the Bible hoping that somehow a magical answer would pop out of the text and solve all my problems. After I pulled my concordance trick and snagged a few passages, I believed that if I read the right verses over and over, even memorized them, they would act like some spiritual performance-enhancing steroid (only legal). My performance in life would improve, and I'd finally be an achiever, a winner, a gold-medal Christian. (I'm still waiting for the gold medals that my wife, kids and friends are going to place around my neck for all the good biblical knowledge I possess and sanctimonious advice I've given them. Well, not really...not anymore.)

For far too long, I treated my life like one ginormous problem to be solved, rather than a journey to be taken. What I was betting on to bring me Real Life was a deeper and more thorough knowledge of the Bible. Somehow that plan just wasn't working for me, and I noticed that it wasn't working for many of those around me either. We've all known "professional Christians" (pastors, priests, missionaries, ministers and church leaders) who know the Bible backward and forward, and yet their lives seem to be moving only backward. A crash was or is bound to happen. It is a great travesty when a Christian leader promotes the abundant life of God and yet completely misses out on experiencing it in his or her own life. I know, because I was one of them. My ministry was growing and thriving, but inside I was not experiencing real Life.

When we live our lives as a problem to be solved with rules and formulas, performances and evaluations, we end up subjecting others' hearts to the system of judgments and decrees that we place on ourselves. Biblical knowledge is a good thing, but do you remember the Pharisees of Jesus' day? They were experts in the Law, the Torah, the traditions, obedience and the observance of the Holy Days (Passover, the Sabbath, etc.) Yet they were so far from the Life Jesus offered. How do I know? The Pharisees, the religious leaders of that day, were the ones who made sure Jesus was executed by being placed on a cross. They couldn't make the leap from being in the center of their own small stories to a wonderful supporting role in the larger one.

If our lives are just problems to be solved, then we have put ourselves in the center of a story that is too small for us. We were created for a much larger role. If you have been in this dilemma, I invite you to abandon the epidemic belief that you just need to "shape up" and "do better." Better performance alone won't solve everything and set you on the right course. This approach leads to chronic spiritual breakdown. The only treatment for such a condition is to abandon this perspective and orientation and trade it in for something better. By doing so, your Life will get larger very quickly. You can never produce the Life you long for or the Life you were meant for, nor can you offer it to anyone else, when your approach is simply to do better, try harder, pull yourself up by your bootstraps and fix it yourself. You can't do it by committing to sin less or be more holy. It just isn't within your ability to do so. These religious "New Year's resolutions" end up on the list of *things I've gotta get done someday*. If we could fix ourselves, we would be the doctor not the patient...we would be the well and not the bucket. We're not the source of Life, but we can be its glorious container.

The Bible is not a manual for problem solving, nor is Christianity a program to follow. Christianity and the Scriptures are invitations into the Larger Story (which we are actually already in) and a promotion to the place that is our part to play—a large and significant one. We are the buckets, and God is the well. Jesus says, *I will give you water and you will thirst no more.* (John 4:14)

LIVING IN THE GLORIOUS COLLISION

Being a Christian might mean many things, but one thing it must mean is that we follow after the Life of Christ and aspire to be like him—for indeed his followers are becoming *like him*. Because of this we must understand how the Two Realms exist and intersect, how they collide, and how to recognize when and where they do. We can actually keep our eyes, ears and hearts open to what God is up to in order to play our role in the Larger Story He is telling. The simplest and most profound answer to the question *What is God up to?* is, He is **restoring** it all.

The progression of the book of Romans tells us much about this work of *restoration*. God removes our sin so He can *restore* our love relationship with Him. God places His Spirit within us to help us on our journey of becoming what we were meant to be—*His image bearers,* His partners, participating in Life and for Life. The Father shows us that we are being grown up into the likeness of nothing less than Jesus Christ Himself (Christ *in me* and Christ *is me* Colossians 1:27, Colossians 3:3, Romans 6:11). We will return to this idea in some depth later. For now, I imagine that for some of you this is good news and for others it could be bothersome. Your image of Christ makes all the difference. If we have wrongly assessed Him as the Pharisees did (and many do today; I have been guilty of it myself), your membership to lostness will be renewed again and again, for you do not yet know your Rescuer.

The image we were created in is the image that the Father is restoring us to. The churchy word for this is *sanctification*. This is the journey He will take us on to recover His glorious image in us. Sanctification actually means "to be set apart." Not in a "flaw that needs to be fixed" nor in a "didn't pass inspection, make him try again" kind of way, but more as a specially chosen and committed way. The Father says, *I choose him. He's got the right stuff. I ought to know, I made him.* You are chosen *by* Love *for* love, and He is committed to the training. The One who knows what you are and can become will do all it takes to see you through.

This collision of realms is where we are invited to live. It's messy, it's confusing, it's hard, and it's constantly moving and shifting—for now. But frankly this is mostly because it is happening far too often *without* our engagement and participation. When storms hit or the weather of life turns, it's one thing to be a passenger and yet quite another to be a part of the crew. When we choose to get involved and engaged, a whole new world opens up. The Scriptures reveal to us how these realms work and warn us to have our wits about us as we move and live in them. Finding our bearings and plotting coordinates and directions from the Author of Life makes for a whole new adventure. And joining this adventure is the first significant move on our part in the rescue and recovery of our Life. The Father lets down the rope, and life changes when we grab hold.

There are Two Realms, and one matters much more than the other. The Spiritual Realm holds the perspective we need in order to see our lives as they truly are. And there are grave consequences if we don't see it or choose to stay blind to the reality we are living in. Once we see, we are invited to more. As our eyes adjust, we continue to become oriented to things we must know from the Spiritual Realm perspective. In the Spiritual Realm, two kingdoms exist. Seeing them, hearing them and orienting our lives around them will explain a great deal as to why life is so hard. This orientation will help us look back upon the journey to this point and realize it has all been worth the struggle, if only for all the steps having led you to this point. As C.S. Lewis said, "I believe in Christianity as I believe that the sun has risen. Not only because I see it, but because by it I see everything else."

CHAPTER 6

TWO KINGDOMS

Obsessed by a fairy tale we spend our lives searching for a magic door and a lost Kingdom of peace.

Eugene O'Neill

But seek first His Kingdom…

Matthew 6:33

After [Christ's] suffering, he showed himself to these men and gave many convincing proofs that he was alive. He appeared to them over a period of forty days and spoke about the Kingdom of God.

Acts 1:3

*O*nce upon a time there was a great Kingdom that stretched far and wide. Everyone living within this Kingdom enjoyed his or her place in it. Everyone and everything that lived within its borders knew Life as it was intended and it was good...very good. It was not always this way. Many of the older men and women of this wonderful Kingdom told stories of its foundation, its great loss, and most importantly its great recovery. They had heard the story from their fathers, who had heard from their father's father.

Now no great Kingdom is without a King. Reigning and ruling over this Kingdom was a Great King who loved well, laughed often and had compassion for those under his domain. Everyone and everything under his protection and provision prospered. All that the King crafted was glorious and made with kindness and care. His Kingdom was created as a unique expression of his goodness, bearing his fingerprints and marked by his royal monogram, his initials not only as King but as craftsman, creator and provider. What all enjoyed the most about Life within the

Kingdom was the deep satisfying sense that they were valued, and each person felt as if he or she were the best of friends with the Great King. They could not help but speak of their encounters with their King, the wonderful things he would share and the special gifts he would bring.

Does this little tale sound too good to be true? Like a children's book or the beginning of some classic fable...so sweet, so nice. A story reserved for bedtime tuck-in or preschool rest time. Have you ever observed children and adults when a story like this is shared? Most of those listening tilt their heads, smile and even nod thinking, *Awww, That sounds so nice. How wonderful.* And yet for a select few, all they can think is *Yeah right, fairy tales.*

This is where I—and so many others—got off course. Dismissing these stories as pretend prolongs our Great Search. By doing so, we misunderstand or mishandle our lives. My friend, author Gary Barkalow, often says, "*The story you believe you are living in will determine how you live.*"

In his book *Epic*, author John Eldredge writes:

> *Life, for most of us, feels like a movie we've arrived to forty minutes late. Sure, good things happen, sometimes beautiful things. But tragic things happen, too. What does it mean? We find ourselves in the middle of a story that is sometimes wonderful, sometimes awful, usually a confusing mixture of both, and we haven't a clue how to make sense of it all. No wonder we keep losing heart. We need to know the rest of the story. For when we were born, we were born into the midst of a great story begun before the dawn of time.*
>
> *A story of adventure, of risk and loss, heroism...and betrayal. A story where good is warring against evil, danger lurks around every corner, and glorious deeds wait to be done. Think of all those stories you've ever loved—there's a reason they stirred your heart. They've been trying to tell you about the true Epic ever*

since you were young. There is a Larger Story. And you have a crucial role to play.

Once upon a time is not just the opening to a Disney movie or one of the Brothers Grimm tales. It is the beginning, the *accurate beginning,* of the Larger Story in which we live. *In the beginning,* a sovereign Holy Trinity expanded and created the domain in which they would reign and rule. Here love and goodness would be the greatest expression of their hearts and character. All they made and all they did was declared good. The Scriptures record that after making man in *their* image, God then declared man *was very good.*

I must admit I have fallen victim to forgetting this core fundamental. As a result, I have settled for a much smaller story. Remember, if the story I am living in revolves around me and I am the main character in it, then I am living in way too small of a story. So let's live large—for this is the Life we were created to live.

FROM TWO REALMS TO TWO KINGDOMS

The LORD is gracious and compassionate; slow to anger and rich in love. The LORD is good to all; he has compassion on all he has made. All you have made will praise you, O LORD; your saints will extol you. They will tell of the glory of your Kingdom and speak of your might, so that all men may know of your mighty acts and the glorious splendor of your Kingdom. Your Kingdom is an everlasting Kingdom, and your dominion endures through all generations.

Psalm 145: 8-13a

Most of us are not conscious of the reality of our own breathing as we take in the oxygen to be processed by our lungs and supplied to the rest of our organs. Neither are we likely to announce that our heart is beating and acknowledge that it is pumping the flow of blood throughout our body, enabling life to be sustained. Seldom are we fully aware that we are seeing or hearing. Yet we use these senses constantly throughout our day, without thinking about how they are performing their functions.

When we do notice our breathing, or that our heart is beating or that we are seeing or hearing, it is usually because the air we breathe doesn't smell right, or our chest hurts or something impedes our vision or hearing. I've never actually seen my heart or lungs (though it is possible with some advanced technology), yet I know they exist. Neither have I seen air, though I know it exists in and around me every moment. Similarly, even if we don't realize or acknowledge that the Two Realms exist, we are still constantly experiencing them and always subject to them. They are pressing in on all sides, at all times.

In the Spiritual Realm there are Two Kingdoms, and understanding these Two Kingdoms will add a layer of new insight into the story you and I are living in.

ABOUT KINGDOMS

For the Kingdom of Heaven is like…

Matthew 13:47, 18:23, 20:1

Jesus starts many of His teaching moments with *"The Kingdom of Heaven is like…"* Before we take a much deeper look into this, let me say…there is no way anyone can cover this most major of biblical themes in one chapter. I invite you, however, to check a concordance for the word **kingdom.** You will discover—from Genesis to Revelation—the relevance, weight and significance that God gives to the elements and concepts of kingdoms.

The idea of a **kingdom** is the way God chooses to reveal and express how the Spiritual Realm works—not only for our past and present, but also for our future. *Strong's Concordance* states that the word **kingdom** appears 162 times in the New Testament alone. Just for comparison, the word *love*—in all its different forms—appears 208 times; *forgive* and *forgiveness* 163 times; *sin*, 174; and *life*, 180. The idea of *kingdom* ranks among the most important themes of the Bible.

I believe we would find more of the abundant Life we are created for and searching for if we would really come to understand the Two Realms and Two Kingdoms. This is the full reality of *where we are*. One might be ignorant, naïve or untrained in the Two Realms and its Two Kingdoms, but the Two Realms and Two Kingdoms are not ignorant nor naïve about us. One Kingdom is inviting us into a true, rich and full Life. The other kingdom is hindering, blocking, accosting, assaulting and doing all it can to pull us down and away from that same Life. One Kingdom is about *Life*; the other, *death*.

When we think of kings and kingdoms, words like these most often come to mind:

ruling	reigning	authority	crowns	thrones
dominion	boundaries	territory	lands	subjects
splendor	domain	majesty	sovereign	lordship

God has chosen a specific way to describe the deeper things regarding where we are and where we live. If we know anything about our physical realm, we realize that a species functions best when it is in the environment for which it was made. Fish do best in the sea. Lions do well on the savannah. And penguins are right at home on the ice. It is no accident that the descriptions, stories, parables and pictures in the scriptures all center on the metaphor and reality of kingdoms. The subject is scattered throughout the Bible. God is using this idea to help us comprehend and understand the environment in which we thrive, where full Life abounds, how we can engage and where we are to search for it.

In the scriptures, Jesus is called many things: *the Christ, the Messiah (Anointed One), the Good Shepherd, the Prince of Peace, the Lion of the Tribe of Judah, the Way, the Truth and the Life*, to name just a few. These names show us a few pieces of the much larger picture God is painting.

God provides these names and titles as glimpses of His Kingdom and His identity so that we can know Him and relate to Him in deeper and more significant ways.

This is not just *ancient* history because it's in the Bible and therefore not *relevant* for today. Drawing that conclusion would be a grave mistake and add to our tendency to become lost. All our human "progress" and technological advancements have no bearing on this realm and its kingdoms except to potentially enhance or further distract our awareness of living within them. The Two Realms and Two Kingdoms are both *ancient* and *relevant*. Therefore, we must know *kingdom* as more than a theory or idea—although that is the trailhead where we can start. By the end of this chapter, I hope to demonstrate to you the importance of knowing the truth about the kingdoms in which we are living. Awareness is always a good thing, but it's only the first step of many to the *experience* it invites us into. Awareness gives us the lenses through which the truth can be seen in order to truly find our way home in the midst of both the good and the evil kingdoms that occupy positions and places in the Larger Story.

GOOD VERSUS EVIL

Nearly all the great stories we love (books and movies, fiction and non-fiction) seem to have an element of good versus evil. Have you ever stopped to wonder why this idea is so present in our most beloved stories? The stories we love to hear and to tell are the echoes of this larger reality we find ourselves in. Deep down we seem to know that there are Two Kingdoms, one that is good and one that is not.

The Two Kingdoms in the Spiritual Realm battle and clash over the most important of treasures—the hearts of men and women.

J. R. R. Tolkien shares this ideology in the epic story *The Lord of the Rings*. The whole of the *Lord of the Rings Trilogy* is the collection of the stories and tales of many lives caught up in the battle between good and evil. Other epic stories that depict this great battle and offer us a reference point to understand the Larger Story include:

    C.S. Lewis' *The Chronicles of Narnia*
    Shakespeare's *Romeo and Juliet*
    Epic films such as: *Gladiator*, *Braveheart*, *Last of the Mohicans*, *Tombstone*, *Sound of Music*, *Ben Hur* and *Lawrence of Arabia*

Each of these stories, in its own way, explores the universal battle between good and evil, freedom and bondage, life and death. All the great stories do.

Disney's whole empire is built on this central theme of *good* versus *evil*. Pick any genre at Blockbuster or Netflix and you are likely to find it; westerns, comedies, love stories, science fiction, drama, even the horror films capitalize on this fundamental reality. We tell the same story of a great conflict, recycling the story of good versus evil again and again. Whether set in galaxies far, far away or somewhere on the yellow brick road, I believe these stories resonate with us because we are all subject to this ongoing struggle in our own lives—whether we are fully aware of it or not.

Author, counselor and teacher, John Eldredge, asks and answers a most significant question in his book, *Waking the Dead*: "Why do all the great stories have a villain? Because ours does." The Two Kingdoms in the realm that matters most are in a great conflict, which is taking place all around us and even within us. They are in a war—a war over and for us. The Two Kingdoms do not negotiate, nor are they ever friendly or diplomatic with one another. Matthew 11:12 says, "From the days of John the Baptist until now, the kingdom of heaven has been forcefully advancing, and forceful men lay hold of it." When we choose to ignore this larger landscape—the true elements in which we live, we will find ourselves in danger. Naiveté will bring confusion, disorientation and a life that will *almost* make sense but leave much to be desired. You do *not* want to live not knowing where you are, who or what is after you, why you are being both hunted and sought after and what it is they want. One kingdom's hope is to go undetected for as long as possible so we will settle for less. For a smaller story. The other Kingdom desires nothing less than to break through, to be seen and even be entered into so that we might live Life to the fullest.

THE GREATER KINGDOM

The Greater Kingdom, the Kingdom of God, Christ's Kingdom, offers, promotes, promises and delivers *Life, freedom, victory, purpose, glory, newness, power, restoration, intimacy and love*. Most of all, the Greater Kingdom extends an **invitation** from its King: *Walk with me, trust me, and come be a part of my family. Be my son! Be my daughter! You will love it here, so walk through life with me. I love you. Please come.*

Two men encounter this Kingdom first hand in the Spiritual Realm, and the Bible records their encounters that we might take to heart the reality of its presence and influence. In the Old Testament it was the prophet Isaiah who was given a vision of the Kingdom of God:

In the year that King Uzziah died, I saw the Master sitting on a throne—high, exalted!—and the train of his robes filled the Temple. Angel-seraphs hovered above him, each with six wings. With two wings they covered their faces, with two their feet, and with two they flew. And they called back and forth one to the other, Holy, Holy, Holy is God-of-the-Angel-Armies. His bright glory fills the whole earth. The foundations trembled at the sound of the angel voices, and then the whole house filled with smoke. I said, "Doom! It's Doomsday! I'm as good as dead! Every word I've ever spoken is tainted—blasphemous even! And the people I live with talk the same way, using words that corrupt and desecrate. And here I've looked God in the face! The King! God-of-the-Angel-Armies!"

Isaiah 6:1-5 (MSG)

Later in his life, Isaiah wrote:

> GOD's *Message:* "*Heaven's my throne, earth is my footstool. What sort of house could you build for me? What holiday spot reserve for me? I made all this! I own all this!*" GOD's *Decree.* "*But there is something I'm looking for: a person simple and plain, reverently responsive to what I say.*"
>
> Isaiah 66:1-2 (MSG)

The apostle John talks of kingdoms, kings and thrones in the last book of the Bible, Revelation:

> *Then I looked, and, oh!—a door open into Heaven. The trumpet-voice, the first voice in my vision, called out, "Ascend and enter. I'll show you what happens next." I was caught up at once in deep worship and, oh!—a Throne set in Heaven with One Seated on the Throne, suffused in gem hues of amber and flame with a nimbus of emerald.*
>
> Revelation 4:1-3 (MSG)

And later in the book, John records:

> *Then I saw Heaven open wide—and oh! a white horse and its Rider. The Rider, named Faithful and True, judges and makes war in pure righteousness. His eyes are a blaze of fire, on his head many crowns. He has a Name inscribed that's known only to himself. He is dressed in a robe soaked with blood, and he is addressed as "Word of God." The armies of Heaven, mounted on white horses and dressed in dazzling white linen, follow him. A sharp sword comes out of his mouth so he can subdue the nations, then rule them with a rod of iron. He treads the winepress of the raging wrath of God, the Sovereign-Strong. On his robe and thigh is written,* **KING OF KINGS, LORD OF LORDS**.
>
> Revelation 19:11-16 (MSG)

Are you are familiar with the old hymns *Crown Him with Many Crowns*

(1852) and *A Mighty Fortress is Our God* (1529)? The composers of these classic hymns wrote long, long ago of the significance of a Kingdom perspective. They unearthed great treasures in this life because they knew *how to look* at the Larger Story and *what to look* for. The vantage point of the Larger Story sheds light, gives context and reveals to us more and more of the perspective we need to live well. That perspective whispers to us the truth, "seeing isn't believing...believing is seeing."

The Greater Kingdom offers our hearts the Truth, which is far more than a proposition or a written word. The Truth is actually a person. Jesus Himself said, *I am the Truth* (John 14:6). And Truth is what we need. If I embrace the truth about who I am, where I am and the goodness of God in my life, the Truth promises to set me free. This *is* the greatest way to live... *freely*. Much must be risked, and long will be the journey to find more and more freedom. God wants to set us free from *all* that entangles us, inhibits us, oppresses us and tries to derail us from Life in His Kingdom.

The apostle Paul writes in the fifth chapter of Galatians to believers who have been freed and yet are now in trouble again:

> *IN [this] **freedom** Christ has made us free [and completely liberated us]; stand fast then, and do not be hampered and held ensnared and submit again to a yoke of slavery [which you have once put off].*
>
> Galatians 5:1 (AMP)

Freedom may be the greatest component of Life. It is when we are free that we are best able to receive as well as offer love. As Paul's letter to the Galatians notes, if that is what Jesus accomplished for us, then it makes sense that it must be what we needed most! Yet often we find ourselves spiraling back or, like the Galatians, tricked back into slavery. It is as if some gravitational pull or evil force is bent on taking us away from the very thing we want and need the most—freedom. This is more true than many of us have been led to believe. There is a force at work against Life and against our desire to find it.

THE LESSER KINGDOM

Some people are like seed along the path, where the word is sown. As soon as they hear it, Satan comes and takes away the word that was sown in them.

Mark 4:15

The thief comes only to steal and kill and destroy.

John 10:10a

This may be one of the most valuable pieces of information in the whole of this book—our pursuit of Life and freedom is *opposed*. The lesser kingdom opposes you and me. It is truly the *lesser kingdom* because it is under the rule of Christ, and yet it exists and has a role in the Larger Story in which we find ourselves. It is the *lesser,* but we put ourselves at great risk if we underestimate its power and influence. This regime, though it is small, greatly impacts the world for evil.

We have born witness to some dastardly rulers in the past 100 years. There always seems to be one on the stage and one in the wings. When I was growing up, it was Castro in Cuba. I also watched the reports on the oppressive rule of Saddam Hussein and his invasion of Kuwait. The constant Middle East struggle over the Gaza Strip, some 360 square kilometers of real estate, seems to affect not only the thousands who live there, but the millions surrounding it. Perhaps the most terrible dark regime we have witnessed over the last century was Nazi Germany's Third Reich led by Hitler. One small country came a few victories short of having the whole continent of Europe under its rule—and we know the Nazi kingdom wouldn't have stopped there. And there are great similarities between Germany's World War II campaign and the workings of the lesser kingdom in the Spiritual Realm. Like Hitler's rule in the physical realm, the kingdom of darkness in the Spiritual Realm produces death, slavery, bondage, fear, guilt, shame, oppression and accusation. In short, it holds its subjects captive.

So how evil is this evil kingdom? First, one must decide whether or not it exists. If you decide yes, then the next issue to settle is what these evil forces are up to. Hitler advanced as far as he did because few believed the rumors, and by the time they were proven true it was too late for most. This is the first strategy of our enemy—stay as covert as possible. How bad do you think these spiritual influences within the kingdom of darkness are? In that pivotal scene from the film *The Matrix*, Neo's future hangs on whether or not he will come out of, or continue to stay in, the Matrix. Morpheus offers Neo *the truth*. But to gain freedom, Neo has to choose to believe that truth. Up until that moment, Morpheus declares, "You have been living in bondage under a lie. All I'm offering is the truth. Take the red pill and see how far the rabbit hole goes. Take the blue pill and stay in wonderland."

What is the power of a lie? What is its strength and impact? Stated simply, the power of a lie rests in the fact *that you believe it.* Jesus calls the ruler of the lesser kingdom the *prince of darkness* and *the father of lies* (John 8:44). What you believe matters. Remember my friend, Gary's, advice, *the story you believe you are living in will determine how you live.*

MADE FOR KINGDOM

Recovering the fundamental belief that we live in Two Realms with Two Kingdoms is crucial to our heart's search for Life. We must find and carry with us this orientation like a survival kit necessary for a long and perilous journey. If we do not possess this survival kit, we are in constant danger of living in captivity or routinely having our lives crushed—like strolling casually into a bull-fighting ring wearing a red shirt. We will bring new meaning to the phrase, *I never saw it coming*. It's a tragedy waiting to happen. Unfortunately, for most of us the tragedy has already happened and the bull has won.

Author and teacher, Dallas Willard, wrote in his book, *Hearing God*:

> *The life and outlook identifiable with the mind of Christ and with life in his footsteps is one that sees the universe as a Kingdom...Some of our greatest problems in understanding and entering into life in the Kingdom of God come from an inadequate appreciation of how that Kingdom—like all Kingdoms—works...*

Being grounded in the fundamentals and equipped with the crucial survival kit, allows us to live well in the Two Realms and Two Kingdoms. This will not only *aid* us in the recovery of what has been lost, but it will also *arm* us in our search for more and more Life. These provisions lead us to the understanding that we need of what is happening all around us. It will help us to know where we are in each moment and in what direction our next best step should be.

LIVING CURIOUSLY

In light of this, I am learning to live more and more *curiously*. I am learning to live in the knowledge that there is more to every situation than meets the eye. To live in the Kingdom and learn how to live there well, we must become curious. We must become men and women who are learners, students committed to a way of Life that moves at a slower pace than the rest of the world.

Living curiously has made me a better father, husband and friend. When the struggles and trials of life come up—whether they're mine or belong to someone I'm close to, Jesus has taught me that time is on my side. But only when I take my time and seek to follow Him through a Two Realms and Two Kingdoms perspective. Question like the ones I'm about to share are better handled with a follow-up question. There is always more going on and often the first question isn't really the one in need of answering. So many of us have uttered these questions or walked along side someone else who—in pain, confusion, anger or hurt—has

expressed their heart's heavy condition with...
> *Why is life so difficult?*
> *Why does my boss always take out his frustrations on me?*
> *Why do we never have enough money?*
> *Why won't they return our calls?*
> *Why is it so hard to love my wife?*
> *Why are the kids so hard to deal with?*
> *Why isn't my life working?*

Living curiously, rather than definitively, is a glorious move any person can make. Investigating a little deeper, *before* launching into a counter attack or declaring some untimely advice, is an act of mature kindness we can offer family and friends around us—not to mention our own hearts. Inviting God into the conversation, escorts you, and possibly your fellow travelers, into a whole new world.

I've been very naive to believe that I'm the only one asking these painful or frustrating questions. Everyone else lives in the same story I do—my kids, my parents, my boss, my co-workers, my neighbors, the teachers at my kids' school, the mechanic who works on my car and the cashier at the store of the last errand I ran. We are all looking for Life. We are all trying to arrange for it. We are all trying hard to find some temporary relief and momentary satisfaction.

INVITED

Only a minority of Christians are passionately pursuing life in an awareness of the Two Realms. Kingdom Living is far too rare. We must bring this perspective and orientation back in this generation. We need to not only find Life but to offer it to others. God *invites* us all to end our search and be caught by His Love and His Life. Engaging, experiencing and participating in authentic Life may be far more important than studying about one. Only with Him, by Him and from Him—in His company and closeness—can we have the Life and Love we were created for.

The 1997 film *First Knight* is the retelling of the legendary story of King Arthur and the Knights of the Round Table. In an early scene, Lancelot enters Camelot showing great strength and cunning by conquering a medieval obstacle course called the Gauntlet. He is the only one to run it successfully and remain unscathed. Arthur, the king played by Sean Connery, is intrigued by Lancelot's demonstration of chivalry and invites Lancelot into the castle for a discussion:

> **Arthur:** Well. Lancelot...you're an unusual man. I've never seen such a display of courage, skill, nerve, grace and... stupidity. Come. (They walk into the chamber of the round table.) Here, every life is precious, even the lives of strangers. If you must die, die serving something greater than yourself. Better still. Live...and serve.
> **Lancelot:** The Round Table.
> **Arthur:** Yes. The High Council meets here. No head. No foot. Everyone equal...even the King.
> **Lancelot:** (Observing the writing around the table, he reads it aloud) In serving each other, we become free.
> **Arthur:** That is the very heart of Camelot, (pointing around the hall) not these stones, timbers, towers, palaces. Burn them all... and Camelot lives on. Because it lives in us. It's a belief we hold in our hearts. (Dialing his passion back down.) Well, no matter. **Stay in Camelot. I invite you.**

Everyone likes to be invited. At times I decline an invitation, or I am unable to accept—but it is always good to be *invited*. Who doesn't like to be invited? Even when the date and time are inconvenient or the inviter is someone you appreciate more from a distance, it *still* feels good to be invited. If you are a parent, you've probably heard from one of your children, *Guess what? Chrissy invited me to her birthday party,* or *Dad (or Mom), Caitlyn invited me to spend the night. Can I?* Invitations make us feel wanted.

Recently some close friends of mine, men I do life with in our little Redemptive Community, mentioned they had played golf just a few days earlier. Granted, I'm not the greatest golfer. (I must say…I always shoot in the 70s, but it's usually because I stop playing around hole 13 or 14). Anyway, they were talking about their day together, some conversations they enjoyed on the course, and some moments when a putt was made or a drive was never found. While they were talking, another conversation broke out—this one in my heart: *Huh, I wonder why they didn't invite me.* I'm actually smiling, nodding at the table and pretending to listen to them, but the volume of my heart's conversation had overtaken the volume of their voices. *They didn't even ask. I asked all of them to dinner last week, and they came. Jim and Tom have been doing a lot together lately. I was friends with Jim before Tom came around. I didn't want to play a stupid round of golf anyway.* To assume I'm alone with my thoughts would not be wise; because I live in this message, I know better.

Though people—even people we consider friends—may not make us feel invited, there is One whose invitation is constant and relentless. *Jesus is the great inviter.* He invites the lame to walk, the blind to see, the bound to be free and the weary to find rest (Luke 4:18). He invites us to His home, to be His friends, to take up His cause, to fight with Him against evil and to advance His Kingdom. Like so many invitations we receive, His comes with the letters *RSVP* at the bottom—*Répondez s'il vous plaît*, a French phrase that translates *please respond* or *respond if you please*. These types of invitations ask for a response either way. Are you coming or not? Are you in or out? Do you accept or decline? And I'm not talking about salvation alone because neither is He.

The Great Inviter is asking for a response. *What do you say, are you in or out, with me or not?*

His greatest offer and invitation is and always will be *Let me help you*. When we accept His invitation—every time we say yes, a shift takes place, an alteration occurs. As significant a move from the black and white of Kansas to the technicolor of Oz. A weighty and tremendous change occurs. A great equipping can take place, and the journey toward Life opens up before us more and more. All because we say *yes, I accept*. I like how The Message presents Jesus' invitation:

> *Are you tired? Worn out? Burned out on religion? Come to me. Get away with me and you'll recover your life. I'll show you how to take a real rest. Walk with me and work with me—watch how I do it. Learn the unforced rhythms of grace. I won't lay anything heavy or ill-fitting on you.*
>
> Matthew 11:28-29a (MSG)

Again, Jesus invites us to receive His Kingdom and Life:

> *He said to them, "Let the little children come to me, and do not hinder them, for the **kingdom** of God belongs to such as these. I tell you the truth, anyone who will not receive the **kingdom** of God like a little child will never enter it." And he took the children in his arms, put his hands on them and blessed them.*
>
> Mark 10:14b-16 (emphasis added)

This is where our initial search for Life finally meets the Great Inviter of Life and the first of hundreds of moments where we will need His way again. The King of a glorious Kingdom has invited us to rest, believe and take up our place in a family as Christ's brothers and sisters. This family has all the privileges and opportunities that await us in His Great Kingdom. He invites us to learn through training and initiation, validation and trials. How else might we grow up into the image we bear but through many moments of invitation? How will you RSVP?

CHAPTER 7

THE ECONOMY OF KINGDOM: WAR

Soldiers, Sailors and Airmen of the Allied Expeditionary Forces:

You are about to embark upon the Great Crusade toward which we have striven for these many months. The eyes of the world are upon you. You will bring about the destruction of the German war machine, the elimination of Nazi tyranny over the oppressed peoples of Europe, and security for ourselves in a free world. Your task will not be an easy one. Your enemy is well trained, well equipped, and battle-hardened. He will fight savagely. .... The free men of the world are marching together to victory. I have full confidence in your courage, devotion to duty, and skill in battle. We will accept nothing less than full victory. Good luck, and let us all beseech the blessings of Almighty God upon this great and noble undertaking.

General Dwight D. Eisenhower, June 6, 1944, Giving the orders for D-Day

Fight the good fight of the faith; lay hold of the eternal life to which you were summoned and [for which] you confessed the good confession [of faith] before many witnesses.

1 Timothy 6:12 (AMP)

Open war is upon you whether you would like it or not.

Aragorn to King Theodin, *The Lord of the Rings, The Two Towers*

The best way to sum up the state of affairs in which we find ourselves is, in a word, *War*. The elements and environments we are subject to in our daily search for Life can only be described as *war*. I believe John Eldredge said it best when he wrote: "We live in a great love story set in the midst of a great battle." If you and I live within this awareness, we will have more than a *chance* at Life—we *will find* Life. More importantly, the Author of Life will find you. Most people live their lives with attitudes and beliefs that are far from those needed on the battlefield.

Howard Hendricks, the great Bible teacher and friend of Jesus, once said: "You can tell a lot about a man by what he complains about. A man who complains the coffee is too cold or the beer to warm is a man who believes life is a cruise ship. A man who complains that he doesn't have enough ammo is a man who knows he's on a battle ship."

Likewise, you can tell through what lenses people are seeing the world when they offer you advice. More often than not, a person's advice says more about himself or herself than it does about actions you should take. A person who tells you to ignore someone might very well be telling you of his pain not yours. A person who declares you should get even or give that person who hurt you a piece of your mind might very well be someone who has very little of his (or her) own mind left.

At 11-years-old, my daughter Abbey is beautiful and full of life. As do most children her age, she believes that the world revolves around her. If you cross her plans, she will throw you in her penalty box—*three minutes for not saying yes to what I wanted!* My wife Robin and I inconvenience Abbey quite often, according to Abbey. She has a hard time grasping that the world doesn't move according to her wishes or commands.

It's amazing how many of us don't step out of this place as we get older. Add 30 years to a life and you can still stand around the water cooler, church foyer, gym parking lot or mall food court and see many 40-something-year-olds still stuck in an 11-year-old's inward bent toward matters of life working out for *them* on *their* terms. There is a small minority, however, that has outgrown this approach to life. A very small minority.

One of the ways the kingdom of darkness succeeds in its campaign against the Life to which God invites us is to offer a false imitation of that life. The forces of evil can use prosperity or success as a prison just as much as it can use poverty or failure.

THE LONG AND BRUTAL ASSAULT

In his book, *Waking the Dead*, John Eldredge writes: "The story of your life is the story of the long and brutal assault on your heart by the one who knows what you could be and fears it."

I have to admit, when I first heard this I was skeptical. *Really? Can that be true?*

But when I came back to it later, I found it to be a very serious possibility for explaining the great deal of the heartache experienced in life. What a weighty proposition…not all the *stuff* in my life is my doing.

You and I have an enemy, an adversary (I Peter 5:8, Matthew 13:39), and there are forces at work against us. If this is true, then the struggles we all experience in the pursuit of Life just came into a much clearer view. When these blinders are off, the whole of my existence is invited to shift from victim to participant, As a participant I am encouraged and actually find myself wanting to engage in defending myself against evil forces and, in doing so, I advance the Kingdom in my life. There is a post that is mine to take up, a contribution for me to make. I can offer my skills, talents, courage and strength as a rightly oriented man. This is not what the enemy wants. Eldredge writes in the book, *Wild at Heart*, *"Your enemy fears you and what you may become."*

By the end of the film *The Matrix*, Neo has journeyed through a great deal. He sees, hears and engages on a whole new level as he learns to wield the power and authority found in his new life. In the last scene of the movie, he steps into a phone booth, picks up the pay phone and broadcasts to the Matrix:

> *I know you're out there. I can feel you now. I know that you're afraid. You're afraid of us, you're afraid of change. I don't know the future. I didn't come here to tell you how this is going to end. I came here to tell you how this is going to begin. Now, I'm going to hang up this phone, and I'm going to show these people what you don't want them to see. I'm going to show them a world without you—a world without rules and controls, without borders or boundaries. A world where anything is possible. Where we go from there is a choice I leave to you...*

CITIZENSHIP-BORN P.O.W

...many live as enemies of the cross of Christ. Their destiny is destruction, their god is their stomach, and their glory is in their shame. Their mind is on earthly things. But our citizenship is in

heaven. And we eagerly await a Savior from there, the Lord Jesus Christ.

Philippians 3:20

But you are a chosen people, a royal priesthood, a holy nation, a people belonging to God, that you may declare the praises of him who called you out of darkness into his wonderful light.

1 Peter 2:9

Citizenship is an amazing thing. All of us on the planet are born citizens of one country or another. Your citizenship depends on who your parents are and where you were born. If you don't like the country you are a citizen of, there is a process you can go through to change it. Obviously, the first step to a new citizenship would be to realize that there is a better place for you—one where the opportunities and possibilities available are worth the work and effort to establish a new life. *Applying* for citizenship is the next step. When you complete the application, you are asked *Why?* Why do you want to become a citizen of this new country?

First and foremost, the central ingredient is probably your desire. You want a change. The list of requirements, according to the U.S. Bureau of Citizenship and Immigration Services, is that you:

> Live five years legally in the U.S. with permit or visa
> Speak the language
> Go through the application process
> Pay the fee ($675)
> Swear the oath

Desire is what fuels a heart to change, not the list of requirements. The requirements are simply the means to an end, the new life longed for. If you lose track of the end, the *why* you want something, your desire will fade. You will lose heart and quickly lose the Life until you're left with either coping, medicating or just plain giving up. *Citizenship*—and all that it offers—is what makes more than 700,000 people apply each year to become Americans. The requirements are the price that must be paid for the privilege and responsibility granted. An individual desires or chooses to leave his or her old country and embraces the new one believed to offer more.

It is no different in the Spiritual Realm. Both kingdoms have citizens, but the kingdom we are born into is not the kingdom in which we must stay. Many people leave their countries of origin due to oppressive governments, rampant poverty or the limitations on their future and happiness.

What if the kingdom that holds my passport and my citizenship papers is the lesser one? What if I'm living under an oppressive regime that will never allow me to find the Life I so long to live? Just as in any country, there are those who have made it work for them. Transferring citizenship is far from what they desire. They have actually carved out a good-enough life, one that makes sense to them and one they have made work. The Jews in World War II weren't the only ones living under an oppressive, deranged tyrant. So were the guards of those awful camps and all the citizens of Germany. Drastic times call for drastic measures. A move can be made. For *Life,* a move *must* be made.

NOT SAFE TO UNDERESTIMATE

If we are ever going to find Life, we must understand the elements and environments in which we are searching. This is not a safe world. There are forces in it that are opposed to the Life we are searching for, and there are things in this environment that are set against us. But just because it is dangerous doesn't mean it isn't also glorious. The Great Barrier Reef is one of the most gorgeous places on earth. It is beautiful and full of all kinds of good ocean life, but don't turn your back! If you don't pay attention to your surroundings while navigating its beauty, it might not be your diving buddy tugging at your arm to show you a cool fish—it might be a shark taking a bite.

Being snuck up on, tricked, lied to or fooled is never good—whether it is a result of bad information or a misunderstanding. Are you familiar with pyrite? It is a very common mineral found in a wide variety of geological formations. It is never misunderstood today, but that wasn't always the case. The brassy-yellow metallic color of pyrite has in many cases led people to mistake it for gold—earning it the name "fool's gold." *Something worthless mistaken for something priceless.* This works the other way as well. *Some things of great value are often underestimated as common.*

I remember when some friends and I were thinking through these ideas and allowing the realities of the Two Realms and Two Kingdoms to take root in our hearts. Once when I was sharing this perspective and orientation at a men's gathering, my good friend, Jim, asked from the crowd: "How did we miss all of this?" You could hear a pin drop. All eyes were on me, and mine were looking to God with a question. *What do I say Father?* My next thought was w*e've underestimated it all.* And that was my response. Jim jumped back in and said, "If this is true, it changes everything, *everything*." He was beginning to see the Larger Story he was already living in—and when this happens, it does change everything. We have underestimated it all, and it is time to be shaken and awaken to the war we were born into. Our life is a battle, and it is time we learn how to fight.

THE CURRENCY OF THE KINGDOM

That if you confess with your mouth, "Jesus is Lord," and believe in your heart that God raised Him from the dead, you will be saved.
Romans 10:9

For God so loved the world that he gave his one and only Son, that whoever believes on him shall not perish but have eternal life.
John 3:16

And without faith it is impossible to please God, because anyone who comes to Him must believe that he exists and that he rewards those who earnestly seek Him.

Hebrews 11:6

What I am inviting you to see is that what a person believes, what he or she puts faith in, the perspectives a person holds, the attitudes and hopes he or she carries, who and what this person trusts and gives his or her heart to, *matters*. **What you believe matters—it matters a whole lot.** What you believe is actually *the currency of the kingdom.* We all have belief, faith and hope to invest and to spend. Handling your beliefs is very much like wealth management; how you spend and invest your beliefs will accumulate over time. They can bring debt, or they can bring equity; it's hard to tell what they will produce on the day you're signing the papers, just like a lot of investments.

Everyone on the planet believes something. Even believing there is nothing or no one to believe in is a belief. We may use other terms for it: attitudes, perspectives, bents or persuasions. The words *I think* can be a clue for spotting beliefs. Not always, but usually, you can swap the words *I think* with *I believe*. But the weightier of the two terms is *believe*.

When I start a sentence with the words *I believe* rather than *I think,* it seems to make what I'm about to say more significant:

I think that the chicken tastes better than the beef.
versus
I believe that the chicken tastes better than the beef.

I think you are the one I should marry
versus
I believe you are the one I should marry.

I think you can do this.
versus
I believe you can do this.

Which is true? I've actually observed my vocabulary change from *I think* to *I believe* in many weightier moments in my life. When I slow down and take an extra second before voicing my thoughts or opinions, I simply ask my heart, "Is this what I *think* or is this what I *believe*?" My opinions and the lighter things in my world usually are best offered or shared with *I think*. The moments in my life when I have conviction, commitment or a weightier sense that "this is true" are when I upgrade to *I believe*. What I believe really matters.

Here's my point: the Two Kingdoms know we have this currency of belief to spend or invest. The economy is organized and orchestrated by God to operate this way. What we believe has repercussions; it has literal benefits or consequences based on how we spend it and where we invest it for Life. It has so much impact that what we believe actually has authority in our lives.

BELIEF AND BLUE JEANS

What matters most is not *if* you invest or spend but *when*. We invest in or spend on the things we *believe* will give us Life. All this happens very much like making a decision in the department store dressing room: *If I buy this shirt or these pants, I will fit in, be accepted and get a little life from my friends. I'll take two pair!* After all, our hearts long for belonging and acceptance. When I experience this, among a host of other things, I feel alive. I have often based my choices on what I believe will bring me the greatest reward or result from the polls and opinions of others.

Let's take blue jeans, for instance. There are dozens of kinds of jeans out there. They are all denim. They all look basically the same and will serve the same purpose. Why do we desire one pair over another? Is it the fit? (Look around. Most of the time that isn't the deciding factor.) Is it the price? Or is it something intangible we think we might gain through this trivial choice?

When I hit seventh grade, these kinds of choices began demanding my heart's attention. I was a typical 12-year-old, living in a middle class family in 1976, and the choices for clothes in our house of three boys were decided at a department store. Sears or J.C. Penney to be exact. I didn't even know there were jeans in the world other than Toughskins until I began to walk the halls of junior high. But there might as well have been signs posted all around school declaring: *Toughskins aren't cool. Get some real jeans.* My mission was clear within the first week—get cool jeans.

And my Toughskins weren't the only thing on the chopping block. From now on, not just any notebooks would do. Pencils needed to be multi-colored rather than plain yellow, tennis shoes weren't for tennis and hair cuts needed to be performed by a stylist instead of your dad. The list went on, and so did my need to invest in new items, promising to improve my status and my life. Funny how much things stay the same. This is what my teenage kids don't realize. They've stepped into a time in their lives that I remember all too well in mine. Technology, clothing styles and hairdos may have changed, but the heart has not.

Speaking of jeans...when my oldest daughter Ashley hit seventh grade, my wife and I barely had time to strap ourselves down before the hurricanes of "fitting in" came storming in. One Saturday afternoon a few weeks into the school year, Ashley came down the stairs with a sales pitch. She was wearing a pair of jeans borrowed from a friend. "Mom, Dad, I need some new jeans like these," she declared while giving a quick half turn as she finished her descent. "Turn back around," my wife requested. When Ashley did, we saw the low-rider jeans of Hollywood on our 12 year-old.

The discussion quickly turned into an argument. In the midst of the whines—*Why can't I have these jeans?*—my daughter made a major blunder. She said: "I don't know what the big deal is; they're just jeans." At which time I stepped into the line of fire—with great wisdom I might add—and said, "Great, if they're not that big a deal then it won't matter if you don't get them." Then there were two seconds of silence just before the explosion of emotions hit the battlefield. **"You don't understand. I need these jeans!"** There it was, the heart of the matter. The brand name will get the applause or approval of others (usually those who have also invested or come to believe in that particular brand of jeans' ability to secure you a place at the cool table). The jeans, like many other things we've come to believe in our lives, are often just the means to a promised end. Get the jeans and you will get cool.

CLAIMS AND AUTHORITY

When we place our belief, trust and faith in something, or someone, we give them power and claim over our lives. Remember the power of a lie? ***It only has power if you believe it.*** Jesus makes it clear that Satan is the *father* of lies (John 8:44). When we believe a lie, *it* has a power over us, *he* has an authority over us. And he then lays claim to a part of our lives that he has no right to.

I grew up in Oklahoma, and in junior high and high school we had to take a class on our state's history. Some of the most significant series of events in its history were the Land Runs. The most famous of these was the first one, held at high noon on April 22, 1889. On this day, 50,000 people of all kinds (some from as far as Europe and Asia) lined up for the race to lay claim to parcels of some two million acres of land. Our lives are like these parcels of land. Who and what we believe determines who has legal claim.

My wife and I have bought a couple of cars during our marriage. Financed is the more accurate term. The contracts require about a million signatures from both of us. Anyone who has closed on a house and felt the writer's cramp from all the signatures and initials knows what I'm talking about. There is even a page to sign and initial stating that these are your signatures and initials! Why? The bank wants to make it *very* clear that *they* have claim to your finances and *will* exercise their authority to get the money on said contract should it come to that. The

Two Kingdoms work on very similar principles.

A DARK MIXTURE

My wife, Robin, and I have had the privilege over the years to counsel and help others discover where they are, who they are and what God is up to in their lives. We see again and again how beliefs, attitudes and perspectives impact a person's heart and his or her search for Life. A while back we were engaged in counseling a friend of ours who I'll call Betsy. While talking about her future, she started unpacking some of the things she was struggling with from her past. She mentioned a season in her life when she struggled with the eating disorder, bulimia. She shared it as if it was one of many little sound bites from her past. We stopped the conversation right there and asked her to tell us more about it. Betsy went on to describe the pressure she felt in high school and college to be fit and in shape. She was a great athlete and actually got a college scholarship to play her sport. All those years in junior high and high school, as she trained, worked out and practiced her sport, her mom and dad would say things like...

> *Have you practiced your serve today? You know there are other girls working hard right now.*
> *Don't eat that, or you're going to get fat.*
> *Betsy, have you run today? Well, you better if you're going to eat all that.*

These packages were delivered frequently to her heart and mingled with feelings of fear, guilt and shame. The enemy had all he needed to work with. What a chemistry set. This dark mixture led her to a desperate place. Betsy *believed* she was in danger of losing her place on the team and that she could gain her parents' love by performing well. There was also the sense of identity she gained as a star athlete, the friendships she made because of the sport, the newspaper articles and accolades. All this made up what Betsy came to believe was the primary source of life for her. This is a powerful poison: the ever-present pressure from well-meaning parents that a child's approval depends upon her performance as an athlete. This lethal combination of fear and insecurity set up Betsy for a terrible fall. She came to believe that her only alternative was to eat and throw up. The greatest tragedy was that, for a while, it worked for her. Betsy lost or maintained her weight and stayed in the starting line up. But over time, this habit began to take its toll on her body, her skills and her energy level. Her investment eventually came to collect. When an anorexic Betsy looked in the mirror, she *believed* she saw an overweight little girl in danger of losing it all. Because of her fear and insecurity, no one—especially those close to her—could tell her differently.

PLAYING THE GAME

Unfortunately, this story line is too common. Why would a high-level professional or an Olympic athlete use performance-enhancing drugs? What do they believe that drives them to break the rules and risk their health? *If my statistics or numbers go up, so do my chances for a scholarship or a new contract. If I can just win this big account, this big game, I'll prove that I'm worthwhile and that I deserve to be loved.* To them, the risk seems worth betting against their current reality (which is often dominated by insecurities and fears at these pivotal times).

Athletics is not the only place we see this common scenario. A high level executive cheats a company out of its retirement funds and pensions. A spouse leaves the marriage that he or she has committed to only to try again with someone else. Look at the magazines committed to informing us of the lives of those in the Hollywood scene. They tell all the latest celebrity gossip: who is seeing who, who is breaking up with who, who's in jail, who's getting out of jail, who's checking into or coming out of rehab. They have all the applause and all the fame, yet so many have unsettled hearts and are lost in their own lives.

Many of the athletes, CEOs and entertainers of our day are awake until all hours, frightened and bored with their lives. We forget the fact that even the icons and heroes of our generation are living in the same story we are. Maybe they have the awards, wealth and fame, but are they settled? Are they happy, and do they live well? John Eldredge once said, "What can a bunch of posers tell you but how to live as posers?" Like you and me, celebrities are searching. The only difference between their lives and ours is that theirs make headlines in the physical realm. Conversely, *all* our lives make headlines in the Realm that matters most.

Great are the number of hearts betting that someone or something will relieve their aches. That new circumstances and new relationships will replace sadness, boredom or loneliness and bring relief and even happiness. Oh, that we would learn from our mistakes. Sadly, it's not just *once in a lifetime* we make these blunders and lose these high-stake wagers. Are we destined to make the same mistakes over and over until our last breath? With all the information out there, you would think people would know that this approach to life is a lost cause and a sure way to a bankrupt heart. What seems to be our common belief is that we are the center of the story. We feel we must take matters into our own hands and make life work for us. We conclude that we deserve more than we have, and it is up to us to arrange for it.

I've worked so hard at following this program and have discovered that it just doesn't pan out. It over-promises and under-delivers every time. Playing this game is more than detrimental; it is dangerous. Just like Vegas, the house wins in the long run.

You may be somewhat *overwhelmed* by all this. If so, I know exactly how you feel. *Overwhelmed* is exactly what I'm shooting for. For if we are not overwhelmed, then we don't realize we need help. If not *overwhelmed*, we will fall into the trap of trying to determine our own destinies and arrange Life for ourselves. We will be lulled into the false belief that we can handle life on our own. *Control* is not your friend; it's your greatest enemy. The kingdom of darkness wants you and me to believe that we *are* capable of controlling our lives and all its components. It wants to put us on the hamster wheel and watch us vainly chase after the prize. That is life in a small story. That is a lie. We live in a large story, *overwhelmingly* large. Being overwhelmed invites us to ask for help.

Let me ask you a question. What happens when you are overexposed to something? Do those who live on the Hawaiian Islands get used to all those incredible sunsets and simply ignore them? Do those who work at Niagara Falls pass by on their way to the vending machines without a second glance? Is Disney's Magic Kingdom still magical for those who dress up in character costumes every day? Or are they tired of the wide eyes and the light in the children's faces when they approach? When did we get so familiar with this story God is telling that it became boring or dull, common, taken for granted or even "manageable"?

TWO KINGDOMS BATTLE OVER THE HEART

All of us desire Life. In our hearts, at our deepest core, we all long and search for *validation, acceptance, significance, belonging* and *worth.* Who doesn't want to be seen, invited, encouraged and applauded? Who doesn't want to belong? This desire is a wonderful thing—it is what we were made for. The one word that encompasses all these longings, wants, hopes and desires set deep in the human heart is *Love.*

When I say, *I love you*, I'm saying, *I accept you. I want to be with you. You are significant to me. I see you.* We didn't *evolve* into this condition. We were designed, created and crafted by God with a longing and a desire to love and be loved. This is one of the powerful ways we bear His image. His invitation is to come to *Him* for the fulfillment of our heart's deepest needs and desires. He designed us so that our hearts are central. The heart is our core, and He actually asks each of us if He can come in and dwell there. This territory is what He longs to occupy and the critical position from which His heart longs to do a work from the inside out.

The Two Kingdoms wage war over our hearts because they know

if you capture a person's heart, you capture the person. The rulers and authorities of the Two Kingdoms are advancing on each of us and are in conflict with one another (Ephesians 6:12, Colossians 1:16). One Kingdom offers Life, and the other offers death. It would be wonderful if these two options were as obviously different as they are so obviously opposed. But it isn't always easy to tell the difference. One is True Life, but the other is a lie, masquerading as life. It is a matter of *authentic* versus *counterfeit*. The kingdom of darkness wants you to accept its substitutes for love and life in order to keep us from True Love and Life.

The temporary relief we feel when we accept these substitutes is always fleeting. We then find we have to arrange, perform or orchestrate it all again. The maintenance program is up to us, and it leads only to unmet expectations, unreasonable demands on ourselves (or others) and eventually to lostness, again. What if we could enter the fight and tip the scale of the war by aiding one Kingdom in the battle for our hearts? This is our opportunity, and what the King of the Good Kingdom is offering us. The God of the Universe desires that we give him our hearts so that He might fill them with True Love and Life.

The enemy of God comes after God's image bearers to thwart that. We were made for intimacy, oneness and connectedness with God. We feel most alive when we are being loved. Our enemy knows this better than we do. He knows where and in whom Life is found. Our adversary is launching an all-out assault to get in the way of our intimacy with God and intimacy with others. In Matthew 22:37, Jesus tells us that the greatest commandment is, *Love God and love others as yourself.* There is a reason this is called the greatest command, and there is a reason we are the most opposed when we seek to fulfill it.

Love makes us come alive because Love is the greatest thing in the whole universe. The Tin Man knew this truth, as evidenced in his request of the great wizard of Oz, "I shall take the heart, for brains do not make one happy, and happiness is the best thing in the world." Our friend of tin knew that one needs a heart to love, it is with a heart one can love and we are happiest when we are loving or being loved. Love is what we were meant for, and love is what God is all about.

When we get ahold of this—or when it gets ahold of us—the tide changes, the momentum shifts and the lost ground of our hearts will be taken back. We become *more* because the deepest needs of our heart are met in abundant supply. When we become more, everything changes; we're fighting a new war. The Life and Love that is looking for you is God Himself. He *is* the author of Life, and He *is* Love. The great mission of God is upon us. This great search and rescue campaign to recover what is most precious to Him is in motion. And what is most valuable to the Father are His children. God has moved heaven and earth to accomplish a mission only He can complete…our rescue!

PART III

THE SEARCH

CHAPTER 8 SEARCH FOR THE HEART
CHAPTER 9 WE'RE NOT THE ONLY ONES SEARCHING
CHAPTER 10 ONE TO SHOW THE WAY

I have held many things in my hands, and I have lost them all; but whatever I have placed in God's hands, that I still possess.

Martin Luther

There is a God shaped vacuum in the heart of every man which cannot be filled by any created thing, but only by God, the Creator, made known through Jesus.

Blaise Pascal

It is the glory of God to conceal a matter; but the glory of kings to search out a matter.

Proverbs 25:2 (NKJV)

What matters to God?

Is it service? Obedience? Worship? Over the centuries, like hit records that come and go, all of these offerings have reached the top of the "theological billboard charts." Jesus answers this question and not like we might think. He doesn't answer it in a sentence or in one particular message He preached. Nor does He unveil the answer in one of His many parables. Jesus answers the question of *what matters to God* with much, much more…*His life*. More than what He taught or said, it was Jesus' life, *all* of His life, that is the answer to the question. The Father matters, and *we matter*. How do I know? When asked what was the greatest commandment, Jesus summarized all the law and all the prophets with this: *Love God and love each other like we love ourselves* (Matthew 22:37). This matters most.

Every person on the planet is searching for Life. The *redeemed* heart of a Christ follower is on a journey. The *unredeemed* or yet-to-be-redeemed heart of a person is also on a journey. Actually our hearts are on more of a mission, an expansive quest. *All hearts are searching for Life.* It might be said that the difference between the two types of hearts is that the *redeemed* heart has found the Source of what it was searching for, *Life.* The *unredeemed* heart still searches. The glorious result of a heart that has found God is that the questions have been answered and the issues of life are now settled. Or at least that's how it is supposed to work. Love settles things. Many a love relationship, many a marriage, once believed so as well. Divorce rates tell us differently though. Hearts fall prey to discontent, unsettledness and distress. They drift apart and the pain drifts right along with them. Why is it all so hard?

As mentioned earlier, I believe the most *Life-giving* substance in the cosmos is love. Love, according to 1 John, is exactly what God *is.* Taking up God on his offer to love us can actually end our search for Life and settle our hearts, inviting them to stop wandering. Sure, we still journey on, but our mission changes. No longer will we be trying to fill a bottomless pit with substitutes and imitations (temporary snacks to a permanent hunger) nor will we place on the hearts of others the burden of filling ours. All we've looked for and all we hope for is provided in abundance—God *so* loves to love you.

A whole bundle of meaning comes with the three little words, *I love you.* It is a large declaration, one that is very, very **validating**. It means you are welcome here next to my heart; that you **belong**; I want **to be with** you; you are **significant** to me; I **accept** you; I see your **worth**; I **value** you and I want to **invite** you to be with me. Look back over those words in bold type. Aren't these the things we all hope for, the things we are searching for?

The next question is *Will it be enough?* Can the rescued heart stay settled, or will it revert back to old ways, striving and arranging for life and love apart from God? I believe this is what author, John Piper, meant when he wrote a definition for sin in his book, *Future Grace.* He writes, "Sin is what we do when we're not satisfied with God." A rescued heart is not immune to reverting back to old ways—old sinful ways. How many of us have experienced some relief or freedom from a bad habit or addiction...for a while, only to fall back into the same rut once again? But a rescued heart is a redeemed heart—one that is free from the penalty of sin and can be free from the power and bondage of sin. But it can only be free if that heart moves forward to new ways rather than reverting back to the old ways of arranging for life and love apart from God.

Not being satisfied with God is what makes us susceptible to bad relationships and bad choices. It also makes us susceptible to using others to have our needs and expectations met, to place on them the burden of feeding our desire for love. Many people try to medicate or cut out this desire all together in order to save their hearts, but this is another kind of death. You won't be successful in that operation. It's like treating a heart condition with Neosporin® and a Band-Aid®. That's not nearly enough. God put desires in the heart, and God desires that hearts come to him to be healed, filled and sustained.

Hearts crave love: *validation, belonging, significance, acceptance, worth and value*. Ever since Adam and Eve were escorted out of the Garden of Eden that fallen day, we've been trying to return to it in order to ease the pain of life outside the garden. Because we live outside the garden, we have a tendency to wander, looking for a something or a someone to rescue us. And *rescued* is what we need to be, again and again and again. When I inventory my heart, I find my deep desires are *to matter, to contribute to something, to be seen, to be encouraged* and *to be invited* (just to mention a few). And when I look back at my life, I have to confess I have gone to great lengths to arrange for these things on my own. I'll try to tip the scale my way by people-pleasing or people-demanding. These are just a couple of my best (actually worst) plays, and I'll run them over and over again in order to gain life for myself. But at best these tactics have temporary results, just like an energy drink or a double-shot latte. They are good for a short burst but then comes the crash, and I have to get back to work, arranging, manipulating and orchestrating my next installment of life. It's what I do when I'm not satisfied with God.

What if the one true supplier *of* Love and Life met my addiction *for*

Love and Life head on? Is there such a thing as a good codependency? I believe there is, and it brings rest and relief to a weary heart.

It has brought rest and relief to mine.

ADDICTED TO LOVE

There was a hit song in the 80s by the recording artist Robert Plant. You 40-somethings might remember it from the early days of music videos—the all-girl band with slicked back hair, dressed in black leather skirts, wearing bright red lipstick. They looked like moving mannequins, stoic and haunting. The song itself was a good one, but it was the video that captured many a teenage boy. I recall the chorus: *You might as well face it, you're addicted to love.*

Every heart—both the ones that have been found, and all those still wandering, wanting and waiting to be found—wants *love*, for love is **Life**.

This reality is a problem.

No one person or even group of people can keep that flow of love coming your heart's way because they are all wanting and waiting for Love themselves. My wife and my kids, my parents and my friends, all are as much in need as I am and as addicted as I am. That is why we must find a Supplier outside of the physical realm who offers an unending hope for an eternal supply of Love that leads to Life. Having my tank full is what allows me to offer love to others from a *fullness* rather than a *neediness*.

To be clear, I'm not saying that we can escape our desire and need for Love and Life or put out to pasture our hunger and hope for it. What I am suggesting is that we can settle the question of who our supplier is, who the primary source of love is in our lives. God is the only one who can handle the weight of this order and meet the desires of our hearts consistently and abundantly. He simply asks that we come around often for the filling. It is then, from full hearts, that we can offer love to others and, in turn, point them to the One who supplies us with acceptance, worth, belonging and value.

But what does God get in the deal? Remember what we were made for? He made us for Himself, to not only receive His love but to return that love back to Him. That is His hope and desire. I'm not saying God *needs* our love. I'm saying He *desires* it, and those are different things.

One might say that everything I truly *need,* I will desire, but not everything I *desire* will I truly need. Every day God extends an invitation for me to be loved, to be a receiver of His love. This, after all, is how we are told we know love—not because we love Him, but because He first loved us. We know this makes sense. Ask any parent who loves more—the parent or the child? It is the parent of course, and over time the child connects to the parent because of what he or she has received. And though the child can't always articulate it, he or she can show it.

I remember when my oldest daughter, Ashley, was about two and a half years old. We were in line at a park, about to ride those little ponies that walk in a circle. She was so mesmerized by the little horses that they might as well have been the Budweiser Clydesdales. Because her eyes were fixed on the horses, she had stopped moving with the line and was now standing beside the man behind me. I watched her, taking great pleasure in the awe she had for the horses. Just then she reached out her arm and put a half hug around the knee of the gentleman who had taken the place I had been standing in. When the man said "Hi there," Ashley looked up and her pleasant smile was quickly replaced by a stunned look of *Hey, you're not my Dad!* Quickly I said "Hey sweetie, I'm right here," at which Ashley immediately offered both arms to me for rescue.

Who taught her which man was safer? How did she learn one pant leg is quite different from another? I believe this is the way and the will of the Father. He wants to show us that He is all we need to cling to by wooing us to Himself with dose after dose of Life and Love. He seems to pursue me more than I pursue Him, to want me near more than I want to be near him. He wants me filled more than I long to be filled. And that is a good thing. Pursued? Brought near? Filled again? What a relief! I seem to need this not just once but more and more like some kind of addict. *Hi, my name is Michael, and I'm addicted to Love.*

CHAPTER 8

SEARCH FOR THE HEART

But the seed on good soil stands for those with a noble and good heart.

Luke 8:15a

I learned God-worship when my pride was shattered. Heart-shattered lives ready for love don't for a moment escape God's notice.

Psalm 51:17 (MSG)

I remember where I was and what I was doing the first time I heard about the significance of the heart. I was sitting in a folding chair, surrounded by 250 men at a retreat in Colorado, listening to the speaker talk about men and the critical need for us to *get our hearts back*.

You know when you go to a restaurant and you are so tuned into the conversation you're having with someone over lunch that you don't hear the background music…then you notice a song you like and now the music is louder than the person speaking? That is kind of like what happened to me in that moment. My mind began to wander as the speaker moved through his various points, and I began having a conversation with myself. I drifted from the audible words of the speaker to the thoughts forming in my mind.

These questions surfaced: *Why haven't I heard this before? Is this right, is this true?* The conversation within continued as the speaker rattled off several passages of scripture about the heart, and another question surfaced: *I wonder how many passages there are about this heart stuff?*

One of my traditional ways of measuring the biblical weight and significance of a subject addressed in scripture is to see how many actual verses there are about that specific word. So, in order to answer these invading and interrupting questions, I flipped to the concordance in the back of my NIV Study Bible.

When I got to the word *heart*, I was stunned. There were more than three columns of verses that reference the heart. I saw *heart* passages from Genesis to Revelation: throughout the Old Testament, the books of the law, the major and minor prophets, the Gospels, the Epistles, and on into the letters written to the first-century church. I remember sitting there in that moment silently yelling to myself, *Oh my gosh, I think this is really important!* And, mind you, the print in a concordance is tiny, eight-point font, and it covered all of one page and spilled onto the next—more than 200 references! I've found that this is a pretty good way to determine if what I'm researching is a major or minor theme in the Bible. *Major* simply means there are lots of scripture references, and *heart* qualifies as a major theme!

Back to me at the conference, sitting in my chair, not paying attention to the speaker. I was stuck in that moment for what seemed like quite a while. Like Ashley with those ponies, I was in awe—and, at that time, almost 40 years old. I reached my arm around the knee of my heavenly Father, and He reached down and picked me up and carried me into *more*. I left that session—and the weekend—awakened, disrupted and wanting more. Little did I know, in the months to come, how major that moment, as well as that word *heart*, would prove itself to be in the recovery of my own heart and the trajectory of my spiritual life.

When I returned home from that weekend, my quest to research the depths of what the Bible says about the heart was before me. My game plan was simple—look up all the passages from the concordance and uncover what each had to say. For weeks I found myself standing over the theological microscope, my eyes fixed on sample after sample. I examined verse after verse, checking the translations from the Greek of the New

Testament and the Hebrew of the Old to investigate each verse's context. How had I missed this all these years—a treasure in my own back yard? It was becoming clearer and clearer to me that the heart matters, and it matters most to God.

Counselor and author, Ted Tripp, offers us this explanation on the heart in his book, *Shepherding a Child's Heart*:

> *The Scripture teaches that the heart is the control center for life...Proverbs 4:23– "Above all else, guard your **heart**, for it is the wellspring of life." The heart is a well from which all the issues of life gush forth. The behavior a person exhibits is an expression of the overflow of the **heart**.* (emphasis added)

The heart is the control center and the overflow. Ah ha! The lights were coming on, and I was beginning to see clearly. Not only were the passages containing the word *heart* bringing me a perspective I never had, the focus of a much larger picture was starting to emerge. The overwhelming conclusion that God was leading me to was that I can't live well in these Two Realms, in these Two Kingdoms, without my heart —my *whole* heart.

LOST IN TRANSLATION

I believe one of the most misunderstood words in the Bible is the word *heart*. Its definition, meaning and significance for the most part have been lost. Similar to misplacing an important document or leaving behind a precious piece of art or jewelry, this is a loss we cannot afford. We must recover the true significance of the heart if we are to journey well in our search for life. More accurately, in our *heart's* search for *Life*.

There are some passages that refer to the physical realm heart and the actual blood-pumping muscle housed in our chest, but the most common definition used for understanding the heart can be summarized by *Easton's Illustrated Dictionary of Biblical Terms*. Regarding the **heart**, Easton's says, "The heart is that center of spiritual activity and all the operations of human life."

The Hebrew language term for the heart—*leb,* and its synonym *lebab*—appears some 860 times in the Old Testament. *Vines Expository Dictionary of Biblical Words* states...

> *The heart is regarded as the seat of emotions, seat of knowledge and wisdom, and can be used of the man himself or his personality. It is also considered the seat of conscience and moral character.*

Here are some significant and noteworthy samples on the heart from the Old Testament:

*Love the Lord your God with all your **heart**.* Deuteronomy 6:5, Luke 10:27

*The Lord searches every **heart**.* 1 Chronicles 28:9

*We will be given a new **heart**.* Ezekiel 36:26

One of the larger questions that always seems to surface in the discussion of the heart is whether it is good or evil. The evidence in scripture refers to the heart as *swayable, impressionable,* and yet *significant* and even *crucial*. The heart is a wonderful and glorious place, vitally important, but also dangerous—a place in the core of a person's being.

PROTECTING THE HEART

The branch and the vine, the clay and the potter, the servant and the master—there is a relationship not just between these things but also *within* these things. These are the metaphors used in scripture to give us a glimpse of our need for connectedness to God. Without the vine, the branch withers and dies; without the potter, the clay remains formless and without function; without the master, the servant has no purpose or guidance; without a son or a daughter, there is no father.

Jesus made these references to everyday relationships to bring some extraordinary spiritual truths down to earth for us. Paul, too, uses this method to unpack an important message in Ephesians 6 when he speaks about the armor of God. He paints the picture of the image of a warrior and outfits him with spiritual armor. Is there really spiritual armor? I believe that if you asked Paul, he would answer, *Are you kidding? Try to make it through this battle zone, through your search for Life, without it! Don't you dare go unarmed. Going into battle naked is a sure way to take some major hits. Look around...casualties are everywhere!* You need armor if you are in a war; in much the same way, there is a vital connection between your life and protecting your heart. You need a heart for life—both the blood-pumping muscle in your chest and the spiritual one that is the wellspring of true Life.

I started to explore this idea, both logically and theologically, with a good friend of mine who is a doctor. It was truly amazing to discover the similarities between the physical and spiritual hearts. The physical heart is integral to a vital organ system, and many parts of this system must function in harmony in order to sustain life. Lungs, kidneys, stomach, brain, spinal cord—all the parts are important, and we see the same idea played out in our spiritual body through scripture. Our minds, our souls and our strength must work in harmony with our hearts to bring us spiritual health and life. The spiritual armor Paul speaks of is vital to protecting our *spiritual* bodies. When you cut off a part of your body, or inhibit it or corrupt it, both the physical man and the spiritual man will function at a sub-par level. Just like the pumping of blood and its flow throughout our bodies depends on a good heart, we must have a healthy spiritual heart at our core to thrive in the Spiritual Realm. The irony is that we tend to give much more attention to our physical hearts that are winding down with every beat than we do to the spiritual heart that is eternal and the dwelling place of a Life that only gets better and better when we tend to it properly.

The heart is susceptible in both the physical and spiritual realms to disease or infection. But one heart is going to have its last beat while the other will live forever. The more we learn how to live from and journey with a whole spiritual heart, the more Life we will experience—in this realm now as well as in the glorious merger of realms to come. The cycle looks like this: more heart equals more love, more love equals more Life, and more Life equals more heart. Block or infect this cycle, and the result will be less and less of each. Less Life, less Love; less Love, less Heart.

JESUS ON THE HEART

Jesus spoke often of the heart. In the Sermon on the Mount (Matthew 5), Jesus makes it clear that He is after more than a *principled* or *dutiful life*, more than a life that simply manages itself by keeping the rules or staying in line. Jesus says in the eighth verse: *Blessed are the pure in* **heart**, *for they will see God.* In their *New Testament Commentary on The Gospel of Matthew*, Walvoord and Zuck state that this passage literally means:"Happy are those who are clean on the inside from sin through faith in God's provision." When we are transformed, our hearts (our cores) are made clean and holy. A few verses later in the Sermon on the Mount, Jesus makes it clear that it is the heart He is after: *For where your treasure is there your heart will be also.* (Matthew 6:21) I believe what he is saying is, *Treasure Me, treasure my Father's Kingdom and treasure this way of Life. You give your heart to what you treasure and what you treasure has your heart.* Don't we know this reality all too well?

Jesus wants His audience to see the heart as the source of their sin-behavior, sin-attitudes and sin-choices. But even more He wants us to see that the heart is the very place He came to inhabit, heal and restore. He does so in order that our same sin-centered hearts can be free of all that once hindered, shackled and weighed us down. If the heart is dangerous on one side of the ledger, then, when transformed, made over and made new, it is glorious on the other side. It becomes the very place in which the Spirit of God resides. The heart of a person, the core of his or her being, becomes the source of godliness and holiness, identity and mission, from deep within.

Here are several other passages highlighting Jesus' teaching about the heart:

> *The good man brings good things out of the good stored up in his **heart**...For out of the overflow of his **heart** his mouth speaks*
>
> Luke 6:45

> *But the seed on good soil stands for those with a noble and good **heart**, who hear the word, retain it, and by persevering produce a crop.*
>
> Luke 8:15

> *For this people's **heart** has become calloused; they hardly hear with their ears, and they have closed their eyes. Otherwise they might see with their eyes, and hear with their ears, understand with their **hearts** and turn, and I would heal them.*
>
> Matthew 13:15

> *Do not let your **hearts** be troubled. Trust in God, trust also in me. ... Peace I leave with you; my peace I give you. I do not give to you as the world gives. Do not let your **hearts** be troubled and do not be afraid.*
>
> John 14:1, 27

Jesus is very concerned with the inside of a person, the core, the heart.

> Vine's Expository Dictionary states: *The **heart** is to be seen as the seat of moral nature, spiritual life, grief, desires, affections, perceptions, thoughts, understanding, reasoning powers, imagination, intentions, purposes, will and faith...the **core**.*
> (emphasis added)

Is it any wonder that the heart has extreme value and significance in the realm that matters most? Jesus is inviting us to a deeper understanding of how He views this treasure within a man or a woman. He is constantly making the point that life is not to operate under the belief that our performance is the key to gaining favor with God. Jesus goes out of His way to make clear again and again that adopting this perspective is detrimental, a desperately wrong turn in life. Performance *for* blessing will get us lost. Performance *from* blessing is what Jesus wants for us and what will ultimately bring us fulfillment.

AN APOSTLE OF THE HEART

Paul makes more references to the *heart* than any other New Testament writer. Of Paul's writings, the book of Romans carries the greatest New Testament inventory of heart passages. The two passages that just might be of the greatest significance are these:

> *... that if you confess with your mouth, "Jesus is Lord," and believe in your **heart** that God raised him from the dead and you will be saved.*
>
> Romans 10:9

> *I pray that out of his glorious riches he may strengthen you with power through his Spirit in your inner being, so that Christ may dwell in your **hearts** through faith.*
>
> Ephesians 3:16-17a (emphasis added)

The heart is central to the message of the Christian Gospel, the Good News. When a congregation or community of believers encourages a non-believer to *invite Jesus into his heart*, the offer is nothing less than *Life*. Jesus said, *I am the way, the truth and the life.* (John 14:6) What was once dead, a life without Christ, is made alive *in* Christ (Colossians 3:1-4, John 10:10). When a person who is spiritually pronounced dead encounters the One who raises people from the dead, Life is the result. Jesus literally enters his or her spiritual heart and revives that person. He indwells them and commits to sustain them. He has started a *new life* in them. This is why Jesus can invite us to come to Him for Life *and* by no other can we have Life though, we may try (John 5:40). As I've mentioned before, our hearts and life are consistently connected in scripture, especially when the subject of scripture has anything to do with how a person is saved from sin. The result is a new state, a new condition, a new man or woman. From death we are brought into *Life*. **That is what we are searching for:** ***Life!*** Try to have life without a heart or a heart without life. They go together and are clearly meant to by design.

HEARTS OVER BEHAVIOR

When my three girls were nine, seven and four (all beautiful like their mother), they began to tutor their dad about engaging with their hearts and not just their behavior. This was a major result of having my own heart rescued by God again and again and the restorative work He is still accomplishing in me. So now I'm discovering I can be a part of the same search and rescue effort for the hearts of others, beginning on my own home front. Regarding my kids, some significant obstacles had to be understood, addressed and removed in my relationship with these precious girls. For too long, all I wanted to give them as their dad seemed to be hindered by all I was wanting and needing to *get* from them. More and more it became evident that much of what I was doing was trying to control their behavior—and worse, my motivation to do this was to make life more convenient for *me*. So often I tried to get them to do what I told them when I told them—and in record time—so we could move on to the next task or just get through the next moment. I would look at things they did, call them close (or sometimes just yell at them from across the room) and tell them what they had done wrong. It was never a question on my part as to what *they* were thinking or feeling. I had determined I already knew and had responded accordingly with, *Do more, be better and try harder.*

The results of this method soon became increasingly clear. *It wasn't working.* You see, I can *make* my children behave, I can modify their behavior with a stern or threatening voice or an ultimatum, and I can get results. This program can work simply because I'm bigger and stronger, and I can intimidate them. I remember as a boy being sent to my room to think about my *bad* behavior or being made to pick something up or do a chore over again. I did it, but you don't want to know what I was saying about my parents in my heart and under my breath. They had my behavior but not my heart. What if we could get both?

I am so passionate about this restorative message about the heart because I have experienced the difference it can make firsthand. As God got hold of my heart, I began to be enabled to offer others, like my wife and three girls, all the new depths of Life and Love I was now experiencing from God. The Father was moving from my heart to my head and remolding me, reforming me, restoring my life to more of what I hoped it could be. More like Him. I heard author Wayne Jacobson once say, "I believe we have it backward. We often say we need to get it from our heads to our hearts; what we really need to do is get it from our hearts to our heads." The more of my heart I got back, the more I came alive. The more I came alive, the more I started to think differently. Restoration of heart brought Life—and the more alive I became, the more I began to see and hear differently. As a result I was beginning to affect for good those on this planet I wanted to love the most.

The revelation I learned about my heart, and in turn about the hearts of my children, was that addressing behavior alone is actually a backward way of approaching our own struggles and those of others. Behavior is the *result* of what is already in our hearts. Behavior may actually be the greatest clue as to what is in our hearts; addressing behavior alone is like putting a Band-Aid® on a broken bone. Going after the heart, seeing and hearing *why* a person does things is a much better way to love someone.

Now this new home-front program of focusing on hearts over behavior was established in early 2000, but it has not always gone well for my wife and three daughters—or for me. We are truly working it out as we go, but it has become the new glorious standard in our home. Why are we so committed to this attitude, perspective and belief? Because it is the closest thing we've found to what God is up to in our lives. The Father knows that if you get a person's heart, you get his or her behavior too. After almost 10 years of practicing this approach, we are beginning to reap the rewards in the way our girls are living and seeing life. Hearts over behavior is simply the better way. Just a few nights ago at dinner with some friends, they were asking us what God was teaching us about raising our daughters. I smiled when my wife said, "We go after their hearts."

GOD HAS A HEART

One of the greatest honors I have as a dad is when someone comes up to me with a big smile and declares, *Hey you're Ashley's (or Hannah's or Abbey's) Dad!*, followed by a compliment about her manners, her skills or her contributions. My wife and I take great joy and pride in moments like that. Now when we are standing among friends, the other parents don't seem to enjoy it as much. Their *Oh, that's nice* smile breaks out. Why is it that we, her parents, take more pleasure out of the compliment than those who aren't her parents? Clearly it is because of our connection to our children. In a very real way, we made them. Yes, like any parent, there are times we'd rather not claim, them but we never deny our connection. Our hearts are for our daughters, and we've passed along not only the shape of their bodies through DNA but also the shape of their hearts through the bestowing of love, guidance and help.

The same principles apply to our relationship with God. He is, after all, our Father, and we bear His image in significant ways—most especially in that we have a heart. As I was studying and researching the overall topic of the heart, it was truly a stunning discovery and an astounding whisper to my own heart that *God has a heart too*. Here are a few of the verses that present this powerful truth:

In Matthew 11:29, Jesus says:

> *Take my yoke upon you and learn from me, for I am gentle and humble in **heart**, and you will find rest for your souls.*

In John 12:27-28, Jesus says:

> *Now my **heart** is troubled, and what shall I say? 'Father, save me from this hour'? No, it was for this very reason I came to this hour. Father, glorify your name!*

In Jeremiah 3:15, God speaks:

> *Then I will give you shepherds after my own **heart**, who will lead you with knowledge and understanding.*

In I Kings 9:3 and II Chronicles 7:16, God tells Solomon:

> *...I have heard the prayer and plea you have made before me; I have consecrated this temple, which you have built, by putting my Name there forever. My eyes and my heart will always be there.*

The story of King David, recorded in both Old and New Testaments, is one of a boy stepping from the sheep pasture to the king's throne. David's life is marked by one of the greatest confirmations, validations and declarations one could ever receive from God. In 1 Samuel 13:13-14, Samuel tells King Saul that God's hand is being removed from him as king and another is going to replace him. Samuel says of the future king, Saul's replacement, *The L<small>ORD</small> has sought out a man after his own **heart** and appointed him leader of his people.* Later in Acts 13:22, it is stated again: *I have found David son of Jesse a man after my own **heart**; he will do everything I want him to do.* (Emphasis added)

God has a heart. Whether or not we must interpret this literally or figuratively, I don't know. I leave that discussion to those who find it necessary to resolve the issue. What I do know is that either way the scriptures are clear; there *is* a heart of God. There is a core, a center to His being, and at times He seems to feel the need to reference it.

Going all the way back to the beginning of the Bible, the first two chapters of Genesis, and the record of how we were created, we might find our greatest clue to the significance of having a heart connected with God. There in the creation account, we learn *we* are His *image bearers* and though there is much more to discuss on the weightiness and significance of that fact, I simply ask that we take this truth at face value. God has a heart, as revealed by scripture, and so do we—those created in His image. That magnificent reality alone makes us valuable and important to Him. When He made us, He gave us a heart of our own— one that was created to connect to His. And when we connect to the heart of God, there is Life. When connected, we bring *His heart* joy. This is what we were designed for and therefore what we really desire—to be connected.

GIVING OUR HEARTS AWAY

This is why there is a battle between the Two Kingdoms. It is for the alliance, allegiance and the affections of one's heart. And we know this, don't we? Look at the friendship formed when a young man and woman meet. When this friendship progresses, dating or courting evolves. Soon the focus turns to the two becoming one. Ceremonies take place —the giving of one heart to the significant other.

> *Do you, Michael, take this woman, Robin, and her whole heart, to love and to cherish 'til death do you part?*
> *I do.*

A heart has been given away, entrusted to the care of another; trusted with the alliance, allegiance and affection of one's own heart. There is a reason the scriptures speak of the church as the bride of Christ and of Him as the bridegroom. This most intimate of relationships is not a metaphor of our relationship, but rather a demonstrative one. What if we were not just loved by God, but rather we were *in love*?

One day I was praying, actually more listening than launching words. I was inviting God to speak to my heart. I asked Him about His love *for* me, like a child who wants to hear her Dad say how important or precious she is to him. Like my girls might ask, *Daddy do you love me?* God, do you really love me? Really? The next whisper I heard in my thoughts was, *I more than love you, I'm in love with you.* I smiled, and I think I actually skipped rather than walked the rest of the day. It was scandalous, and it was good. I might be one of His favorites, you might be too. Ask Him. Go on…ask Him.

This is why God is so fiercely *for* us and tender *with* us. We matter to Him. When Christ searches for and rescues a person, the recovery of significant things comes next. Change would be an understatement—*transformation* is what truly happens. The man or woman who was once dead in sin is now alive. That is truly a transformational work of Christ. The question is then: Is the heart still evil and sinful, hard (like a stone) and wicked, after one is transformed and steps into the family of God? When a person—by repentance of sin and acceptance of God's provision for sin—is justified to God, is he or she still wicked and sinful at the core?

Scripture states that the work of Christ revives, reshapes and restores us from our inside (the heart) out. Would Jesus then, in the form of the Holy Spirit, reside in a predominantly or even remotely evil, sinful place? Scripture clearly states that *He comes to dwell in our **hearts.*** (Ephesians 3:17, Romans 8:11, I Corinthians 3:16) Maybe you're asking *Is this figurative?* I would extend caution when walking on that ice. Be careful not to label *figurative* what biblical evidence points to as a *reality*. Mysterious is different than figurative. And if it is figurative then what weight and significance can be placed on it? If the heart were, contrary to scripture, evil even *after* it is redeemed then the residence of God in us wouldn't be fit for Him. But the Bible tells us that His majesty and holiness dwells in the temple in the holy of holies—our hearts. (1 Corinthians 6:19)

According to the scriptures, the heart is the home of our deepest, most personal life—the heart is where the real you resides. Therefore a man is *designated* or described by the orientation of his heart. Consider these examples from the Bible:

    A Wise heart (1 Kings 3:12)
    A Pure heart (Psalm 24:3-4 and Matthew 5:8)
    A Praising heart (Psalm 9:1)
    An Upright heart (Psalms 11:2)
    A heart of Integrity (Psalm 78:72)
    A Good and Noble heart (Luke 8:15)
    A Forgiving heart (Matthew 18:35)

The heart is also the seat of conscience (Romans 2:15) and, in its unregenerate, natural state, it is wicked (Genesis 8:21) and therefore can and does contaminate the whole person. If the well is polluted, the water will be bad; if the root is infected, the fruit will be also. God knows this, and that is why we must go through a heart transformation (Ezekiel 11:19 and 36:26) before we can truly have the relationship with God we were created for. He recognizes our deepest need and does something only He can do—rescues us, then transforms us. He cleanses, heals, softens and restores us—this is why the Gospel is such good news. Really good news!!!

This is both our reality *and* our forecast. We're not home yet. The significance, magnitude and weight of God's search and rescue efforts are still greatly underestimated. Our condition is far worse than most of us know, and yet the good that God is up to in our lives is far, far greater than we've understood or been led to believe. There are reasons for that, and we must continue our journey in hopes of seeing, hearing and being found, *again and again*. And while we search, we must know we are not the only ones searching. As in any epic story, there are forces far larger than us searching as well.

CHAPTER 9

WE'RE NOT THE ONLY ONES SEARCHING

All our lives we search for someone who makes us complete. We choose partners and change partners. We dance the song of heartbreak and hope all the while, wondering if somewhere, somehow there is someone searching for us.

Unknown

Now the serpent was more subtle and crafty than any living creature of the field which the Lord God had made.

Genesis 3:1a (AMP)

We look upon the enemy of our souls as a conquered foe, so he is, but only to God, not to us.

Oswald Chambers

This story is not near as safe as you and I have been led to believe.

John Eldredge

In *The Lord of the Rings*, Frodo and Sam find themselves traveling in circles on their journey to Mordor and the quest to destroy the Ring. Their frustration levels rise above their weariness when they realize they are lost. From different vantage points on the mountains where they roam, they can see the dark and evil lands they must enter, but time and time again they set out from their position only to descend, then climb again and find themselves no closer to their destination than they were before.

>**Sam:** This looks strangely familiar
>
>**Frodo** (exasperated)**:** Because we've been here before. We're going in circles.
>
>**Sam:** Uh! What's that horrid stink, I wonder if there's a nasty bog near by. Can you smell it?
>
>**Frodo:** Yes, I can smell it…We're not alone.

This is one of many significant moments in *The Lord of the Rings*

Trilogy. While Sam and Frodo are searching for Mordor, others are searching for them. The jealous, vengeful creature, Gollum, who once possessed the Ring, is after them, and he isn't the only evil searching for the two little hobbits. Platoons of Orks and Urk-hai, the goblin servants of the Dark Lord Sauron, are also on patrol, searching and hunting for the two companions. If that isn't enough drama, Sam and Frodo's friends, the fellowship of the ring, are hanging onto hope that they too will find and soon rejoin the lost members of their fellowship. There is a lot going on. So it is with our lives.

SEARCHING AND BEING SEARCHED FOR

As stated earlier, we are all searching. The alarming reality is that as we are searching, there are things searching for us. I remember being about 11 years old and *not* out looking for a magazine with pictures of naked women. It wasn't on my boyhood heart's to-do list that day—*mow the lawn, pick up my room, have grilled cheese for lunch, find pornography.* But that magazine found me. My story is an unfortunately common one among men in regards to pornography. It is paralleled by the story of little girls, when the subject is that of beauty and appearance. An accusation comes along with the glamour magazines—*you don't have enough to offer.*

I work with the hearts of men and women, committed to helping them recover their deep hearts so they might live freely. I hear countless stories of what has attacked them, what has attached to them and encumbered their hearts in the search for Life. Somewhere in all our stories, harmful things have found us and clung to us in ways that are draining, weakening and hindering us in our mission to find the Life we were meant for and the Life we deeply desire.

Both of the kingdoms are hoping to attach to us, resulting in our attachment in turn to one of them. Remember, one Kingdom is *for* us and the other is *against* us. One Kingdom is Life-giving and the other over-promises and under-delivers. Both are working hard to convince us that they are offering Life. One can deliver Life while the other is death in disguise, offering bondage as its actual product. The methods and schemes of the kingdom of darkness take Life away. In John 10:10a, before the promise of abundant Life, Jesus says...

"The thief comes only to steal and kill and destroy."

Our enemy knows how God designed us—to need Him and each other. The enemy slips in to use this *need* to his advantage. The worst collisions of all are when two life-draining forces (two people) find each other and attach. You can easily predict the outcome. It's not pretty. Our enemy knows this and is constantly working to put us in harm's way by having us either feed off of others or be fed upon.

There is another reality in motion that we must give time and attention to, another movement within the Larger Story. While we are searching, on the lookout for something or someone that will give us Life, there are forces at work searching for us. One is ready and able to give us our heart's desire, the other is hell bent on keeping us from it. There is a Life that is searching for us. But death is also on the prowl.

PREDATOR AND PROTECTION

We are all searching for Life, wanting our lives to matter, to make sense, and we need someone to tell us so. We're wired that way, and there truly is a way for our deep longings and desires for Life to be met.

> *...I Myself, will search for My sheep and will seek them out. As a shepherd seeks out his sheep in the day that he is among his flock that are scattered, so will I seek out My sheep; and I will rescue them out of all places where they have been scattered in the day of clouds and thick darkness.*
>
> Ezekiel 34:11-12 (AMP)

God searches for us, offering and inviting us into Life in Him and with

Him. All the while, there is another who is searching too. Actually *hunting* would be a better word. We see this theme played out in story after story. Dorothy finds out there is a wicked witch after her shoes and trying to spoil her mission to get home. Neo battles the agents and their attempts to control the prisoners of the Matrix. Maximus fights against Commodus in order to free all of Rome. And eventually the three little pigs all hole up together, stoking the fire in the fireplace, just in case the wolf gets any more sinister ideas.

Peter writes in a letter to the church, "That our adversary prowls around like a roaring lion, searching for whom he may devour." (1 Peter 5:8) **Yikes!** Why in the world is this verse in the Bible? There is a predator in our story? He's looking for his next meal to devour and that meal is *me*? For most of my life I lived naively, without understanding or practicing this reality. And then, when I learned of it, I continued to live in a state of denial. But unaware and untrained is no way to go through life. When I finally awakened to the truth that there *is* an adversary intent on me settling for a counterfeit life, my journey changed and so did my search for Life. I am still reaping the benefits of this awareness and training, because God has upgraded my heart's understanding of the story in which I live.

For too long I was living as lunch, being consumed again and again by the enemy and his counterfeit life. I'll never forget an explanation of a passage in first Peter by a wonderful pastor, Dr. Tony Evans. He wondered how a person would get devoured by a roaring lion. He explained that the roar is the warning people need to hear so they can either defend themselves or retreat to another location. So how can somebody not hear that there is a lion roaring close by? "I'll tell you how," Evans said. "They don't hear the roar of the approaching lion because their ears are tuned to their own voice. Because they are self absorbed, they are deaf to the danger that lurks nearby."

Dr. Evans continued, explaining, "The secret to not being eaten up comes in the verses of 1 Peter preceding the dire warning of the roar, where it says to '*Clothe yourselves with humility....Humble yourself....*

Cast all your anxiety on him (God) because he cares for you.' " (1 Peter 5:5-7) "Pride is not just a beating of the chest and a *look at me* attitude," shared Evans. "Pride is simply looking inwardly for solutions to life, a self reliance of any kind and that makes us deaf to the roar of our adversary."

If the only voice we hear in the story is our own because we believe we are both author and center of the story, then we will be found—but by a ruthless and evil prince rather than by the kind heart of God. This prince is a sinister hunter who runs a dark kingdom and already has far too many trophies. I know this great hunter well and have the teeth marks to show for it. I am glad to say that escaping his clutches was another one of the rescues in my life. Staying out of his way is now part of my mission. God is training up those who long to be a part of His abolition force, freedom fighters leading others to the safety of His Kingdom. You have to be free yourself in order to lead and love others to safety. There is always a pull of the enemy, and as God's liberators we can't afford to underestimate it.

THE GRAVITATIONAL PULL

We are all are subject to the pull of gravity, even if we're not all that familiar with how it works. I know I don't often think about it; I just live with it. So describes my life prior to being given new eyes, ears and heart.

I played college basketball at a small NAIA school in Oklahoma. I was just good enough to make the team, and I was determined to work hard in order to be *somebody*. I loved the game. Ever since junior high, the pull of the game became more than a healthy force that kept my feet on the ground and gave me exercise, a group of friends and some fun things to do on Friday or Saturday nights. The harder I worked, the more the feeling crept in that *this game owes me*. The more I practiced, the more I found I had to prove my abilities and needed, even demanded, opportunities to show I had what it took.

At one point in my junior year of college, I broke into the starting line-up. All my hard work had paid off. It was then that I found I couldn't shut off the constant pressing, striving and proving I had made my default over the past several years. I was great at chasing the dream, but not very good at possessing it. The pressure became too much and after a few games I was replaced in the starting lineup and went back to coming off the bench. And so I returned to the only method I knew to deal with the pain and to remedy the heartache I felt—*more work, more practice, more devotion.* I have to confess—this had become my plan for much more than just basketball at that point.

Late one night in the midst of this wreckage, I went back to the gym alone to shoot. Several minutes into the workout, hitting jump shot after jump shot, I began to get angrier and angrier. I finally collapsed to the floor in angry tears. All the whispers of the enemy bombarded me in this climactic moment. All I had come to believe was being put on the table. *This game owes me. I've sacrificed. I've done all the work. I love this game.* My next thought came as more of a rebuttal—as if God was invading the gym and protecting me from the enemy, who like a shark had smelled blood and was circling me. I believe God was whispering straight to my heart, *"The game doesn't love you back."* The Jealous Lover of my heart had made His heart known. More tears came but this time they were not of anger but relief. The great break-up began, and the relationship I had been in with this game for the previous 12 years came to a glorious train-wreck ending. I went into the gym under the heavy weight of a gravitational pull toward anything that might give me Life (applause, recognition, validation, acceptance, worth, belonging) and went out of the gym having lost a hundred pounds of spiritual weight. One relationship severed, and another one now free to advance.

A game isn't the only thing that can pull us down with fierce force. Any hobby or interest has the ability to become an obsession. Most often though it is another person that will have the binding effect. Doing whatever it takes to make Mom and Dad proud, giving anything to show a special someone that we aren't lacking and don't fall short—these are all symptoms of a sickness. A sickness that if left untreated will leave us barely alive. A girlfriend, teacher, coach or parent, all with their own heart's gravitational dilemmas to work out, can be so destructive when the forces in our lives collide. There is only one answer. Turn to the One who isn't subject to the gravitational pull but who instead wants to set us free from its power and devastation. God has freedom on His heart all the time because that is what love does. Pure, unconditional, unadulterated love *frees us!*

TWO KINGDOMS WAR

In any epic battle, there are three parts:
>The one being oppressed
>The one oppressing
>The one coming to set things right and restore freedom

As mentioned before, Two Kingdoms are warring for the alliance, allegiance and affection of your heart. One kingdom brings ultimate oppression while the other offers ultimate freedom. What makes all the battles fought *over me* unique is that I actually get to participate. I get to have a say in which kingdom is victorious in my life. Ultimately, the God who longs to liberate *could make* us come to Him for Life and Freedom. He *could require* us to side with Him, but how freeing would that be? That would just be another form of oppression.

Satan and his network of underlings actually have limited authority in this world and especially over those who belong to God—he only has the power we allow him to have. The honor bestowed on us in the Garden continues to be our greatest honor today—the ability to choose, to have free will. The decision is ours. This is what C. S. Lewis describes in *Mere Christianity* as the great risk of God. I have included this quotation at length as not to lose any of its significance, impact and weight:

Christians, then, believe that an evil power has made himself for the present the Prince of this World. And, of course, that raises problems. Is this state of affairs in accordance with God's will or not? If it is, He is a strange God, you will say: and if it is not, how can anything happen contrary to the will of a being with absolute power?

But anyone who has been in authority knows how a thing can be in accordance with your will in one way and not in another. It may be quite sensible for a mother to say to the children, "I'm not going to go and make you tidy the schoolroom every night. You've got to learn to keep it tidy on your own." Then she goes up one night and finds the Teddy bear and the ink and the French Grammar all lying in the grate. That is against her will. She would prefer the children to be tidy. But on the other hand, it is her will which has left the children free to be untidy. The same thing arises in any regiment, or trade union, or school. You make a thing voluntary and then half the people do not do it. That is not what you willed, but your will made it possible.

Of course God knew what would happen if they used their freedom the wrong way: apparently He thought it worth the risk. Perhaps we feel inclined to disagree with Him. But there is a difficulty about disagreeing with God. He is the source from which all your reasoning power comes: you could not be right and He wrong any more than a stream can rise higher than its own source. When you are arguing against Him you are arguing against the very power that makes you able to argue at all: it is like cutting off the branch you are sitting on. If God thinks this state of war in the universe is a price worth paying for free will—that is, for making a live world in which creatures can do real good or harm and something of real importance can happen, instead of a toy world which only moves when He pulls the strings—then we may take it is worth paying.

In 1979, Bob Dylan wrote a song that circled back again and again to the line, "Well it may be the devil or it may be the Lord but you're gonna have to serve somebody." Where we go, or to whom we go, to receive Life, is an expression of our beliefs. We go where we believe there is a chance to get what we need. That is why it is a matter of faith. There is no way around it. If we declare *there is no God* and we are self-reliant, or if we say *there is a God* and we become interdependent, either way it is our belief in motion—our faith exercised. Our wills declared.
Who you bet on matters a great, great deal.

FOR YOU

Nothing in the universe feels as good to our hearts as being loved. It is Life. Life and Love are connected. They were designed that way. God, the Greatest Being in the cosmos, describes Himself in a word—Love (1 John 4). He is that Being and the creator of all Life in the universe, both in the spiritual and physical realms. It can be said that whenever and wherever love is being experienced or expressed, God is there. Love doesn't exist without Him. And only with Him is there love. What is most amazing is that He is not like a store or a vending machine to which we go to get things. Rather, He is much more like a delivery man with glorious packages He longs to present and from whom we can receive.

Think about it: *what if* there was a person—even better, three persons—who longs to make it so that you are never alone, always seen, always wanted and constantly invited? A person who sees to it that you are appreciated and even sought after. Can you imagine someone who wants to not only share the holidays with you but also the every-days of life? Someone who is not only strong enough to rescue and deliver you but who can also protect and provide for you. A Father who will be beside you the rest of the journey home and beyond. Someone who is so crazy about you that He is willing to die for you. Someone wanting to be your friend in celebrating the good times and comforting you in the bad times. Someone who knows you need *a lot* of help and who is willing to counsel, teach, guide and comfort you on your journey. *What if?*

There is a God—Father, Son and Spirit—and He wants to do all this in a million different ways over a multitude of moments in our lives *and* in the lives around us. This is amazing news. But *what if* there was a force committed to keeping us from the very relationship we were created for and need the most? What if this force plants seeds of doubt that lead us to fear and away from trust and love? What if we were duped into believing a lie that keeps us from all that is offered by the Father, Son and Holy Spirit? *What if?*

ALL THAT IS AGAINST YOU

If we take a look around, we can see the wreckage of lives that can't or won't give heed to the Two Realms they live in. Or they can't see the Two Kingdoms that are at war over their hearts in the Larger Story and the crucial roles that are theirs to play. The greatest accomplishment of our enemy is that we live *disoriented*. In living disoriented, we settle for too little. The reason most people live this way is that captivity is all they've known and they've settled for it. Or they *underestimate* their story, the Larger Story and all of the history that leads to their moments on the grand stage. We underestimate the larger realm (the Spiritual Realm), the Great War and the value that has been placed on us by the One who made us for Himself. For Love. For Life. We underestimate the forces against us. We underestimate the enemy and, as Eldredge says about our enemy, *he fears what we might become*.

In reality, there are three forces of evil working, plotting and conspiring together against us in our journey and great search for Life. These three forces make up the *unholy trinity*. Satan is one, but it is the other two that so often seal the deal.

The second force we're up against is *the world.* Jesus said in John 12:31 that Satan is *the Prince of this world.* Our enemy has a domain, a place in which he wields an influence, and that place is sure to be a hostile environment. It's like we're living in enemy-occupied territory or always playing on the road as the visiting team. Living in North Carolina, I think of it as being like 20,000 of Duke's Cameron Crazy basketball fans filling UNC's Dean Dome for any game the Tarheels play. Just try to tune out the Cameron Crazies and don't let them get to you. Good luck.

Paul warns us to be *in* the world but not *of* the world. Peter shares his concerns that we live with a lion on the loose looking for whom it may devour. The apostle John writes this to the early church:

> *Don't love the world's ways. Don't love the world's goods. Love of the world squeezes out love for the Father. Practically everything that goes on in the world—wanting your own way, wanting everything for yourself, wanting to appear important—has nothing to do with the Father. It just isolates you from him. The world and all its wanting, wanting, wanting is on the way out.*
>
> 1 John 2:15-17a (MSG)

The third and final evil we have to contend with is what scripture calls *the flesh*—a bent toward focusing inward to make life work. It is a tendency to exercise a fierce independence and to go it on our own rather than following God. It goes by other aliases*: the false self, fallenness, the old man, the sin nature.* Author Brennan Manning calls it *the great impostor,* and Eldredge deems it the *poser* for men and *fallen Eve* for women. All are expressions of a counterfeit life that is a threat to us on our search. It is a threat that comes from the inside, a traitor within, that wants to align with the world and with Satan's forces against what is true, right and good. And so it comes down to *Who do we trust?* Sadly, one thing that much of life has taught us to embrace is to trust no one but ourselves.

Vine's New Testament Dictionary of The Bible describes the two conflicting natures in the heart this way:

> *Human depravity is in the heart, because sin is a "principle" which has its seat in the center of a man's inward life, and then corrupts him or defiles him. The other side of the coin, Scripture regards the heart as the sphere of Divine influence, where the real man or woman resides, where the work of God takes place, where our true character lies and the place that God is after when He comes after a man or woman bringing him or her to Himself.*

This is a clear picture of the incredible substantive value of the heart, why it is the subject of internal conflict in a person's life as well as the battle that takes place in the Spiritual Realm for its attention, affection and allegiance. Eternity is at stake, and there is a connected relationship between our hearts and eternity. Ecclesiastes 3:11 says that he says *put (set) eternity in their hearts.*

Remember John Piper's statement, *Sin is what we do when we're not satisfied with God.* The reality is that we need rescuing from this flesh *and* the evil one who is trying to play us like a puppet. Our fallen condition is cause and validation enough to merit a rescuer, a Savior, in the Larger Story in which we live. So, like a super hero who comes in the nick of time to pull us from the clutches of the villain, Christ steps in. With fierce strength He comes between us and the destroying evil that would capture us. The **big** question is this will we go with Him, our Rescuer, or choose to stay with our captor?

BEING FOUND

And so, it is not *if* we are found, but *when* and *by whom* that is most important. There is a finder who has *paid a fee for us*, a ransom; and there is a finder who has a fee *for us to pay*, a debt of insurmountable expense. The *Dictionary of New Testament Theology* explains:

> *God opens a man's heart (Acts 16:14) and lets his light illumine the heart (2 Corinthians 4:6). God bears his witness to man by sending into his heart the Spirit of the Son (2 Corinthians 1:22). When this Spirit takes up his dwelling in the heart, man is no longer a slave to sin, but a son and heir of God (Galatians 4:6). God pours out His love into his heart (Romans 5:5). Through faith Christ can take up residence in the heart (Ephesians 3:17).*

The process of our search and rescue begins at the heart and in the heart. God targets our hearts. When a person places faith and trust in Christ as his or her Savior, things change. *Everything* changes. A missing person has been found. When a missing person is found, things change. When God finds us, we are changed at the deepest level—in our hearts. It is at that moment, when we believe, that we are not only found, but transformed. *Made over*. Our old nature is replaced with a new one. We are no longer a *slave* but a *son or daughter*. Trust and faith in Christ, wrapping our arms around His neck and letting Him whisk us to safety, is far more than getting us out of harm's way. It is a rescue of heart, a transformation of identity and an equipping for victory through the authority of the One to whom we have now given our allegiance. Anything less would be a partial saving, "mostly" rescued, "for the most part" set free. Paul puts it this way in 2 Corinthians 5:17: **Therefore, if anyone is in Christ, he is a new creation; the old has gone, the new has come!**

    Remember Nicodemus, the religious man, and his encounter with Jesus in the alley under the shadow of the night? He asks, *What must I do to be saved?* Jesus tells him (and us) in John 3:3, *You must be born again.* And in that *rebirth* we are given the essential gift, a new piece of equipment that makes our new Life possible. In order to have a new **Life**, we are issued a new **Heart***!* (Ezekiel 11:19 and Psalm 51:10-14) This surgery doesn't come cheap. It has a great price—a ransom price—one that our enemy didn't want paid and does not want us to know has been made available. After all, ownership gives authority. Our enemy would rather not give us up—but again, that isn't up to him. He rules by lies and intimidation. The prisoners he holds, he holds by their conditions and will more than his own. It is a prison without fences and a cell without walls or a door, and yet far too many remain imprisoned. Getting out is and has always been up to us.

RANSOMED

We have two dogs in our home. Mine is a beautiful hunting dog from South Dakota named Arwyn, after the Elven princess in *The Lord of the Rings*. A good friend gave her to me as a very special gift. My daughters' dog, Zoe, is a cockapoo (just writing the name *cockapoo* gives me the willies). Now if someone broke into my home and stole Zoe and pinned a ransom note on the door that read, *One million dollars left in a bag on the porch by midnight tomorrow, or the dog gets it,* I would honestly have to tell you that I would write back and say, *Enjoy the dog*. But if someone broke into my house and kidnapped one of my daughters, the amount on the ransom note wouldn't matter—I'd pay. Whatever it took and whatever I had to do, I'd pay.

My car has been broken into twice in my lifetime. Both times the vehicles were in my driveway. It is a sickening feeling to walk up to your truck and see the window bashed in and the mess of glass scattered inside. It is a violation that sticks with you. All crimes violate their victims—some in far worse ways than the break-in of a car or home. One of the worst crimes I can think of, and I pray I will never experience, is the kidnapping of a child. Reports of kidnappings hit the evening news more often than any of us want to see: *Eleven-year-old Stephanie Grant is missing*. The pictures on milk cartons remind us that not all loved ones are safe. In our hometown, we now have interstate media boards, and the other day it was flashing an *Amber Alert*. All of a sudden my lunch appointment didn't seem so important. Kidnapping is larger than just someone being lost—someone has been taken. And yet, I don't have that difficult of a time going on with life as usual after seeing those milk carton pictures or driving under an Amber Alert sign or watching a few minutes of the news. Not because I'm insensitive or uncaring, but because I'm not attached. If it were a friend's child, on the other hand, I would join the search team, offer my bank account, canvas the neighborhood—I'd do whatever I could to help. And if it were one of mine who was lost or taken, I would exchange my life for one of my girls in a heartbeat. Because I *love them*. Because they are *mine*. God sees us in the same way according to scripture. Paul writes...

> *He wants not only us but **everyone** saved **(rescued)**, you know, everyone to get to know the truth we've learned: that there's one God and only one, and one Priest-Mediator between God and us—Jesus, who offered himself in exchange **(ransomed)** for everyone held captive by sin, to set them all free.*
>
> 1 Timothy 2:4-6 (MSG, emphasis added)

Matthew records Jesus' words...
The Son of Man came not to be waited on but to serve, and to give His life as a ransom for many [the price paid to set them free].
Matthew 20:28 (AMP)

Unfortunately not everyone who has been ransomed and given a way to freedom takes it. There are many who over time have been conditioned to stay with their oppressor.

When the Civil War in our country ended in April 1865, the four-year conflict that killed more than a million soldiers and civilians was finally over. The end also brought the *official* abolishing of the slave trade that had been in our country for decades. What do you think happened to the majority of those who had lived in slavery for four and five generations? What changed for them with the signing of the Emancipation Proclamation? Very little. Even a few years later when the Thirteenth Amendment made slavery illegal, life for many did not change. The only life they knew was that of a slave. They had heard of freedom, some had even made their own attempts at getting it by running away and had suffered horrible consequences when recaptured. For those who did muster the courage to run and keep running, the life they led was one of a fugitive. They were not yet truly free. Someone still had the authority to return them to slavery. But the war ended all that! When the announcements were made, the fliers were posted and the newspapers reported that slavery was abolished, do you know what most of those slaves did? They stayed. Their status changed, but their lives didn't. For many, change still seemed impossible because the institution of slavery had more power than their newly declared freedom. Freedom was fought for and won, but the reality of it still had to penetrate the hearts of the enslaved.

This story of slavery sounds piercingly familiar. Though made free, they stayed in the life they knew, the life they were accustomed to, the life they had known as normal. The nation of Israel decided they wanted the same thing just a few days on the other side of the Red Sea and out from under Pharaoh's tyranny. *We were better off back in Egypt; how are we going to live now?* (Exodus 16:2-3) It was going to take some time. Being searched for, found and rescued from a life of slavery is a truly glorious event and provides the essential ingredients to being set free. There might be only one thing more important than being set free, and that is being *shown how to live freely*. There is good news. We are not alone. There is One to show us the way.

CHAPTER 10

ONE TO SHOW THE WAY

Jesus tapped me on the shoulder and said, "Bob, why are you resisting me?" I said, "I'm not resisting you!" He said, "You gonna follow me?" I said, "I've never thought about that before!" He said, "When you're not following me, you're resisting me."

Bob Dylan

Follow me, I'll show you the way.

Jesus

Rescues can take many forms—blocking someone from falling off a ledge, pushing someone out of harm's way, carrying the hurt or unconscious to safety, or warning someone who isn't aware of the imminent danger threatening them. For all of us though, Jesus' rescues come with the invitation, *Follow me.* Someone enters into our story, and He knows some things we don't. He knows some things we have forgotten or some things we haven't yet learned. Frequently in the Gospels, Jesus dealt with people's physical and spiritual problems, usually both at the same time. Jesus often used stories or parables in hopes of getting His message past their intellects and into their hearts. Even with Jesus, not all His rescue attempts were successful. There were many people in the first century who watched His life from close range but still refused to sign for the packages He was delivering.

    A few years ago a friend shared something with me that has echoed in my heart and mind ever since. He said, "The effect Jesus had on people was usually one of three things: inviting, intriguing or disrupting." That is so good that I have shared it with many others since then. The impact Christ had on those around Him was often drastic. One person is elated, usually the one who found healing and forgiveness. Others are filled with anger and resentment, usually because of when or where Jesus healed. Jesus' teaching brought relief and hope to some, while others in the crowd at the same time were offended. How a person reacted seemed to depend on the condition of his eyes—*how they saw* Jesus' life and teachings; the condition of his ears—*what he heard* Him saying; and ultimately condition of his heart—*whether his heart was soft and open* or *hard and closed*. Everything Jesus did was to demonstrate the way in which we could live if we would only see, listen, understand and engage with our deepest part—our hearts.

When the religious experts of the day challenged Jesus with the question, *what is the greatest of all the commandments*? Jesus didn't respond from Exodus 20 where the Ten Commandments reside. Instead He responded with a commandment in Deuteronomy 6:4-5: *Love the Lord your God with all your heart, soul, mind and strength and love your neighbor as yourself. There is no commandment greater than these.* (Matthew 22:37, Mark 12:28)

Now, if this is the greatest of all the commandments wouldn't it make sense that we are able to do what we are being commanded to do? And given the authority of who is giving the command, isn't it conceivable that it might be difficult to achieve? Finally, if this is our most important goal and mission in life, then doesn't it stand to reason that it will be the most opposed by our enemy (the unholy trinity)? Considering these factors, doesn't it make sense that we will need a lot of help to pull it off?

Much of what we learn in life we learn by example—from someone's demonstration. So Jesus modeled for us what it looks like to love God and love others, inspiring His followers to do the same. Jesus showed us the Life we can and were created to have through the example of His own life. He showed us that this life is more than a commandment to fill; it is a new way to live, a new way of life, that is accessible for us. We can take our cues and directions for living this way from Jesus' life. He doesn't just leave us with some rules, like a *MapQuest* printout to follow (which ought to say at the bottom "good luck"). He actually *shows* us the way.

Jesus lived all that He taught, and He invites us to live the same way. The ministry He engaged in He passed along to us as well. Remember the passage in which Jesus says, *even greater things will you do than these*? It is tucked away in John 14:11-12, in the middle of a conversation Jesus is having with His disciples prior to His last days. Jesus announces that He has to go away, but He says this:

> *The person who trusts me will not only do what I'm doing **but even greater things**, because I, on my way to the Father, am giving you the same work (the same life) to do that I've been doing. You can count on it.*
>
> John 14:12 (MSG, emphasis added)

For most of us non-pilots that sounds like being put in the cockpit and told, *You fly this one; you can do it.* Whoa, I don't think the passengers are going to go for this! And yet when we move to the book of Acts, which propels us to the other side of Jesus' last days, we see the early Christians testing their wings and taking flight. The disciples are living the life Christ lived and doing the things that He did—all in His name, His power and His authority. All connected to Him, to be sure, but that is the point: *A life that Christ has rescued is a life that can be lived like Christ.*

FOLLOWERS OF THE WAY

Look at the disciples' lives. Jesus healed the blind, the sick and the lame. The disciples healed the blind, the sick and the lame. Jesus taught about the Kingdom of God and how it worked. His disciples taught about the Kingdom and how it worked. Jesus said He was and is the way. The disciples declared far and wide that Jesus was and is the way. Jesus *made* disciples (followers, learners). The disciples went out and made more disciples. Jesus' message might be summarized this way: *Be like me and help make others like me. I showed you how to Live and how to Love. Now you go show others how to Live and Love. You can do it. I'll be with you every step of the way.*

Jesus gives this charge then returns to His Father. The apostles break the huddle and move out—equipped with Jesus' teaching. Being inhabited with the Spirit, they live the life He established and offer it to all they meet. As was true with Jesus, the disciples met and spoke to many who were not receptive to their message. As with Jesus, the disciples' great mission is met with resistance. If you know the story, then you know these faithful followers all paid a tremendous price for love and loyalty to their Savior. All the apostles died martyrs' deaths, not only for what they believed but for how they lived. They died for the Life and Love of Jesus because it was better than anything this world could offer.

Jesus was persecuted. The disciples were persecuted. Jesus was beaten. His disciples were beaten. Jesus was run out of town. They were run out of town. Jesus was killed for claims regarding His relationship with God. His disciples were killed for their claims and relationship with Jesus, who was and is God. (John 14:9-11)

During these early years of the church, a term surfaced to describe Christ's followers (His disciples and those who came to believe through their ministry). The church was booming in the first century; the Gospel of the Resurrected Christ was on the move. Those remaining outside the message, predominantly the unbelieving Jews and the majority of Romans and Greeks, sought to define this baffling subculture. Those outside looking in, labeled the Christ followers with a term they considered belittling and derogatory: *Christians*, which meant *little Christs*. Instead of being offended, the believers embraced this name because that is exactly what they aspired to. In its earliest years, Christianity's adherents also became known as "Followers of the Way." (Acts 19:9; 19:23; 22:4; 24:14; 24:22). This name had its roots deep in Jesus' teaching. In John 14:3-6, Jesus says this:

And if I go and prepare a place for you, I will come back and take *you to be with me that you also may be where I am. You know the way to the place where I am going." Thomas said to him, "Lord, we don't know where you are going, so how can we know the way?" Jesus answered, "I am **the way** and **the truth** and **the life**. No one comes to the Father except through me.* (emphasis added)

There are two major truths being revealed here as the Spiritual Realm mixes with the physical realm once again. Jesus is first of all showing His disciples the road they need to travel in order to meet up with Him again. Then, from a physical realm orientation, Thomas asks the question all of them must have wanted to ask: *Where are you going? I didn't get any directions! I don't know the way!* In response, Jesus explains the second major truth: *I am the way. You know me, so you know the way!*

Now, when I think of *a way*, I think of directions to a destination, I think of *MapQuest* or my GPS unit laying out my route and each turn I need to take. When I think of *the truth*, I think of a principle, an accurate statement. Del Tackett, teacher and author of *The Truth Project,* said that for many people, "Truth is that which conforms to reality." When I think of *the life*, I think of time and the collection of moments that make up my past, my present and those to come in the future. But *my* definitions are not what Jesus was talking about. He is intertwining all three ideas and revealing the reality that all three—the way, the truth, and the life—are wrapped up in *knowing a person, in knowing Him.*

If you get close to Jesus, you find the way, the truth and the life. If you distance yourself from Jesus and get far from Him, you get lost.

THE REAL OFFER

Today's Christians can be described in many different ways, both positive and negative. But I believe that one of the most applicable descriptors may be *committed*. Commitment is a good thing, and we are instructed in God's Word to be committed to Christ. Let me ask you though, if you asked your spouse to describe your marriage in one word, what word would you hope to hear? What if he or she said, *Oh, that's easy, 'committed*. Committed is not a *bad* word to describe a marriage, but is it the *best* word for an intimate, connected and special union between two people? Committed is certainly one characteristic of a good marriage, but if that is the best description we have for a marriage then we may be missing the forest for the trees. I can think of three or four words I would much rather hear used to describe my marriage: *beautiful, thrilling, passionate, intimate…in love.*

In the letters written to the first century church—the church that started right after Jesus' resurrection, we see and hear about a relationship between God and us that is much more about being *in love* than being *in service*. It is much more about *intimacy* than about being *committed* out of a sense of duty. Love and service can be connected, but they should never be confused. Both my wife and I have had jobs in which we served others. She waited tables in high school and college. I mowed lawns. Yes, there was compensation for our efforts, but I didn't *love* those whom I served. Now, my wife often sets the table at our house, serves our family food and clears away the dishes afterward—not because we pay her, but because she loves us. I often mow the lawn—not because anyone gives me a check, but because it is part of showing care and love for my home and family. That's the difference between love and service. Love can enable us to serve, but serving seldom makes us love.

God has put people in our lives to teach us how to love and, in turn, that love inspires us to serve. Robin is not in my life to serve me or for me to serve. Ultimately, Robin is in my life to teach me how to love. My kids are in my life to teach me how to love. Others are in my life to teach me how to love, and I am there to teach them. Loving and serving have a connection, but it doesn't go both ways. As if Jesus weren't't enough to show us how to relate to God and others, He continues to give us hundreds of other opportunities to broaden our view, widen our ability to hear and invite our whole hearts to engage in Life and Love with the Father. He does all this so we might *first* love Him and then, out of that overflow, serve Him—not the other way around.

EXAMPLES NOT EXCEPTIONS

The people in the Bible are more than characters in a story. They are regular folks thrust into the middle of a stage, offering the drama of their lives as examples for us to see and follow (or not follow, as the case may be). Dallas Willard writes this in his book, *Hearing God*:

> *God's visits to Adam and Eve in the Garden, Enoch's walks with God and the face-to-face conversations between Moses and Jehovah are all commonly regarded as highly exceptional moments in the religious history of humankind. Aside from their obviously unique historical role, however, they are not meant to be exceptional at all. Rather they are examples of the normal human life God intended for us; God's indwelling his people through personal presence and fellowship.*

For the longest time, I viewed the lives of the men and women in the Bible as special ones, qualified ones. I saw these people as blessed, unique and deserving of such interaction with God, people who were to be revered and placed on earned pedestals of honor. I saw myself, on the other hand, in the world of "not-quite" and "almost." I believed if I could just get it together, try harder, put in more time and effort with God, then maybe, just maybe, on my best day, I might have a shot at the "blessed" life. If this doesn't sound familiar to you in any way, then you can skip to the next section. But for me, it was an amazing discovery, almost scandalous (again), to even *think* that the stories in scripture were given to me not as exceptions to the rule, but as examples of what Life with God can be for me—and for all of us. When examined more closely, I came to the startling conclusion that these were indeed normal folks, more like me than I had ever realized before. The characters in the scriptures were everyday people—yahoos like me! Mary was a young girl living in a Jewish community that would not look kindly on an unwed teenager's pregnancy. Peter was an outspoken, blue collar worker who left his nets to become a fisher of men. Moses was an adopted son, who was a great disappointment to his father Pharaoh. The list goes on and on; they were all normal men and women, boys and girls, but they entered into extraordinary moments because God stepped on stage with them. The Bible is full of stories of regular people encountering and experiencing God because He wants to reveal to us what it looks like to walk with Him. And He does so in a thousand different ways through a thousand different stories.

I had the opportunity to hear counselor, teacher and author Dan Allender speak at a two-day conference, and I'll never forget what he shared about the people in the Bible. He said that the stories of people's lives with God in the Bible are there to help us understand how we can relate to God and how He relates to us. Then he made a correlation between us and the people of the scriptures, stating that our stories are linked and connected with those in the Bible stories. Like Jacob, Allender said, we will (if we haven't already) wrestle with God. We too will swindle our brother out of his birthrights and blessings. Like Jonah, we too will turn and run from God when what He asks of us seems too hard or is against our personal opinion. Like Peter, we will find ourselves denying Christ in spite of intentions and declarations that we never will. Like Samson, we will use our strength for our own purposes and find it taken from us. Like James and John, we will seek to put ourselves first in the Kingdom of Christ.

And so, the stories of the Bible are really our stories. They invite us to see ourselves in the lives of those who have gone before us. The invitation is to see these men and women of the scriptures as real people, not just as ancient characters in stories beyond our experiences or understanding. If we view them as true but irrelevant to our lives, we'll miss out on so much, on seeing the movement and hearing the voice of God in our lives. But when we learn to see their stories and dramas as the stories and dramas of our lives as well, we can begin to gain insight into our own lives and our own search for Life.

INVITATION VS. INDICTMENT

I believe this perspective will change our view of the Bible; God's Word is an invitation to Life not an indictment. Look at the beautiful 11th chapter of the book of Hebrews. Sometimes called the "Hall of Faith," it is like a heavenly Hall of Fame. But unlike the Football or Baseball Hall of Fame, which is reserved for the exceptional and gifted, the Hall of Faith seems to say to us, *If these people can do it, so can you*!

The inductees to the Hall of Faith are not the kind of people you might expect to find on an illustrious list. They were schemers, self-preservationists, liars, adulterers, cowards, excuse-makers, cheaters, manipulators, disobeyers, complainers—in other words, they struggled and failed just like we do. These people are listed because we can all relate to them and because—in spite of their stories, their flaws, their pasts and their choices—they chose to have faith in the God who could rescue them and bring them Life. Many of them were rescued many times over. And we can be invited into Life with God as well, no matter our failings, flaws or pasts. All the saints of old will testify to that and are actually cheering us on:

> *Therefore, since we are surrounded by such a great cloud of witnesses, let us throw off everything that hinders and the sin that so easily entangles, and let us run with perseverance the race marked out for us.*
>
> Hebrews 12:1

Both in the Old and New Testaments we find a host of folks who really weren't that special and who definitely wouldn't be described as *qualified* for the missions they were given. Most stories captured in scripture seem to feature people who often missed the significant point God was trying to make in their lives, at least initially. The misunderstandings seem to outnumber the times when they actually got it. Take the disciples for instance; they were *always* in need of extra tutoring from Jesus after the sermon or the parable was over and the multitudes had gone home. And yet Christ chose them specifically to be the men entrusted with His ministry after His time on earth was done.

In terms of information and theology, the disciples knew *far* less about God than we do. They often had it wrong with the information and theology they *did* have. Some folks, a small number for sure, were quite faithful to Jesus through and through. But they were confused, unsure and discouraged at times, just like you and me. Christ's followers were doing the best they could with what they heard and saw Jesus say and do. They, too, were simply a group of people, lost, hurting and oppressed. They wanted and desired direction, relief and freedom. That's not just my description by the way, that's what Jesus said of them as well. Early in His ministry, right after the wedding at which He turned water to wine, Jesus is in the synagogue, and He is handed the scroll of the book of Isaiah to read. He reads these words:

> *"The Spirit of the Lord is on me, because he has anointed me to preach good news to the poor. He has sent me to proclaim freedom for the prisoners and recovery of sight for the blind, to release the oppressed, to proclaim the year of the Lord's favor." Then he rolled up the scroll, gave it back to the attendant and sat down. The eyes of everyone in the synagogue were fastened on him, and he began by saying to them, "Today this scripture is fulfilled in your hearing."*
>
> Luke 4:18-21

In other words: *This is what I've come to do because this is who you are, where you are and what you desperately need. More than you know.*

Nothing has changed since then, surely not the mission of Jesus nor the people who need it. His was not a period mission, confined to a day or a season in the first century, but a true mission for all generations since as well as those to come. The prisoners need freeing, the blind need to see, and the broken need repair. We all are in need of transformation—irreversible change! Those who respond with an acknowledgment and admittance of their need for help, find help—the kind of help that matters most. Not physical realm help but Spiritual Realm help. The people of faith mentioned in scripture seemed to possess a common neediness and a desire for help, whether or not they were willing to admit it. Like I've said before, not much has changed. God shows up for those who cry out to Him. Our requests for help and direction are the ingredients that seem to most move God. His desire is to show us the way, the truth and the life. Whether I cry out or whisper, I believe He says, *I can work with that. It's going to take a lot of work. But it's going to be worth it, and it's going to be great! Follow me. I'll lead you home.*

PART IV

REORIENTED

CHAPTER 11 RESTORATION: LIVING NEWLY
CHAPTER 12 OVERWHELMED
CHAPTER 13 TRAINING - THE GOOD THAT GOD
IS UP TO IN OUR LIVES

In his book, *Waking the Dead*, John Eldredge suggests that most people are basically *disoriented*. That's a good word to describe a person's general state or condition when lost. It's one thing to state the obvious to a person whose hand is on his head with blood seeping between his fingers: *Hey, you're bleeding! Oh my gosh, you're hurt*! It's quite another to respond to an emergency situation, pull the wounded and bleeding to safety, bandage wounds and nurse the injured back to health. Lost hearts need people who know what to do and are willing to help, not those who can only state the obvious. *Why* someone is lost and hurting could be much more important than the simple reality of the condition. *It takes one to know one*, as the old saying goes. People with reoriented hearts are the best ones to help those with disoriented hearts, because they have "been there." They know from experience what being rescued is all about.

We have lost a lot of things on life's journey...generally: *who I am, where I am* and *the good that God is up to in my life*. When any or all of these components of our life's journey get lost, it shows. Oh we might try to cover it up with our hands, turn the other way or even declare with a shaky confidence: *I'm all right. It's just a flesh wound.* I'm with Eldredge. I believe that most people—*especially* Christian people—live *disoriented* lives, and I believe the overarching reason is because *we have underestimated everything*. We've underestimated our value and worth. We've underestimated the villain in our story and just how real evil is. We have misunderstood and underestimated the great God who is the hero in our story. And we have little or no clue as to how His Kingdom operates here and now. We've *underestimated* all the characters and all the themes of not only our own story, but the Larger Story that our story has been dropped into. We can see the sad effects of this misunderstanding, the effects of our overarching underestimation. Simply take a look around. *It's killing us.*

Consider all the confusion, suffering, discomfort and inconvenience we seem to live with every day. We settle for this rather than the joy, happiness, peace and rest our hearts long for *and* which seem to be at the top of God's promised benefit package. *Is* there really abundant *Life?* Where? When? Why is there such a discrepancy between the life that we long for and the life we settle for? Why is one the usual and the other the occasional exception?

In the story of God, the work of Christ was not merely to die for our sins—though it *is* a very good thing to have our records erased and sins removed from us as far as the east is from the west. The offer of God by the work of Christ is far more than just forgiveness. It is *Life*. An abundant, full and super-sized *Life*! God desires something for our hearts and lives that is significantly more expansive than forgiving us and sending us on our way. Far too many Christians believe that the offer of God is only some great pardon, accompanied by a heavy-handed rule book for our time of parole, all in an attempt to make sure we don't do it again or else!

Yes, the cross and its forgiveness are great things, significant things, to be sure. But if that is what the Gospel has been reduced to, then we have settled for a gospel too small. The cross is just a part of the whole story. Now, I can just imagine the critics coming to the edge of their seats upon reading those statements. Good. I've got your attention. Look at it this way: forgiveness is the toll booth, and God, in his infinite love and kindness, reaches out and pays the toll for everyone so we can move forward.

For God so loved the world that He gave His only begotten son.
John 3:16

The toll is costly. He pays so we can move forward on the road of *Life* that has now been afforded us. We're not to stay parked at the toll booth. The cross is the means by which we can now enjoy:

    What we were made for...Life!
    What we lost...Life!
    What we have been desperately searching for...Life!
    And what is searching for us... *Life*!

God *is* a relentless pursuer. He searches for us, finds us and rescues us so we can join Him on the great adventure of *Life*. The Life that is now, and the Life that awaits us. As C. S. Lewis said, life that is "further up and further in." This *is* the great adventure...*Life with God*. Can you imagine what it would be like to be rescued, healed, restored and turned loose to be fully alive? And now on a great mission, in a grand partnership, with God? St. Irenaeus nailed it when he said, "The glory of God is man fully alive."

In these last few chapters, I want to offer encouragement and guidance for the glorious things that come next. Think of it as a forecast of the *further up and further in*. After the initial search and rescue of our hearts comes something so beautiful and so wonderful a couple of chapters won't do it justice. But these chapters can spur us on and give us the awareness and orientation we need to participate and partner with God in His great recovery and restoration of our lives. The *rescue* is truly a great work in and of itself—but it is only the beginning. It is just the first of many rescues we will need. Once we are rescued and reunited with the One who loves us most, a new relationship begins—one that might best be described as learning how to *live newly*.

There is a great scene in the film *The Mask of Zorro* where the senior Zorro (played by Anthony Hopkins) comes upon a man named Alejandro (played by Antonio Banderas) who will become his successor. At their initial encounter, Hopkins' Zorro rescues the younger one, who is soon to be his apprentice, from a certain death. I love Zorro's line in Alejandro's rescue: "You would have fought bravely and died quickly. The captain is trained to kill, you seem trained to drink." It is at that point the apprentice's invitation is extended, and Zorro takes Alejandro back to his old hideout in the cliffs. As the two begin the next leg of their journey together, the senior Zorro knows all the training that will be needed in order to move forward in the great adventure that awaits them; Alejandro doesn't have a clue. The senior Zorro prepares to assess his pupil's knowledge and skill. When Alejandro draws his sword to show he is ready to go, Zorro asks him: "Do you know how to use that thing?" To which Alejandro replies: "Yes, the pointy end goes into the other man." The senior Zorro then says: "This is going to take a lot of work."

I know this to be true in my own life. God is training me how to live newly and, as in the case of Alejandro, it is going to take a lot of work.

CHAPTER 11

RESTORATION: LIVING NEWLY

And we, who with unveiled faces all reflect the Lord's glory, are being transformed into his likeness with ever-increasing glory, which comes from the Lord, who is the Spirit.

2 Corinthians 3:18

The cure for all ills and wrongs, the cares, the sorrows and the crimes of humanity, all lie in the one word, "love." It is the divine vitality that everywhere produces and restores life.

Lydia M. Child

And the God of all grace, who called you to his eternal glory in Christ, after you have suffered a little while, will himself restore you and make you strong, firm and steadfast.

1 Peter 5:10

Welcome to life.

Chile's President Sebastian Pinera
To the first miners who emerged

R̲estoration, by nature and definition, is the ability to make old things new again. *Webster's* turns up this definition:
> *The act of restoring or state of being restored, as to a former or original condition...*
>
> *the replacement or giving back of something lost, stolen.*

I find two things significant about restoration. The first is an appreciation for the value of something which can only come from an understanding of its original condition, what it was made for and who made it. The second is the commitment of the restoring craftsman to the work involved in the restoration. The best restoration craftsmen are those who value the article needing to be restored. If the article is not valued – or loved – then it is unlikely the craftsman will make the effort to restore it. It is significant to recognize *what something is*, but recognizing *what something can* or *will be* goes beyond significance...it is *glorious*. The One who knows this best is the Original Craftsman. What a glorious restorer He is.

SEARCH and RESCUE

Sharing in the life of my daughter, Ashley, at age 16 has its joys and its heartaches. As she matures through the rough waters of high school, I am noticing things she does as a high school sophomore that are similar to things she did in kindergarten. At age five, she would organize her stuffed animal friends for tea parties; at 16, she loves to organize dinners out with her sophomore friends. As a young child, she loved stories and all the Disney movies; as a high schooler, she still loves stories and is my movie date for *The Lord of the Rings*, *Harry Potter* or *Twilight*. Since learning to read, she has loved to read out loud; now she not only loves to read, but she loves to write.

Several months ago she picked up my old guitar. In just a few weeks, she had surpassed my capability by having down a dozen cords and strumming to familiar beginner guitar songs. A few more weeks and she announced she had written a song! Now I have to admit, my expectations were along the lines of *Michael Row Your Boat Ashore* with a few new words. But in reality, the song spoke of a teenage girl searching with all her heart for life and love. I was amazed and proud and encouraged. When Ashley was small, she performed concerts for us, singing her heart out on our staircase or fireplace hearth. Now she writes songs and sings her heart out on stage and in recording studios.

In his book *It's Your Call*, Gary Barkalow writes that a person's glory is the "weightiness, splendor, or effect of his or her life." A calling, he says, is something that "has always been true of a person." Singing and performance have *always been true* of Ashley, so it is not hard to see her stepping into a career as a songwriter or performer. What she *is* and what she *might become* are being unveiled to her mom and me right in front of our eyes. Sure, there are trials and errors, passing fads and meager attempts. But in the garden of her heart, her glory is being cultivated and refined. It is here that *who she is* comes forth and what she is to offer the Kingdom is honed, trained up and presented. There is Someone in her story, just as there is Someone in yours and mine, for whom nothing in the journey comes as a surprise. He knows what we will become, and He follows our development with pride and joy. The scriptures tell us it is His good pleasure to partner and participate with us in our glorious unveiling. Scripture is clear that God is up to something good—not just in the universe or the world but in the hearts and lives of individuals. Each heart and each life is being restored to the Creator's original intent. This is what God loves to do.

> *Long before he laid down earth's foundations, he had us in mind, had settled on us as the focus of his love, to be made whole and holy by his love. Long, long ago he decided to adopt us into his family through Jesus Christ. (What pleasure he took in planning this!) He wanted us to enter into the celebration of his lavish gift-giving by the hand of his beloved Son. Because of the sacrifice of the Messiah, his blood poured out on the altar of the Cross, we're a free people—**free** of penalties and punishments chalked up by all our misdeeds. And not just barely free, either. **Abundantly free**! He thought of everything, provided for everything we could possibly need, **letting us in on the plans he took such delight in making. He set it all out before us in Christ, a long-range plan in which everything would be brought together and summed up in him, everything in deepest heaven, everything on planet earth**.*
>
> Ephesians 1:4-10 (MSG, emphasis added)

LES MISERABLES

I was 24 years old when I first saw the play, *Les Miserables*, in 1988. I had no idea what I was about to encounter. Victor Hugo's classic story is set in the days just before the French Revolution. It spoke to my heart as it has millions of other hearts and invited me into a new chapter of my own personal revolution.

When the 1998 film version came out starring Liam Neeson as Jean Valjean, I couldn't help but think it was going to be a nice attempt but fall short of the musical and the book. Oh, how I loved being wrong. This film is *my* story because I am all the characters in it. I relate not only to Jean Valjean on his journey to become a new man but to Inspector Javert, demanding justice and morality. Javert imposes the law on himself and all those around him with a pharisaic presence, judging everyone and finding them lacking compared to the high standards of the law only he self-righteously keeps. I also relate to Fantine who does all she can to arrange for a better life for her child. Always coming up short, she stoops to the point of selling her hair, her teeth and even her body through prostitution to make ends meet. And then there is Cosette, the wonderfully naive little girl who needs to understand the larger story of which her story is a significant part. I am all the characters, and all their stories are right out of the scriptures. Can you imagine the cast listing? Peter as Jean Valjean, Caiaphas the high priest as Inspector Javert, Mary Magdelene as Fantine, and Michael Thompson as Cosette. I could be any or all of these characters, what about you?

An early scene sets the trajectory for the larger story; it happens when Jean Valjean is found. The scene opens with Valjean trying to sleep on a street bench when he is interrupted by a woman who pokes him with her cane and provokes him to knock on a door down the street to request shelter. (How much more than *incidental* her act was to the whole story.) Valjean knocks on the door and is met by a bishop, a good man who sees and hears people's hearts. To the surprise of Valjean, the bishop invites him into his home for a meal and a bed to sleep on. At dinner, Jean Valjean sarcastically thanks the bishop for the meal and the bed, claiming he will be a "new man" in the morning.

But Valjean, still hard from 19 years in prison, is feeling desperate in his newly paroled life. In the middle of the night, he dreams of prison torment and wakes to arrange life for himself. He gets out of bed and, on his way out of the house, steals the bishop's silverware. Valjean assaults the bishop in the process of fleeing, only to be caught and brought back to his host the next morning. We pick up the scene here:

>**Captain of the Guard** (to the bishop): I'm sorry to disturb you. I had my eye on this man.

Bishop: I'm very angry with you, Jean Valjean.
Madam Gilot: You caught him.
Captain of the Guard: What happened to your eye, Monseigneur?
Madam Gilot: Thank God!
Bishop: Didn't he tell you he was our guest?
Captain: Oh, yes, after we searched his knapsack and found all this silver...he claimed...that you gave it to him.
Bishop (pause): Yes. Of course I gave him the silverware. (To Valjean) But why didn't you take the candlesticks? That was very foolish. Madam Gilot, fetch the silver candlesticks. They're worth at least 2,000 francs. Why did you leave them? Hurry! Monsieur Valjean has to get going. He's lost a lot of time. Did you forget to take them?
Captain: Are you saying he told us the truth?
Bishop: Of course. Thank you for bringing him back. I'm very relieved.
Captain: Release him.
Valjean: You're letting me go?
Captain: Didn't you understand the bishop?
Bishop: Madam Gilot, offer these men some wine. They must be thirsty. Thanks. (Madam Gilot and the guards move from the garden into the house leaving the bishop and Jean Valjean alone. The bishop with his black eye from the night before approaches Valjean who is bewildered and has the hood of his tattered coat up over his head. The bishop places both his hands on Valjean's hood and pulls the hood back.)
Bishop: And don't forget...don't ever forget, you've promised to become a new man.
Valjean (still confused): Promise? Why are you doing this?
Bishop: Jean Valjean, my brother, you no longer belong to evil. With this silver, I've bought your soul. I've ransomed you from fear and hatred. Now I give you back to God.

Who wouldn't want to be pardoned like this and then *restored*? How can a novel written in 1862 capture our story so succinctly? Whether in the 400s, the 1400s, 2020 or generations to come, human needs, hopes and desires are the same. As long as there is a person with a heart, there is a person who is longing and looking for both Love and Life. And as long as there is a human heart, there is One who longs to restore it and freely provide all that heart is looking for.

Yet we get caught up in the revolutions of our day—whether it be economic, industrial or national, or set in a much smaller venue like my house, my family and my friends. The scope of my story may not be large and important to the next chapter of human history, and yet maybe it is. It was Edmund Burke who once said: "All that is necessary for evil to succeed is for good men to do nothing." One brave act of a bishop altered the course of not only one life but—as the story of *Les Miserables* goes —*thousands of lives*. One courageous step on any of our parts might alter the steps of another, maybe even dozens, possibly thousands. But no one will be more importantly and profoundly impacted by your courageous steps than you.

> *Therefore if any person is [ingrafted] in Christ (the Messiah) he is a new creation (a new creature altogether); the old [previous moral and spiritual condition] has passed away. Behold, the fresh and new has come!*
>
> 2 Corinthians 5:17 (AMP)

Getting a new start and receiving a new identity didn't come without cost for Jean Valjean. Freedom is never free. Someone steps up and pays. Someone makes it possible, and our freedom always comes with a price. Maybe someday we will accept freedom because it has been paid for and is waiting for us, like a package under the tree on Christmas morning. Christ *gave* His life so we could *have* His life. It was and is an incredible swap—one offered to heart after heart, generation after generation. From one individual's heart (God's) to another's (ours) is an invitation to lay down one life, pick up another one and be free.

SWAPPING PLACES

Many great stories share the message of offering life and freedom through sacrifice. Maximus gives his life for his men, Rome and the safety of a boy in *Gladiator*. Jack ensures Rose has a way to escape the bondage of aristocracy and live through the sinking of the ship in *Titanic*. Even *Ol' Yeller* fights off a rabid wolf, sacrificing his life for that of his beloved boy, Travis. To live newly and be restored, we must realize we have value, significance and importance to the one sacrificing on our behalf. In the Bible, the eighth chapter of Romans pulls all this together: Christ became like us so that we could become like Him.

> *God went for the jugular when he sent his own Son. He didn't deal with the problem as something remote and unimportant. In his Son, Jesus, he personally took on the human condition, entered the disordered mess of struggling humanity in order to set it right once and for all.*
>
> Romans 8:3 (MSG)

Verses 28 and 29 state:

> *That's why we can be so sure that every detail in our lives of love for God is worked into something good. God knew what he was doing from the very beginning. He decided from the outset* **to shape the lives of those who love him along the same lines as the life of his Son**.
>
> Romans 8:28-29 (MSG, emphasis added)

What a swap, what an exchange! He became like us so we could become like Him. His life in exchange for ours! Now this is bound to raise some questions: *Is it good to become like Jesus? What's He like? Do we want to be like him? Is it possible?*

There are many great qualities and attributes of Jesus. He was an amazing man, the God-man (Son of God, Son of Man in the Gospels) who knew *who He was*, *where He was* and the *good the Father was up to in His life*. He understood his identity better than anyone. He knew where He came from and where He was returning to, and He wants us to join Him in His great mission – the search and rescue of others.

Don't get me wrong here. I'm not referring to an evangelistic crusade to save souls. I'm talking about rescuing the millions of believers who are struggling. Jesus' rescue of us does more than get us out of harm's way. His work is not simply helping us avoid the crashing waves of life and placing us safely inland where hurricanes can't reach us. He searches for us, rescues and restores us again and again so we can join His mission. Truly, He doesn't *need* any of us. But He does seem to *want* us. Most often He chooses to work *with* us to see that those who have gotten lost are brought to safety. This is what Jesus meant by the shepherd leaving the 99 in his flock to go after the one who has wandered off.

He rescues us so we can be free men and women who have tasted *Life* and want more. Men and women who, living *newly*, naturally want to help those who are lost and in need of rescue, whether it is their first rescue or somewhere in the triple digits. Men and women who are, with every rescue, becoming more and more of a liberating force, abolitionists, search and rescue teams. We are the ones to carry on the mission of the One who searched for, rescued and brought us to freedom. We are and are becoming His apprentices, His co-heirs, His mighty ones. After all, the battle is large and far from over—for those who are free and especially for those who are yet to be free. The sooner we can grow up and be restored, the sooner we can offer help to others. The image you and I are being "grown up and restored into" is much more than most of us were taught in Sunday School and church. The image we're being matured into is all we dream we might become some day. It's no coincidence that all we long to be has been before us and *is* for us all the time. All we long to be, He is.

YOUR IMAGE OF HIM

One of my favorite stories is that of a boy observing a great artist at work, a sculptor standing over a large piece of granite. For several minutes the boy stands and looks on quietly. As the sculptor moves around the large piece of rock, the boy adjusts his position so he can see what the artist is doing. When the sculptor stands back to examine his work after chipping and chiseling away a few pieces, the boy leans in to inspect the most recent improvements.

> The silence is broken when the boy asks, "Sir, what are you doing?"
>
> "I'm sculpting," comes the artist's reply.
>
> "What are you making?" the boy asks.
>
> With this, the sculptor pauses and smiles at the boy, giving him his full attention. "I am sculpting a great lion," says the artist.
>
> The boy smiles because all boys like lions, and he says, "A lion, really?" Then looking thoughtfully at the large block of rock, the boy says, "It doesn't look like a lion. How are you going to make it into a lion?"
>
> With a dramatic pause for effect the artist answers, "Yes, that's the question isn't it?... I'm going to chip away everything that isn't the lion."

I love that story! A great sculptor at work patiently, even lovingly, restoring, laboring to remove everything in the way of the image beneath the surface. I love it because it inspires me. It brings me hope that God is working *with me*, not just on me, to advance my ability to bear His image with ever-increasing glory (2 Corinthians 3:18). You see, there is no question of *if* I'm being restored; it's *to what* I am being restored that really matters.

When I was young, I dreamed of being an astronaut, a fireman and a solider, usually all in the same day. Now let me ask you, when you were five, 15 or even 30, and someone asked you who you wanted to be when you grew up, would your answer have been Jesus? Mine either, until recently.

My orientation regarding who Jesus *was* and the image I held of Him was more akin to a servant having a duty or obligation. That is what I thought I had signed up for when I signed on to my Christian faith. Serving was the goal rather than a journey and adventure encompassing my own personal transformation—a remaking of me into the greatest, strongest, kindest, fiercest, bravest, most compassionate, caring, determined, sacrificing, loving person ever to have walked the planet. That's a guy I would *want* to become. But that wasn't the guy I had learned about or imagined in all those years of attending church. Maybe I wasn't listening or maybe it wasn't shared well—either way, I had Him all wrong.

Most people have seen pictures of Jesus rendered by different artists. There is the sunken-eyed, long-haired, sad and upward-glancing portrait. There is one where He is depicted on a cloud 30 feet above everyone and the empty tomb with the rock rolled away. Another familiar picture shows Him on the cross between two other guys who are in the dark while Jesus is cast with a glow about Him. Over the centuries many have offered their rendition of His image. What if they were wrong or not *fully* right? Take a picture of anyone on a given day and it may or may not represent them well.

From all the images I can remember seeing of Jesus, I have imagined Him as very somber and serious, desperate and even a little disheartened. I recall always being able to pick Him out of the crowds; He was the one wearing the white robe, usually having a glow around His head, distinguishing Him from the others in the scene. None of this really stirred my boy's heart; I never thought to myself, *I want to be like the one in the white robe*. Rarely have I known of any man who aspired to become the nicest guy in the world or any woman to live out her days sacrificing for the lives of others. And yet that is what most Christians seem to have settled for. Have we ever stopped to consider why? If those of us who are being transformed into His likeness, His image, really don't like that image very much, isn't something wrong with the picture? Really, really wrong?

The accurate image of Christ has been lost. How can Jesus' closest friends while He walked this earth be so transformed that they would all go to their deaths to further His Kingdom and His cause? Is it out of obedience, servanthood or maybe even fear of what would happen if they didn't? It had to be something else—something that would sustain them, something that Jesus possessed more and better than anyone else, something that had them saying in the huddle, *I want to be like Jesus*. They must have experienced something far beyond His teaching, though the modern church often believes teaching alone will do the trick or make the difference. No, Jesus' friends experienced something they needed and were looking for; something that set their hearts at rest; something that made men strong and courageous, just like Jesus, and made women vulnerable and beautiful and free.

THE SECRET INGREDIENT

You can tell a lot about people by what and how they pray. What if the most significant person ever to walk the planet revealed what was most important to Him by what He prayed for, longed for and wanted to arrange for? Would that be a clue to us about what is most important? Yep, a *big* one. Jesus leaves all kinds of clues in the scriptures as to His heart and what is important to Him. He makes statements throughout His life, as recorded in the scriptures, revealing what He was here to arrange for (His purpose), what He was longing for (His mission) and what He

was praying for (His desire):
> *I came to set the captives free and give sight to the blind.* Luke 4:18
> *I came to give my life a ransom for many.* Matthew 20:28
> *I came to seek and save that which was lost.* Luke 19:10
> *I came that they might have life and have it to the full.* John 10:10

When asked the greatest commandment, Jesus basically said, *love God and love others* (Luke 10:27). Jesus was an expert at both and was training up an army of others who would become experts as well. In Jesus' prayers, we see and hear his heart. Now, the Lord's Prayer is great–it was Jesus' answer to His disciples' request in Luke 11:1 to teach them how to pray. Experts get one kind of answer, beginners get another. The Lord's Prayer is Jesus' answer for the beginners, a prayer on par with where their hearts were. But this fierce love Christ has for the Father and the almost scandalous love He has for us is best revealed in the prayer Jesus prayed near the end of His life. A person's last words are always filled with great depth and importance, and Jesus' were no different. Just before He demonstrated the impact of his fierce and scandalous love at the cross, He prayed the following prayer found in John 17 from The Message:

> *And this is the real and eternal life: **that they know you**, the one and only true God, And Jesus Christ, whom you sent…*
>
> *I spelled out your character in detail to the men and women you gave me…Holy Father, **guard them as they pursue this life** that you conferred as a gift through me, so they can be **one heart and mind as we are one heart and mind**…*
>
> *I'm not asking that you take them out of the world But that you **guard them from the Evil One**…*
>
> *In the same way that you gave me a mission in the world, I give them **a mission in the world**. I'm consecrating myself for their sakes so they'll be truth-consecrated in their mission. I'm praying not only for them but also for those who will believe in*

*me Because of them and their witness about me. The goal is for all of them to become one heart and mind— Just as you, Father, are in me and I in you, **So they might be one heart and mind with us**...*

*The same glory you gave me, I gave them, so they'll be as unified and together as we are— **I in them and you in me**. Then they'll be mature in this **oneness**,...*
I have made your very being known to them— who you are and what you do— and continue to make it known, so that your love for me might be in them exactly as I am in them.
John 17: 3-26 (MSG) (emphasis added)

Jesus' prayer gives evidence of what He most wants and what we most need. His words bring into focus the crucial things we need to recover, the things we will be lost without. When the Son of God prays to God the Father, he asks to know God intimately; protection against evil and harm; oneness with God and others; a mission in the world (love); and a connectedness to and union with God. This is what Jesus prayed for in His last days, and this is what is most important to Life. This is what He prayed for, so it must be possible. This is what He prayed, so there must be a reality in which these things are still to come. This is what He prayed at the end of His mission *for His mission*, so His mission isn't over. It may actually be just beginning.

END NOTE FOR CHAPTER 11

Over the past few years, the passage of scripture in John 17 has become more and more significant to me and my heart's journey for Life. I struggled to give you a portion or the important parts alone. I believe in this case more is better—so I've included the whole passage from John 17. I encourage you to find a quiet place, take a seat and have the words of Christ pour over your heart like cool water on a hot day. It is as if we get to eavesdrop on a conversation between a father and son. I believe they actually want us to listen in on their hearts for our hearts. My prayer is that you see, hear and engage in His words and expressions, His hopes and prayers, in all He has to say to you, me and all who matter most to Him.

JOHN 17 FROM THE MESSAGE

[1] Jesus said these things. Then, raising his eyes in prayer, he said: Father, it's time. Display the bright splendor of your Son So the Son in turn may show your bright splendor. [2] You put him in charge of everything human so he might give real and eternal life to all in his charge. [3] <u>And this is the real and eternal life: That they know you, the one and only true God, And Jesus Christ, whom you sent.</u> [4] I glorified you on earth by completing down to the last detail what you assigned me to do. [5] And now, Father, glorify me with your very own splendor, the very splendor I had in your presence before there was a world.

[6] <u>I spelled out your character in detail to the men and women you gave me</u>. They were yours in the first place; then you gave them to me, and they have now done what you said. [7] They know now, beyond the shadow of a doubt, that everything you gave me is firsthand from you, [8] For the message you gave me, I gave them; And they took it, and were convinced that I came from you. They believed that you sent me. [9] I pray for them. I'm not praying for the God-rejecting world but for those you gave me, for they are yours by right. [10] Everything mine is yours, and yours mine, And my life is on display in them. [11] For I'm no longer going to be visible in the world; they'll continue in the world while I return to you. <u>Holy Father, guard them as they pursue this life that you conferred as a gift through me, so they can be one heart and mind</u> [12] <u>as we are one heart and mind.</u> As long as I was with them, I guarded them in the pursuit of the life you gave through me; I even posted a night watch. And

not one of them got away, except for the rebel bent on destruction (the exception that proved the rule of Scripture).

[13] Now I'm returning to you. I'm saying these things in the world's hearing so my people can experience my joy completed in them. [14] I gave them your word; the godless world hated them because of it, because they didn't join the world's ways, [15] just as I didn't join the world's ways. I'm not asking that you take them out of the world But that you guard them from the Evil One. [16] They are no more defined by the world than I am defined by the world. [17] Make them holy—consecrated—with the truth; your word is consecrating truth. [18] In the same way that you gave me a mission in the world, I give them a mission in the world. [19] I'm consecrating myself for their sakes so they'll be truth-consecrated in their mission. [20] I'm praying not only for them but also for those who will believe in me Because of them and their witness about me. [21] The goal is for all of them to become one heart and mind—Just as you, Father, are in me and I in you, So they might be one heart and mind with us. Then the world might believe that you, in fact, sent me. [22] The same glory you gave me, I gave them, so they'll be as unified and together as we are— [23] I in them and you in me. Then they'll be mature in this oneness, and give the godless world evidence that you've sent me and loved them in the same way you've loved me.

[24] Father, I want those you gave me to be with me, right where I am, So they can see my glory, the splendor you gave me, having loved me Long before there ever was a world. [25] Righteous Father, the world has never known you, but I have known you, and these disciples know that you sent me on this mission. [26] I have made your very being known to them— who you are and what you do— and continue to make it known, so that your love for me might be in them exactly as I am in them.

CHAPTER 12

OVERWHELMED

Look carefully then how you walk! Live purposefully and worthily and accurately, not as the unwise and witless, but as wise (sensible, intelligent people), making the very most of the time [buying up each opportunity], because the days are evil.

Paul writing to the Ephesians 5:15-16 (AMP)

I have a friend who loves the expedition stories of Lewis and Clark, the great American explorers. In a recent conversation, the two of us compared our own journeys with God to the adventures of this legendary pair. Learning to live newly is like a great exploration into uncharted lands, an adventure in walking with God.

Although most of our world's physical landscape has now been charted, our journeys are still a lot like Lewis and Clark's. They took one step at a time, re-calibrating and reassessing their position periodically. Taking in all that was around them at any given point, they chose to stop and survey their surroundings. At this point it is safe to say that most of us have journeyed a long way. But unlike Lewis and Clark, we do not travel *away from* home but *toward* home.

We've all heard the expression, *A picture paints a thousand words*. I'm sure my word count is beyond a thousand at this point, but it's time to supply a picture—one that will serve as a map or a guide for our journey toward home.

Maps and GPS units are only helpful when they are laid out on the table or turned on and working. When we keep them in the glove compartment or the box they came in, they don't help…they can't help. The map I am going to unfold on the following pages will be flat and one dimensional, as most maps and GPS screens are, but it will reference things that are neither. Maps depict borders, boundaries, bodies of water, routes, bridges, exits, cities and towns—all references helpful for orienting us to our location so we can create a navigation plan. Now, making a plan is one thing and executing it is another. Who hasn't heard "recalculating" from the voice of a GPS unit? In other words, *you've made a wrong turn and your course must be re-navigated.* Just like points of reference on a map or GPS screen, the diagrams on the next pages are an attempt to illustrate the borders and boundaries of our lives and the best way to navigate our hearts safely through them.

These illustrations attempt to map out *where we are, who we are* and *the good that God is up to in our lives.* It will be helpful to remember that we live in a Large Story, a great love story set in the midst of a great battle. This backdrop of the Larger Story sets the stage for us to consider and explain the environment in which we find ourselves living, the great intersection of the Two Realms. As mentioned in previous chapters, there is the lesser realm, the *physical realm,* and the greater realm, the *Spiritual Realm*—the one that matters most.

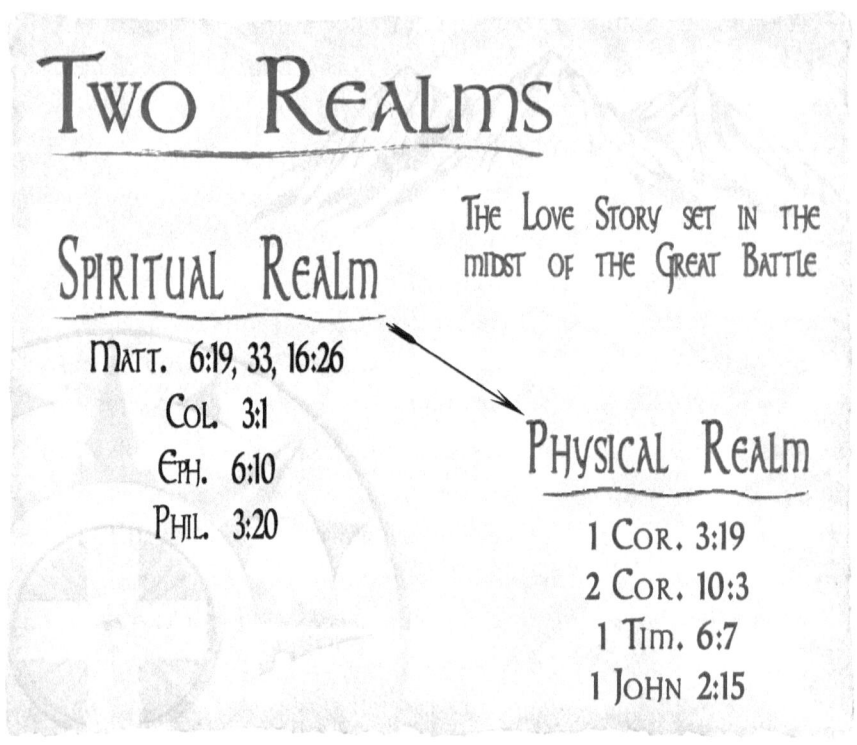

TWO REALMS

As we live within the grand and dangerous intersection of the Two Realms, giving our attention and consent to the realm that matters most is like having Lasik surgery. What once was fuzzy and unclear can become 20/20.

Just because you haven't been around the globe doesn't mean you don't live on a very large planet. Likewise, the story we live in is bigger than what we see and have experienced. The physical realm is important, but there is so much more going on in the Spiritual Realm—and it actually has power and sway over the lesser physical realm.

Two Kingdoms

Kingdom of Light → Kingdom of Darkness

JOHN 18:36	My Kingdom is not of this world
MATT. 3:2	John the Baptist: Repent, the Kingdom of Heaven is near
MATT. 27:11	Pilate asks Jesus- Are you the King of the Jews?
MATT. 6:33	Seek first the Kingdom of Heaven

The parables Jesus taught, tell of the Kingdom...
 MATT. 13:24 The Kingdom of Heaven is like...
 I PETER 2:9 That you may declare the praises of Him who called you out of darkness and into His wonderful light
 COL. 1:13 For He has rescued us from the dominion of darkness and brought us into the Kingdom of the Son.
 PHIL 3:20 Our Citizenship is in Heaven the Kingdom of the Son. (EPH 2:19)
 REV. 19 He is the King of kings

TWO KINGDOMS

Now in the realm that matters most, there exist **Two Kingdoms**: the kingdom of darkness and the Kingdom of the Son (or Light). These kingdoms are at war over something worth fighting for—the alliance, allegiance and affection of our hearts. Remember, the heart in biblical terms describes the core, or the very center of a human being. It is the deep, true place set by God in the inner sanctum of men and women. Similarly, from the biblical perspective, a kingdom is the environment in which we live and the economy that exists within it.

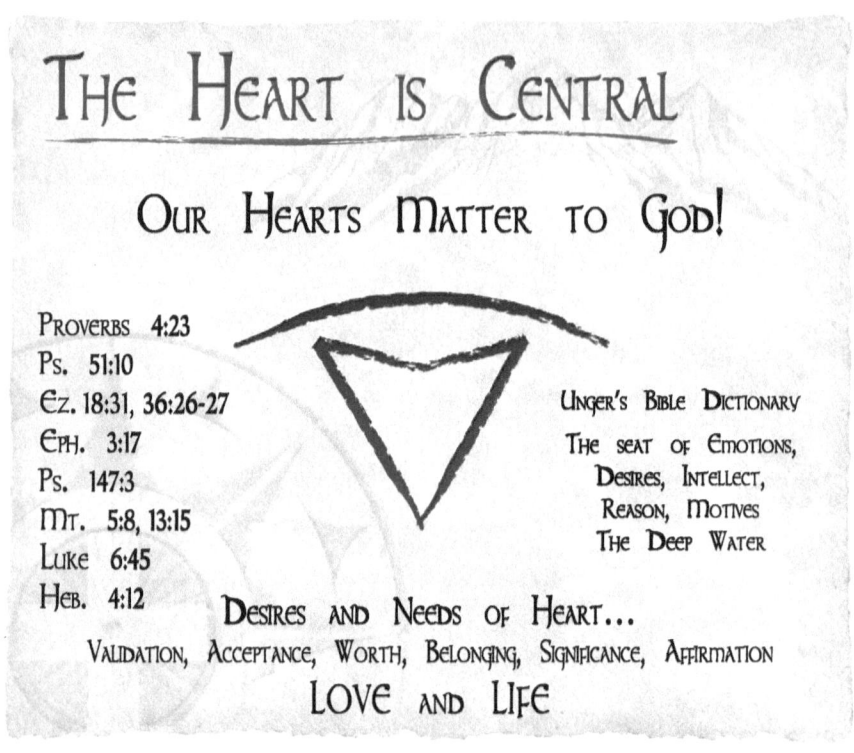

THE HEART IS CENTRAL

The heart is central in the battle between the two kingdoms. An individual's heart is the very source from where a person chooses his or her side, which kingdom he or she will align with and be a citizen of. The heart is more than the repository of our feelings. It is the place where desires, intellect, emotion, reason and motives reside. This is why when you capture a person's heart, you get *the whole person*. Both kingdoms know this and are therefore engaged in a heated battle for our hearts. Remember, every heart in its core longs for and desires Love. The things I've done, and still do, to try to arrange for some attention or affection in my life aren't pretty. We all feel and experience love at the times in our lives when we feel and experience validation, acceptance, worth, belonging, significance and affirmation.

The times I feel most alive are the times I am either receiving or offering the components and ingredients of love. When any one of us says and does *life giving* things for someone else, we are fulfilling the very mission for which God made us: *To love God and love one another*. We are participating in the Larger Story in a hands-on way, with a Kingdom orientation, making a difference, delivering special God-packages and helping change lives. As Jesus said: "...whatever you did for one of the least of these brothers and sisters of mine, you did for me." (Matthew 25:40)

SEARCH and RESCUE

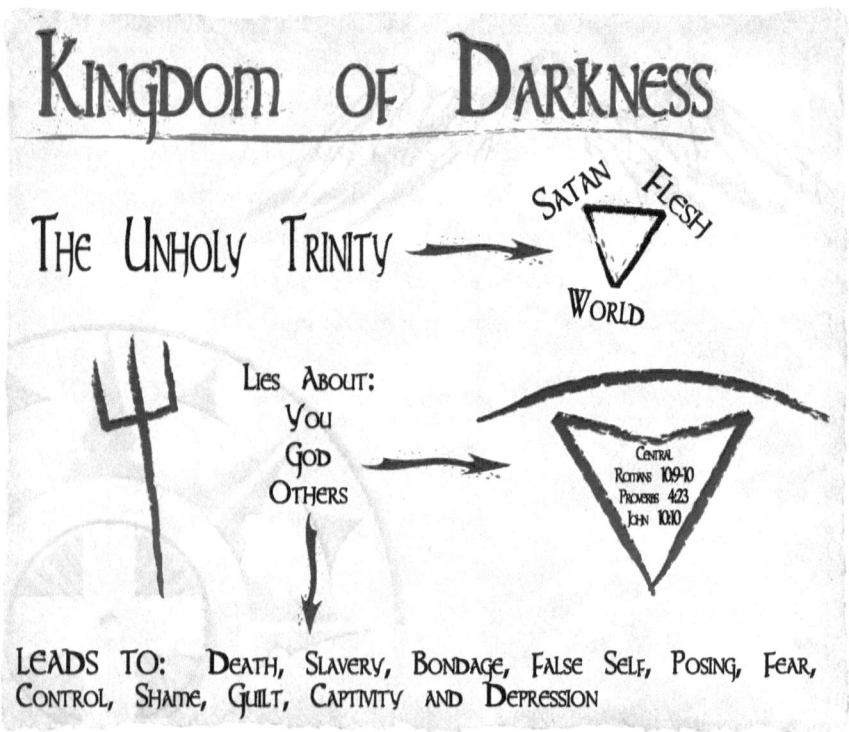

THE KINGDOM OF DARKNESS

There is a stark contrast between what the Two Kingdoms are offering the hearts of men and women; it is as different as life and death. The kingdom of darkness is offering lies, a twisting of reality and truth, that when believed will act as an infection—inhibiting love, binding life, and creating havoc on and in a person's heart. An infected person can become so lost he will either succumb to the pressure and wilt or, possibly even worse, rise to the situation and conclude he is master of his own destiny able to make life happen on his own. Either way the enemy wins; whether the person believes he has failed or succeeded, he becomes captive to a life of performance that will need to be repeated again and again the rest of his days unless there is healing and restoration. There is a part of us, a fallen part, that wants to believe the lies and make allowances for self promotion, self provision and self protection.

In John 12:31, Jesus calls Satan *the prince of this dark world*. It is the world and its great oppressive prince that work in scandalous partnership to bring hardship, heartache and glimpses of hell on earth to the hearts of those who are naïve, ignorant or in denial of evil's very existence. Satan and the world accomplish this dastardly feat with just enough maintenance and gentle pressure to virtually go unnoticed and thereby never tip their hand. It's as if we are drinking a drop of poison a day, just enough to keep us ill and living with an impaired immune system. And, most sinister of all—we're not aware of our captivity, yet we are being restrained to a marginal existence in a prison we ourselves have aided and participated in building. A jailbreak is our only hope!

Why Jesus Came – His Search and Rescue Mission...

Luke 4:18	Heal the broken hearted, sight for the blind, freedom for the prisoners (Isaiah 61)
Luke 19:10	Seek and Save that which was Lost
John 10	That we might have Life
Matt 20:28	Give His life as a Ransom
Gal 1:4	Rescue us from the present evil age
Col 1:13	Rescue us from the dominion of darkness
I Pet 5:10	Restore Us to Himself and make us strong, firm and steadfast

Rescue, Ransom, Redeem and Restore Luke 4, Isaiah 61

THE MISSION OF CHRIST: WHY HE CAME

The term "missional" has become a popular one in our culture. To be missional means having an intentional significance or purpose. Companies create mission statements either to justify what they do or remind themselves of what they want to do. Military and special forces units move from one mission to the next. Within a personal or corporate mission are objectives that, when accomplished, contribute to the fulfillment of the mission. When the mission is rescuing a lost person, the rescue team must accomplish several things:
- Identify the location of the lost, missing or captive person
- Deploy to that position
- Engage with the enemies holding the person
- Rescue and recover the person

- Provide any medical care or treatment needed
- Safely deliver the hostage or victim to a place of restoration, rehabilitation and rest
- And finally, reunite the person with loved ones.

This is the mission of Christ: To **search, rescue and restore**. This *is* the good that God is up to in our lives!

God's great *rescue* of us is essential to His great *restoration* of us. Our initial rescue is by the Father who sends the Son to ransom and recover those He loves–*us*! Not only is it His heart to redeem us, but it is even more His heart to restore us. John Eldredge describes this in his book, *Waking the Dead:*

> *So we now receive a new nature and a new heart, our second man. We have been made alive with the life of Christ. Just as we received our sinful nature from Adam, so we now receive a good and holy nature from Christ (Romans 5:14-19). It has always been God's plan not just to forgive you, but to restore you!*

God's Kingdom is the one we have always been intended to live in and to get Life from. God created us to be at our best and settle the issues of who we are by being with Him and living with Him, the King of kings. To live with all those who are His sons and daughters, our brothers and sisters who by our new birth are fellow citizens of His Kingdom, is now—and will be—a glorious thing. Jesus' life was a declaration of whom and what is most important. He fights for us that we might know Him, not just theologically but experientially. It is in the knowing that we find Life. The offer of the Gospel is much more than forgiveness. Don't get me wrong...forgiveness and reconciliation are great things, but they are only the means to an end. The end is Life; and the larger gospel is nothing less than a great invitation to Life. When we are *rescued from the dominion of darkness and brought into the Kingdom of the Son whom God loves and in whom we have Life* (1 Peter 2: 8-10), then true *Life* begins. And from there, the best part of all, it continues forever.

SEARCH and RESCUE

KINGDOM OF THE SON

The Bible speaks of light and darkness as a constant reality, and we are invited to choose whether to live in spiritual darkness or light. Is it any wonder that the Kingdom of Light and the Kingdom of the Son are synonymous? They're like the The Motor City and Detroit. Chocolate Town and Hershey...Graceland and Memphis...The City that Never Sleeps and New York...Tinsel Town and Los Angeles. The scriptures link together Light and the Son. Jesus said, *I am the light of the world* (John 8:12) and *I have come into the world as a light* (John 12:46). Do you see the connection? By light we see, and *Jesus* is the Light.

What we see can be an invitation or a confirmation. We've all heard the expression, *hind sight is 20/20*. It is the present that so often sheds light on the past. This holds true in the offer of the Larger Gospel. Like the old hymn says, *I once was blind but now I see*. Cataracts aren't just physical realm issues. When we don't see or don't see well, the odds of getting lost increase exponentially. The Great King, Jesus Christ, and His Kingdom offer us a life we can't conjure up, arrange for or make happen on our own. All the needs we have in life and for life have an Author and Creator whose supply store is always open. Wait, I'll do you one better—His *heart* is always open to supplying all we need. Our currency is belief. What we believe matters. The Great King invites, even pleads, *believe in me and I will set you free!*

So what does all this add up to? What does the map of all this look like? Pull together all the variables from the Two Realms and Two Kingdoms in one illustration, and what do you get? (See map on next page)

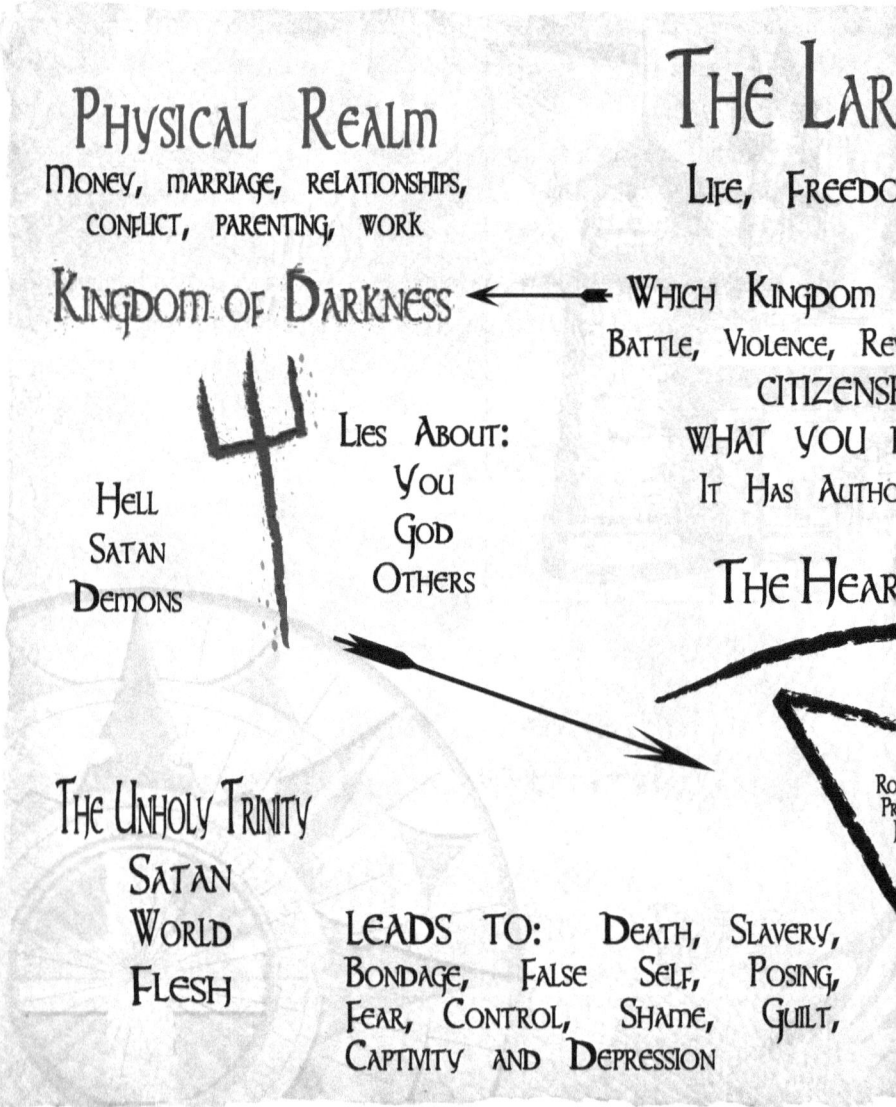

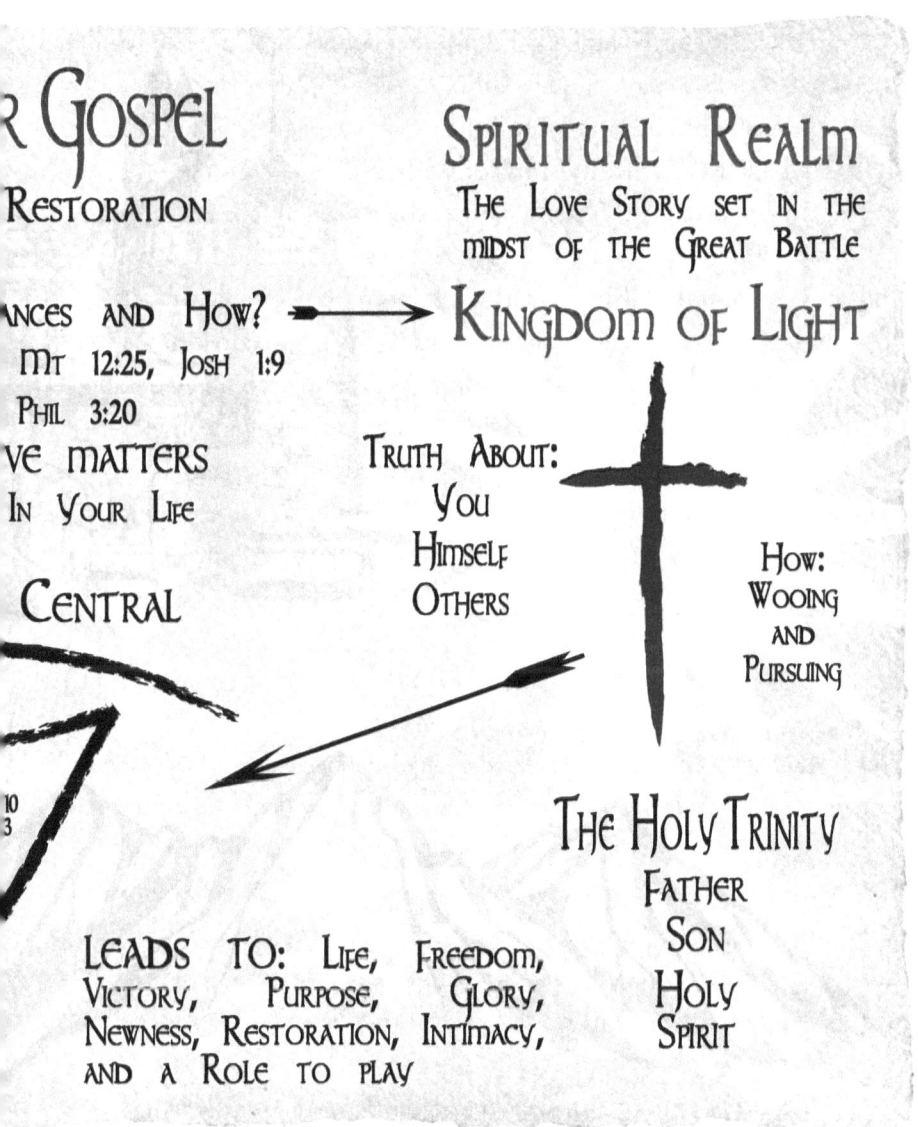

Whoa! Look at that. It is like a map, pulled from the glove compartment and opened up, taking up both driver and passenger seats. When did we begin to think we could control all of this? This is the territory we travel and the story we find ourselves in the midst of; this is *where we live*. This is the Larger Story that defines our value and our role, the part only we are uniquely gifted and equipped to play, *who we are*. And, most glorious of all, this is the story that enables us to see, understand and experience *the good that God is up to in our lives*.

This picture also gives us critical insight we need to face that which opposes us. The unholy trinity (Satan, the world and the flesh) is in the story, at least for now. It won't always be this way, but for now we will certainly be lost if we underestimate our enemy. When we are lost, we settle for a lesser life, a part too small. And we are subject to the frustration that results in drinking too much, eating too much, sleeping too much, working too much, complaining too much and judging others far too much. But once we get our bearings, we're able to help others. There is quite a lot going on in the Two Realms. Kind of *overwhelming,* isn't it?

OVERWHELMED

Now if you've stayed with me this far, then it is my hope that you have landed right there, at *overwhelmed.* John Eldredge in *Waking the Dead* writes:

> *If you're not pursuing a dangerous quest with your life, well, then, you don't need a Guide. If you haven't found yourself in the midst of a ferocious war, then you won't need a seasoned Captain. If you've settled in your mind to live as though this is a fairly neutral world and you're simply trying to live your life as best you can, then you can probably get by with the Christianity of tips and techniques....We need God intimately and desperately.*

When did we begin to believe we could control the Larger Story and all the elements within the Two Realms and Two Kingdoms? There seems to be a gravitational pull for me to attempt to control my life. You probably know the feeling I'm talking about: To be in charge, call the shots, keep it all together and, like the old commercial says, *Never let 'em see you sweat.* As I often like to ask folks who are still on the self-help treadmill, *how's that working for you?* We cannot control these Larger Story variables and characters. Rather, we are subject to them, contend with them and are invited to choose which to align with and which to fight against. Choose unwisely and, well...just look around; casualties are everywhere. Choose wisely, and there is One who promises to guide us safely home. Truly, this earth is not our home. The day I stepped into this reality was a very good day, one that set up many more good days to come. I didn't say they were easy; there were and still can be hard days, but they are good.

WHEN ONE MOVES, THEY ALL MOVE

I have to let you in on a little secret, one that I didn't discover till walking in this Larger Story for a few years. The more I saw, the more my orientation adjusted, the more free I became. The more God took me into my own history, the more my history was rewritten. The more God took me deeper into study and understanding of a component on the map, an element in this new reality of Two Realms and Two Kingdoms, the more the whole thing expanded. In other words, you can't gain ground in knowledge and experience in one element without it affecting all the others. For example, when I teach this, each person listening hears something a little different. Individual hearts pick up on different things. Listeners collect the dots, then they start connecting them. Some hearts discover a battle they've been oblivious to. Others catch onto the mission of Christ and confess they've had Him all wrong. On one occasion when my wife and I were having dinner with friends and the conversation turned to this map and orientation, one woman said, "All this focus on your heart; it seems a little selfish." This particular friend is a dietitian, an expert at nutrition. I wonder how she would have reacted if I had said, "Feeding yourself sounds a little selfish, don't you think?" Now I'm not claiming to be an expert at living this way, but I can say I've seen this from the macro and the micro levels in my life and many lives around me. And just like eating right and a little exercise can help a person live better, recognizing the Two Realms and Two Kingdoms is helpful and significantly aids us in a better way to experience Life.

I always thought it odd when flight attendants would say in their pre-flight announcements:

> *Now, if for any reason we should experience a loss of cabin pressure, oxygen masks will drop from overhead. Pull tightly on the cord to begin the flow of oxygen and place the mask over you nose and mouth and breathe normally, then help children and others with their masks.*

My initial thought was *yeah right, who's going to put his mask on first then help the kids*. I always felt noble as a father when I would smile protectively at one of my daughters sitting next to me on the plane during those announcements. *Don't worry honey, Daddy will take care of yours first*. I'm sure you're two steps ahead of me here. If those masks ever drop, you can guarantee that something has gone wrong. It is not a selfish pursuit to mask up; it is a necessary one in order to be of help to my loved ones and even total strangers for that matter. And so it is with the emphasis on your heart and getting it back, on becoming whole hearted. It is with a whole heart that we live and love well. To focus on the recovery of our hearts is not selfish; it is necessary, especially when it comes to helping others find the Life and Love they are searching for and Who is searching for them.

When we discover or uncover, expand or deepen our understanding of one of the Larger Story elements—God's love, our significance and value, the enemy's evil, the unholy trinity or the mission of Christ—then all the other elements will move with it. A clearer picture of God's love for me makes me realize I'm more valuable to Him than I knew. The relationship I was created to have and experience with Him is one thwarted by an enemy who would rather I not live connected and intimate with my Father. For when I begin to live this way, others will watch, see, hear and sense that something is different. And if they will walk out of the concentration camp as I did, they will also experience a new freedom and life. Living in a new Kingdom under a gloriously kind and loving King means bad news for the old kingdom ruled by an evil and sinister prince.

One of the greatest expeditions a heart can enter into is learning how to live anew as a Kingdom citizen and not be pulled back into old ways. It will also be the greatest battle a heart will know. If you want this Love and this Life, you're going to have to fight for it. It will not be easy, it will not be quick, and you are going to need *a lot* of help.

Living newly, with a *new normal,* is the hope and mission of the Spirit of God. As the Spirit works in and partners with the hearts of those connected to Him, *living newly* will be the reality. This new life will not be one in which we do everything right from now on, but rather we will know the One who is there to help us after we've done something wrong. It's going to take time to learn this new way to live. After placing our life in the hands of the Author of Life, is it possible that we will stumble or struggle? Will we get lost again? You bet! But it will be without the previous aftershocks of our mistakes—the guilt, shame, fear, condemnation—when the best we could expect after blowing it was groveling our way back to some remotely safe place to lick our battle wounds. Can we be taken captive again? Can we lose sight again? You bet, but not like before. The wrong turns we make, the poor decisions we execute, are and will be redeemed. We are to *work out our salvation* (Philippians 2:12), and God is with us and for us as we do. He will provide ways for us to go where we've never gone, choose what we hadn't known was available and live in a way we didn't know was an option!

CHAPTER 13

TRAINING: THE GOOD THAT GOD US UP TO IN OUR LIVES

I imagine myself before God whom I behold as King. I imagine myself as the most wretched of all, full of sores and sins, and the one who has committed all sorts of crimes against his King. Feeling a deep sorrow, I confess to Him all of my sins, I ask His forgiveness, and I abandon myself into His hands so that He may do with me what He pleases. This King, full of mercy and goodness, very far from chastening me, embraces me with love, invites me to feast at his table, serves me with His own hands, and gives me the key to His treasures. He converses with me, and takes delight in me, and treats me as if I were His favorite. This is how I imagine myself from time to time in His holy presence.

Brother Lawrence,
Practicing the Presence of God

There was a reason the shepherds came to the manger and the Magi followed the star (Matthew 1 and 2). There was a reason Satan offered Jesus the kingdoms of the world (Matthew 4:9) and a reason Jesus decided He would take them another way. There was a reason the 12 disciples followed Jesus (Matthew 4:19), and it wasn't what they had originally thought. There was a reason the religious leaders of Jesus' day didn't follow Him, and it was for the same reason the disciples did. It was because of who He claimed to be. There was a reason Pilate asked Jesus if He was King of the Jews (Matthew 27:11), and Jesus didn't deny it. And there was a reason Jesus was put to death on a cross.

    The reasons for all of this were far more than political and far more than physical realm, though those involved with Jesus attributed these things to these limited understandings. Jesus wasn't running for office; He was declaring one: King. Revelation 19 forecasts the Second Coming of the King of kings because Jesus is King and He is coming back. And, by the way, His reign as King doesn't start when He comes back. In Matthew 28:18, the risen Christ declares: *All authority in heaven and on earth has been given to me*. Jesus has always been King of the Spiritual Realm, and with His resurrection He conquered death and offered a ransom for His people. He reigns over it all now. What a good King He is. Good kings *provide for* and *protect* those living under their rule. Jesus offers us a provision and protection that we cannot purchase or pick up for ourselves. We can't arrange this provision for ourselves like we buy a cart full of groceries. We can't order this protection as we would a new security system for our house. When we try to take control of our lives in the Larger Story, we begin to assume a role that isn't ours. Jesus reigns over all, including our lives; He is in control. Our vain and even comical attempts at mutiny act as an internal drive system for our lives. These attempts actually *run* our lives, and when we attempt them, we play right into our enemy's hands.

God's provision and protection are things that can only come from Him; we have to trust Him, place our faith in His goodness and believe He will come through for us because he has a reliable track record. When we wander off and go blind and deaf to the Author of the Great Story, we take on a part that isn't ours to play. Yet, He comes for us every time. He knows it's only a matter of time before we will need comfort, relief and restoration. He is a patient King; love begins with patience (1 Corinthians 13:4).

FORGETTING

I once heard this quote about believers in Christ, and I've never forgotten it:
> *The problem with most believers is that they tend to remember the things they should forget and forget the things they should remember.*

Our journeys with God will require us to forget certain things. Paul tells us he *forgets what is behind and strains toward what is ahead* in his letter to the Philippian church (Philippians 3:13). If you know Paul's story then you know he had some forgetting to do. Now the kind of forgetting we need is not the kind that erases our memory. This forgetting is not an amnesia by which we have no recollection of certain times in our lives and the messages they carry with them. Instead, we choose to forget that old way of life and the lies associated with it. Remember, what we believe matters; what we believe has authority in our lives. Forget the indictments and accusations, the diminishment and discouragement, the guilt and the shame, all the woulda's, shoulda's and coulda's. This will be part of joining God in our restoration. We've got to get rid of all the crap before we can pick up the good stuff. And friend, I'm here to tell you... the good stuff is really, really good. But I believe there is only so much square footage in a heart and when the bad stuff is occupying space, the good stuff isn't. Exchanging the bad for the good is what God is up to in our lives—an exchange program. We give Him the mess, and He redeems it and restores us.

In the movie *The Legend of Bagger Vance*, Matt Damon plays Captain Rannulph Junuh, the only survivor of the men from Savannah, Georgia., who fought together to World War II. Junuh feels responsible, guilty and ashamed, and he chooses to try and hide in response. The narrator of the film describes Junuh's return home: *Confused, broken... and unable to face a return to a hero's welcome... Junuh just disappeared... Hopin' to forget... and to be forgotten.*

Early in the story a young boy, Hardy Greaves, goes looking for Junuh one night to invite him to represent Savannah by playing in a golf tournament with Bobby Jones and Walter Hagen. Hardy finds Junuh in a smoky shack where he is playing cards and drinking whiskey. Hardy enters the shack but, seeing the men drunk, thinks it might not be the best time:

> **Hardy:** Maybe I should come back when you're not so "busy."
>
> **Junuh:** Busy? I thought you were gonna say "drunk." But I'm not busy and I'm not drunk. There ain't enough whiskey in Georgia to get me drunk enough.

Hardy: How drunk is drunk enough, Captain Junuh?
Junuh: Good question. Sit over here, I'll tell you what drunk enough is. Aaron, can you find the young man a bottle of Nehi?
Aaron: I expect I could...just as long as I take my money with me.
Junuh: Now the question on the table is how drunk is drunk enough? And the answer is, it's all a matter of brain cells.
Hardy: Brain cells?
Junuh: That's right. Every drink of liquor you take kills 1,000 brain cells. But that don't matter, cuz we got billions more. First the sadness cells die, so you smile real big.

Then the quiet cells go, so you talk real loud for no reason at all. That's okay, because the stupid cells go next...so everything you say is real smart.

And finally... come the memory cells. These are tough to kill.

This *forgetting* that happens in the Christian life is not about killing brain cells, but rather that we forget the lies we have believed and exchange them for the truth being revealed to us. The truth about me, about God and about others. We open our hands to reach for the new, and the old falls out. We make room to receive and embrace the new, and we forget the old and untrue. Unfortunately our enemy is crafty; when we unsubscribe to the lies he worked so hard to deliver to our hearts, he fights to keep our hearts bound. His usual tactic is to freshen up the old lies, but if that bodes unfruitful, he tries sending us new ones that we might agree with, subscribe to and live under.

This is why the apostles wrote letters to the first-century churches. All of the churches have their plusses and their minuses, and every letter – whether from Paul, Peter, James or John – addresses the same sort of thing. Like caring and equipping big brothers, they share from experience:

> *Don't do that. Why are you doing that again? That's not who you are now, that's consistent with who you **were**. Stop that old stuff, let the new stuff lay hold of you again!*

By the way, all the letters mention the enemy and offer warnings not to underestimate the prince of this dark world. Just as there are some things we should forget, there are some things we shouldn't.

REMEMBERING

My mom and dad did a great job of taking pictures of me and my siblings while we were growing up. Digging up those old family photo albums always brings a smile to my face and a warmth to my heart. My wife and I have been a little obnoxious when it comes to taking pictures of our kids and making albums, either on the computer or of the old-fashioned kind. My kids love looking at the chapters of their lives and seeing with each turned page where they were and who they were with. A couple of years ago we transferred onto DVD all the home videos we'd kept in shoe boxes. Now we plug in one periodically, and it's just a matter of time before all three girls are in the living room offering commentary and laughing, and my wife and I are tearing up.

Mark Twain once said, "What is human life? The first third a good time; the rest remembering about it." Every year, my dad and I take a group of men pheasant hunting in South Dakota. When my Dad welcomes the men, he tells them it's no accident that they're there. With a smile he tells of the glorious time that will unfold over the next few days. And every time, tearing up, he says, "Let's make a memory."

Israel as a nation was charged with the crime of not remembering, not only once but on many occasions. Conversely, the thief on the cross next to Jesus was tuned in; he petitioned: *Jesus, remember me when you come into your Kingdom* (Luke 23:42). He knew the future was about not reliving the past.

In 1988 I started to journal. You know...write things down, log them on pages, and chronicle my heart's interaction with God. At first, my entries were more of a collection of lists and phrases, kind of like a grocery list or a bunch of sticky-note reminders to myself about the news of the day. After a couple of years, the entries became more conversational, archiving my walk with God rather than the daily news. I am amazed how the filled journals have collected, but what is even more amazing is how they help me remember God's provision and protection in my life. It is good for my heart to get them down and browse through them from time to time. They help me know today, from the experiences in my past, that He is with me, for me, and has me on a journey of life and for Life.

> *So, what do you think? With God on our side like this, how can we lose? If God didn't hesitate to put everything on the line for us, embracing our condition and exposing himself to the worst by sending his own Son, is there anything else he wouldn't gladly and freely do for us? And who would dare tangle with God by messing with one of God's chosen? Who would dare even to point a finger? The One who died for us—who was raised to life for us!—is in the presence of God at this very moment sticking up for us. Do you think anyone is going to be able to drive a wedge between us and Christ's love for us? There is no way! Not trouble, not hard times, not hatred, not hunger, not homelessness, not bullying threats, not backstabbing, not even the worst sins listed in Scripture: They kill us in cold blood because they hate you. We're sitting ducks; they pick us off one by one. None of this fazes us because Jesus loves us. I'm absolutely convinced that nothing—nothing living or dead, angelic or demonic, today or tomorrow, high or low, thinkable or unthinkable—absolutely nothing can get between us and God's love because of the way that Jesus our Master has embraced us.*
>
> Romans 8:31-39 (MSG)

Too often, Christians immerse themselves in programs, missions, duties and chores but miss intimacy, oneness and connectedness with the One who has set them free. It is much easier to serve someone than to be in love with them; but easier is clearly not better. In the movie, *The Notebook*, a main character, Noah, is speaking to the doctor who is handling the Alzheimer's case of his true love, Ali. He says, "I read to her and she remembers." She remembers by hearing of past events, and this helps her connect with who she really is. Love has the power to heal that service alone does not. We are invited to remember what we were made for...*Love*.

FORGIVENESS

How often do we remember the mistakes, shortcomings or blunders in our stories and consequently live with large, if not extra-large, amounts of guilt, shame or regret? I used to chalk this up to human nature, but I know better these days. Regret, one of our enemy's greatest strategies, keeps us barely living in the present, carrying the heavy weight of past losses and the echoes of their pain and discouragement. Regret can be brutal. We wish things could have been different in our lives—either things we have done that we shouldn't have or things we didn't do that we should have. And seldom are we the only person involved in these situations; they almost always involve others. The source of the regret is either something we've done or said to others or something others have done or said to us. This is a sinister thing the enemy lays hold of for evil. The quickest way to unearth what is lying toxic just below the surface of our heart is to ask questions of God such as:

Father, who has wronged me in my life?
Jesus, who makes my pulse race or heart skip a beat when they enter the room?
Holy Spirit, when I think of someone's life and its impact on me,

who does guilt and shame seem to accompany?
God, who do I need to forgive?

Forgiveness is the antidote for regret. The Father has made this wonderful provision in life for *real life*. Forgiveness is not the same as *excusing* someone's behavior; the process and application of forgiveness is much more substantial. My friend Tom has spent the past five years moving toward forgiving his father. He is almost there, and a relationship that was seriously strained has now become life giving for both of them. But Tom hasn't stopped there; because he has gone with God into the depths of his heart and emerged healed and restored, he is experiencing more and more freedom with his wife, sons, daughter and friends. And that is the best way to live—free! The freedom to love is so often made possible and amplified through forgiveness.

Let me take a moment here to speak to anyone reading this who has experienced a severe, possibly even life-threatening, trauma. Perhaps you have witnessed or endured abuse, molestation, rape or worse. The most horrible of circumstances are not beyond our God's capacity for redemption, forgiveness and healing, but I highly recommend you seek the ministry of a compassionate Christian counselor for help confronting such grievous situations.

BEING WATCHED

Sports teams around the country at almost every level from high school to college to pro do something that would be helpful for the rest of us to do. In preparation for a game, each team sends out scouts to investigate the opponent. What are these *spies* looking for? Their opponents' strengths and weaknesses, tendencies and habits.

During my years of playing college basketball, the manager of our team was one of my best friends. The team manager is the guy who arrives at each game before the players, stays after the players leave, picks up after them, does the laundry, sets out the uniforms, and so on... what a thankless job. One morning, after we had played a game the previous night, I went over to the field house—our home court gym—to help my friend finish some of the post game chores left from the night before. We were scooping up towels and uniforms and throwing them into the big laundry bins. He asked me to hit the visitor's locker room to see if they had left any towels. I pushed the big cart down the hall and through the doors to find there were a few more towels to collect. But that wasn't all I discovered. As I picked up the towels, I noticed something on the rolling chalkboard standing in the middle of the locker room. What do you think I saw? Remember, I am in the enemy's territory. There, listed on the chalkboard, were the names and numbers of my team, some descriptions of what we did well and what they wanted to exploit, and the assignments of their players who were responsible for covering ours.

> *Smith #32: post, strong inside, likes the right side, keep off the boards, put a body on him and he'll quit, don't block out and he will jump over you.*
> *DeLaney #24: forward, quick off the dribble, likes to penetrate, give the shot but honor the penetration, we want him to shoot outside.*
> *Thompson #14* (that's me): *point guard, likes to penetrate, good passer, fair shooter from three, put full court pressure, make him speed up/out of control, make him go left.*

I stood there, taking it in and pondering their scouting report on me. My first thought was...*I can go left!* But after my initial defensiveness, I realized the value of this information. How did the other team get this information and come to these conclusions? They had watched me play. They had seen, heard and even experienced my game, from previous years right up until that moment. They recognized my strengths, what I could do well, and they were committed to thwarting it, shutting it down, controlling it and getting me out of those areas of strength. When

I thought back to the night before, I realized that what I had experienced was far more calculated than random. And the same is true in the Spiritual Realm.

The sooner we embrace the fact that our lives have an opponent, an enemy, the sooner we can defend ourselves against him and take back lost ground from the one who has embezzled so much. I wonder what the spiritual opposition, the enemy of my heart, has written on his locker room wall. What has he planned against me and the life I long for and desire? I wonder how I might be able to *overcome* his plans, as passages of scripture tell me—"I am an *overcomer*." (Romans 12:21, Revelation 2, 1 John 2:13)

ALIGNMENT

The weight and significance of what we *experience* in our lives matters. But what matters a few degrees more is how we interpret our experiences. Our interpretations stick in our hearts. Each person's life experiences are categorized, classified and filed away. The files never go inactive; the messages of those files come up regularly or randomly but with great consistency or at the most inopportune times.

Living with some of the interpretations we've accumulated over the years is like trying to drive a car that is severely out of alignment. The potholes on the road of life and the things we have hit or run over create a lasting effect on our tires, their treads and our alignment. As we motor on down the road, driving out of alignment, we struggle to steer the car, fighting with all our might to keep the wheels on the road and out of the ditch. Whether or not we end up in the ditch, over an embankment or, even worse, over the proverbial edge depends where we're going in life, at what speed, who's in the car with us, and who's on the road with us at the wrong time and place. It's hard enough just to get my heart safely through the day. But with the road full of "heart traffic," a short drive can feel more like demolition derby, spinning around in circles, always bracing oneself for either hitting someone or being hit. This is not the way we were intended to live.

The things we experience and how we interpret them lay down records in our minds. Even when we are mistaken in our interpretation, we live as though our inaccurate conclusions are true. The enemy knows this and tries to work it for his agenda with such things as separation, bondage, fear, guilt, shame and death. Memorizing a bunch of Bible passages or adopting an author's philosophy is ordinarily not enough to counter these powerful mental records.

I like what author and teacher Wayne Jacobson says: *We need to help people discover the truth for themselves.* Helping others discover truth is not my mission, or the small group's mission, or your Sunday school class' or even your pastor's mission. But it is the mission of God in our lives. What if the pastor, Sunday school teacher, men's ministry leader or even the best-selling author has more to learn? What if he (or she) doesn't have it all together yet? Or is living with parts of his, (or her), life out of alignment? Could it be?

When something happens in our lives, who better to take our questions to than the Guide, Counselor, Teacher and Comforter—the Holy Spirit? If we will, most of the work has just been done. Bringing our questions to God is always better than drawing our own conclusions. Authors write books about what they've learned for many good reasons, but my heart may not be receptive to their advice at the particular time and place I read their books. Haven't you found a passage of scripture that is good at a particular time in your life but great when you read it again a few years later? What changed? The passage didn't, we did. Living with curiosity, asking questions, is an amazing way to live. Our questions can actually help us keep our hearts in alignment with God's.

TRUE AND MORE TRUE

Knowing the truth and experiencing the truth are two different things. The good that God is up to in our lives is best understood by experiencing that He is indeed good. Now you may get a forecast or announcement that God is good. But until you "taste and see" for yourself, it's a truth or a promise made that hasn't quite come true. Until it does, a heart and a life can only hope. But when it does, a heart and life will be altered. Amazing things happen once a life knows through *experience* that God is good, that He is in love with the hearts and lives of his people. And that He has a plan to transform his people into the glorious individuals He designed them to be. Once those concepts leave the brochure and become the reality, a heart and a life are changed.

The Bible is true. Stories and passages in the scriptures about people, their hearts, and God and His heart reveal truth to us and provide a framework for our own experience. Then when we experience the truth in our own day-to-day lives, we are able to recognize it. The stories of the Bible are true examples, not exceptions, of what life with God looks like. As truth is experienced, it becomes more real to us and more and more true.

Recently my youngest daughter asked me if I didn't like "Lane" anymore; Lane is a horse I rode on many trail rides with her. I asked her why she thought that. "Well, you don't ride anymore," she replied. This is an example of how we come to our own conclusions about our experiences; we make interpretations or declarations that quite often are not true. The truth is my back had been out of whack and riding my favorite horse wouldn't help me recover. It was not my horse I didn't like, it was the pain. What if, instead of making declarations, we asked questions of ourselves and others? Consider the example of a young person who is overlooked and not invited to a birthday party or sleepover. Did that ever happen to you? If so, how did your heart respond? When it happened to me, I was likely to respond with thoughts or silent declarations like: *I didn't want to go to that stupid party anyway. I never really liked Johnny. He was never really my friend!* It is wild how we first try to protect ourselves and then retaliate, all within our own mind.

Looking back, I didn't ask questions often enough—especially of my Mom and Dad. I was embarrassed by these kind of adolescent episodes, and somewhere along the way I picked up the belief that my parents would be also. Childhood turned into adolescence; the stakes rose and so did my insecurities. I didn't ask questions because somewhere deep down, I truly believed that the inviters who overlooked me were right: I didn't belong, I wasn't wanted and I would have to stay on the outside looking in. The seeds of those lies, planted early in life, produced great crops over the years, well into my 30s and 40s. I learned to be afraid of the answers, so I learned not to ask the questions; I learned how to be whatever was needed to get invited. And if I still wasn't, I could always fall back on the mental back-up plan, *I didn't want to be Johnny's friend anyway... he's a jerk.*

As I got older, I learned to hide the shame or embarrassment, the hurt and the anger. I got quite good at hiding. If there was a diagnosis for my coping technique, it would have been *Highly Functional Hider and Poser*. Like every coping technique, it wasn't working, it wasn't sustaining me, but I knew no other way...until the Father searched me out, rescued me and brought the healing to my heart that would set me on the road of recovery.

Who other than the loving God who created me and came to rescue me would care more about showing up and revealing the truth about who I am, where I am, and who He is? When Jesus was talking with—or, more accurately, rebuking—the self-righteous Pharisees, He had much life-offering advice to give:

> *Don't bargain with God. Be direct. Ask for what you need. This isn't a cat-and-mouse, hide-and-seek game we're in. If your child asks for bread, do you trick him with sawdust? If he asks for fish, do you scare him with a live snake on his plate? As bad as you are, you wouldn't think of such a thing. You're at least decent to your own children. So don't you think the God who conceived you in love will be even better?*
>
> Matthew 7:7-11 (MSG)

Jesus' mission included showing us the heart of the Father toward us. If we miss God's heart, we will misunderstand Him.

INCONVENIENCE?

I lived a long time with a lie lodged in my heart, a wrong belief and philosophy regarding *trials* in my life. Let's call trials what they really are, *inconveniences*, things not going the way I want them to. For many years, I believed these inconveniences were God's way of showing me how far I had to go, just exactly how bad off I was. I wrongly thought God was either getting even with me or punishing me with these inconveniences. I didn't question the truth of this conclusion. I didn't want to search out an answer; I wanted relief and comfort downloaded. I didn't want to talk with God about the issues in my life but rather wanted Him to fill my order. I wanted him to make things smooth and easy so I could get on with my life and not be inconvenienced. I expected him to either fix the situation for me or clear the difficulty out of the way so I could move ahead.

Because I believed God to be sovereign, there was only one possible conclusion for the things that didn't go right in my life: God was inconveniencing me. *Now* I know this couldn't have been further from the truth. But when you live in a small story that revolves around you, with others as supporting cast members, this is the only conclusion available to be forced upon God or anyone else who is not complying with your wishes. The truth is that God is not inconveniencing me. He is *inviting* me to participate with Him in the great mission of my life, training me for the mission and equipping me to walk with Him in oneness, intimacy and connectedness. Walking intimately connected to the Father is a large mission in a Large Story. And it requires a large step of faith to know that things are not always as they seem. *Just because things aren't going well in my life doesn't mean they aren't going according to plan.* In the stories of those in the Bible, things often got worse before they got better. The Peter in the gospels is a different man than the Peter who wrote First, Second and Third Peter. Oh he is the same guy—but different; 30 years of walking with God will do that, it will make you different. That's my hope—same ol' me—but different.

Too often we believe the subtle lie our enemy tells us: If something is successful, it must be of or from God. If it is not successful, then it is not from God and something is wrong. But that is not what the stories of the Bible tell us. What looks like a horrible failure to us may be a success in God's eyes. Was Jesus' brutal death by crucifixion a failure? Many of the stories of the Bible would have found an editor's trash can if the stories were meant to be a collection of human successes. The Bible is a collection of stories about God, not us. He is the center of the story, and yet we are crucial to the whole of it. Why? Because the One in the center of the story says so. It comes back to this: Do we trust the heart of the Father for us and toward us? Trials and struggles have a huge purpose and benefit in our training and maturing. This is the good that God is up to in our lives. Training us and growing us up into an image—the glorious one we had originally before sin entered the world. That image is the one He is restoring. The image we are being conformed to is that of Christ Jesus himself (Eph 1:11). He showed us how to live and invites us to follow his example. Learning to live as He did is the invitation God is determined to deliver to the doorstep of our hearts. Again and again and again.

INVITATION!

The number of life's moments I have misunderstood, mishandled, mislabeled and misdiagnosed along my journey (not to mention in the lives and journeys of others) is so large it's embarrassing. About 10 years ago, I had a change of heart that has since saved me time and time again. Living in the Two Realms and Two Kingdoms, I've learned to slow down. Living slowly offers the invitation to ask questions of God. When an awkward situation comes up, I ask, *What is this, God?* And I ask questions of others, *What did you mean when you said that? Could you give me an example of what you mean?* Slowing down doesn't change the actual speed or busy-ness of life, but it gives me the ability to call a "time out" or anticipate two steps ahead. When I am living fully aware, fully oriented and fully engaged in the Larger Story, moments of time can seem to be suspended, even linger.

It is the glory of God to conceal a matter; to search out a matter is the glory of kings.

Proverbs 25:2

There is something revealed about the heart of God in this proverb. At times it seems God conceals things from us. Answers aren't always obvious. Why would God conceal a matter? Why would He play such a seemingly mean trick? God desires to be sought after, and He paints light brushstrokes of this character trait on the canvas of Scripture...

> *And you, Solomon my son, get to know well your father's God; serve him with a whole heart and eager mind, for God examines every heart and sees through every motive. If you seek him, he'll make sure you find him.*
>
> 1 Chronicles 28:9 (MSG)

> *When you call on me, when you come and pray to me, I'll listen. "When you come looking for me, you'll find me. "Yes, when you get serious about finding me and want it more than anything else, I'll make sure you won't be disappointed.*
>
> Jeremiah 29:12-13 (MSG)

> *A time will come, however, indeed it is already here, when the true (genuine) worshipers will worship the Father in spirit and in truth (reality); for the Father is seeking just such people as these as His worshipers.*
>
> John 4:23 (AMP)

> *It's impossible to please God apart from faith. And why? Because anyone who wants to approach God must believe both that he*

*exists **and** that He cares enough to respond to those who seek him.*
Hebrews 11:6 (MSG)

God doesn't *need* to be sought after and pursued, He *desires* to be. Yes, love and intimacy are aimed at an object, the object of His affection. I used to think that God oozed love, and if I could get in its path I might enjoy some. But now I know I am in the crosshairs of His rifle for love and intimacy and He seeks after me constantly. How remarkable. The Lion of Judah is after *me*? Now that's the lion I want to be devoured by.

In Mere Christianity, C. S. Lewis describes the great love God has for his people and the cost of making it possible:

The happiness which God designs for His higher creatures is the happiness of being freely, voluntarily united to Him and to each other in an ecstasy of love and delight compared to the most rapturous love between a man and a woman on this earth... And for that they must be free. Of course God knew what would happen if they used their freedom the wrong way; apparently He thought it worth the risk.

Love and risk cannot be separated. We set ourselves out there *wanting*, *desiring* and *hoping* for someone to love us. Guarded, but hopeful. That describes me when I proposed to Robin. I went out on a limb, took a chance, hoping she would accept my offer of marriage. The risk paid off, I did not regret it and the memory of that moment will last a lifetime. Now, if God is inviting me into a moment, then I want to step into it —whether He calls me to *come with Him* to a quiet place or to *go with Him* on a search and rescue mission. If He is inviting me into a moment to *be still*, I'm in. Being *together* is the hope and desire, His and mine, no matter what the outcome might be. Whether the outcome is failure or success. It's about being with Him.

BACK TO THE WELL

Back in the summer of 1976, a boy in Seattle, Wash., was rescued from a life of addictions and sorrow, darkness and bondage...most of them in his future, mind you, but gloriously rescued just the same. This wouldn't be the only rescue; the rescue count in his life is now up in the thousands. You see, when someone is rescued they are pulled from danger and taken to safety...for a while. A person can wander off in the wrong direction, or a threatening someone or something can wander in the direction of a person. We've all bumped into things in our life's journey, and we've all had precarious people and events bump into us.

This boy grew up in a war-torn country, and yet, like many do in these places on the planet, he learned how to live with fighting or hiding, to get by and make his circumstances work for him. He found "normal" somewhere in the day-to-day. Some days the war would move in his direction, and he would become a casualty or be captured. Other days his curiosity or compulsions would move him toward the battle with often the same results.

Can you imagine having freedom, being safe, only to fall back into an old well, stuck in its little prison for a time? You would think a person would learn. Some folks do manage to learn to avoid the holes or at least they try to. They put a flag in the ground or some of that police tape around the crevice to remind them where the danger is. But the dark places seem to move, and the flags and tape get pulled up over time. There's not a question of *if* we will fall but *when*—we will all fall at some point—and a heart needs to learn the invaluable lesson of where help comes from and what the rescue looks like when it happens.

The young boy in my story journeyed far in his life, and it is well documented that he was rescued in seven American states and two foreign countries.

Some 20 years later, this boy has become a man, is married with kids of his own, and he is rescued again. This time, he is offered a position on the rescue team. Can you imagine that? Taking someone prone to getting lost and making him a part of the Search and Rescue team? And yet, that is exactly what happened. Those who have been scared, lost, alone and hurting know what it's like to be out there, ashamed of being lost and yet hoping to be found. They often make the best rescue team members because they don't give up. Yes, once in a while a Search and Rescue team member wanders off or, in the pursuit of another life, gets bumped into and thrown off course. It happens. These are the hazards of the role.

Now, if you're a bit confused as to whether I'm speaking of the metaphoric or literal, sharing from a Spiritual Realm or physical realm perspective, then you are on the right track. As you've probably guessed, I am the twelve-year-old boy who grew to be a husband, father and rescue team member.

I am so grateful to God who knows what I need and is committed to my growth after all these years. Being an apprentice, a learner who isn't especially skilled or pre-disposed to rescue work, has actually been the greatest rescue training of all. There is too much to *control* in this Larger Story, and yet *contributing* is quite a different matter than control. I'm in training everyday, and I have a secret to confess. I'm not in the training for what I can learn to do; I'm on the Search and Rescue team *to be close to the King*. I'm particularly fond of Him and I know for a fact that He is particularly fond of me. I'll tell you another secret: He's told me I'm one of His favorites and I'll bet that you are too. He's coming for you again and again. Life and Love are searching for you. My advice and encouragement to you…let yourself be found.

EPILOGUE

WHERE DO WE GO FROM HERE?

W here do we go from here? We live! We live restored, more aware, better oriented, in training. We live more true to who we really are, where we really are, knowing–not speculating about–the good that God is up to in our lives. We live more and more like Jesus did. Our new way of life is more than simply enduring and surviving; it is Life abundant and full. Why would Jesus say He came to bring that to us if it wasn't attainable? Why all the fuss to make arrangements and adjustments if this Life is not possible? God has made this way of living both possible and attainable, not because it pleases Him but because He is pleased with us.

So where do we go from here? What does this Life look like? We learn to live with questions, overwhelmed and to call on the One who has an endless stash of comfort and direction. We look to God for pre-*life-moment* preparations and post-*life-moment* interpretations. We listen for God's voice, accept his packages and discover his clues. We engage in the Great Adventure; and when we're tossed around, or worse, crashed landed, we ask for help.

And He helps every time we ask.

In 2007, twenty years after her rescue as a baby, Jessica McLure was interviewed on the TODAY show. Here are a few of the lines from the transcript recorded by Mike Celizic:

> *Not until she was five years old—more than three years after the rescue effort that captivated the nation and the world—did she learn her own story. She was watching an episode of "Rescue 911" about a little girl trapped in a well and was moved to tears by it. She asked about the girl and was told it was her.*
>
> *Jessica pulled back her bangs to show (Matt) Lauer a diagonal scar on her forehead, the most visible of the several she carries as a result of her ordeal. It marks where her forehead had been rubbed raw against the well casing during the two and a half days she was trapped, while scores of rescuers drilled a parallel tunnel and connecting shaft through solid rock to rescue her.*
>
> *The scar might be erased by plastic surgeons, but Jessica has decided to keep it. "It shows who I am, and the fact that I am here and that I could have not been here," she told Lauer.*
>
> *She endured 15 surgeries in the years after the incident to repair injuries she suffered.*
>
> *Lauer asked her if she's ever been able to understand why so many people became so emotionally involved in her rescue and her life.*
>
> *"I explain to myself that I believe that people cared so much because they would hope that somebody would care that much about them," she said. "In a way, helping me out and caring about me helped them out."*

Jessica's story is my story; it is all our stories. The men trapped in a Chilean mine are just like us. Before their ordeal began on August 5, 2010, each of them was "any man" reporting for work. We've all fallen into a "hole" at some time in our lives. We've all needed to be searched for and rescued. And, like Jessica and the Chilean miners, we have been. And when we enter into a relationship with our Rescuer, the mishaps are much less traumatic because we know Who to call on for help. As we move ahead and help others in their journeys, we help ourselves.

LIVING IN TWO KINGDOMS...

In our new life, we find our bearings with the perspective of the Two Kingdoms. Those around us trying to live without this orientation end up casualties of war, taken down or out by the calculated assaults of the enemy, the one Jesus himself referred to as a *thief, murderer, prince of this dark world* and *the father of lies*. Jesus came to earth for **us**—to **search for, rescue, recover, heal, and restore us and then set us free!** We're that valuable to Him, that important, that worth it. It is no small mission to bring us back to Life (John 10:10, Luke 19:10, Galatians 5:1, I Peter 1:3-4, Galatians 4:3-7, Luke 4:14-21). But it is a mission that He specializes in and engages in everyday, all day.

But now that we have this Life, we know we live in a Larger Story where the Author has assigned each of us an irreplaceable role. We understand that He walks with us, and He invites us to walk with Him into the glorious unknown where the best is yet to come. Sounds a lot like the folks who had their stories chronicled and archived in the Bible, and our stories can matter as much as theirs. We understand in this new Life that, just as there is a holy trinity of Father, Son and Spirit who is fighting for us and for our lives, there are enemies in this world in which we live. We must contend with the enemies on the outside, Satan and his fallen angels, and the ones on the inside, the flesh, the old nature.

The enemies oppose the *Life* God has for us. The unholy trinity of Satan, the world and our flesh form a league of villains that conspires to bring wreckage, wounding, damage and lostness into our lives. But Christ has come to rescue and restore us. With Him, we have a chance; with Him we are victorious. We don't fight for victory, we fight from victory. *Greater is He who is in us than he who is in the world.* (I John 4:4) We have entered into the fight with Him to take back the lost ground of our hearts.

Battling for the alliance, allegiance and affection of our hearts is an essential part of this new life, and it takes time—the kind of time that compares to getting the Nazis out of Europe. The initial counterattack began when we partnered with Christ for the regions of our hearts too long occupied by evil, and the battle to restore our hearts can take years. Sanctification, our "growing up," is often a drill of three steps forward, two steps back.

The Hero of the story, Jesus, heals and restores us as we desire and respond to His beautiful, valiant and timely offers. We no longer need to live as if we're captive. Nor do we need to live as if we don't require rescuing or can somehow, someway save ourselves. We have left behind these old orientations that bleed and get infected like untreated or poorly cared-for wounds.

Though we were born as citizens of one kingdom– a fallen one, Jesus has rescued us and given us citizenship in another, the higher one. *But our citizenship is in heaven. And we eagerly await a Savior from there, the Lord Jesus Christ.* (Philippians 3:20) Jesus came once to set the prisoners free (Isaiah 61, Luke 4), and He is coming back to take us home. Jesus told his disciples this:

> *In my Father's house are many rooms; if it were not so, I would have told you. I am going there to prepare a place for you. And if I go and prepare a place for you, I will come back and take you to be with me that you also may be where I am.*
>
> John 14:2-3

The life that God will set in motion from the end of days as we know them to the beginning of eternity is described in Revelation, the last book of the Bible, a book steeped with future events and kingdom concepts. Chapter 22 provides a beautiful picture of the *Kingdom restored*. More than God's people will be restored; God's entire creation was lost and it will be reclaimed and restored in the end! John, the book's author, paints the picture describing a literal place:

> *Then the angel showed me the river of the <u>water of life</u>, as clear as crystal, flowing from the throne of God and of the Lamb down the middle of the great street of the city. On each side of the river stood <u>the tree of life</u>, bearing twelve crops of fruit, yielding its fruit every month. And the leaves of the tree are <u>for the healing</u> of the nations. <u>No longer will there be any curse.</u>*
>
> *The throne of God and of the Lamb will be in the city, and his servants will serve him. They will see his face, and his name will be on their foreheads. There will be no more night. They will not need the light of a lamp or the light of the sun, for the Lord God will give them light. <u>And they will reign for ever and ever</u>.*
>
> Revelation 22:1-5 (emphasis added)

IT MAY GET HARDER

C. S. Lewis wrote in *The Case for Christianity*...
> *God has landed on this enemy occupied world in human form… Now is our chance to choose the right side. God is holding back to give us that chance. It won't last forever. We must take it or leave it.*

The invitation of God that leads to Life graduates to training on how to live that life. Jesus' commands are actually possible to live out:

> *Love one another as I have loved you.* John 13:34
> *Love your enemies and do good to them.* Luke 6:35
> *Love God with all your heart, soul mind and strength.* Luke 10:27, Matthew 22:37
> *Be courageous.* Matthew 14:27
> *You, dear children, are from God and have overcome them (evil spirits), because the one who is in you is greater than the one who is in the world.* 1 John 4:4

We have been rescued and made free. The enemy has lost us; we are no longer in the P.O.W. camp. But as is the case with most villains, the evil one of our story doesn't give up easily. He is no mere minor league player or junior varsity team member; he's an ancient foe, hell bent on thwarting what you and I were made for —intimacy and connectedness with God and each other.

To date, our adversary has had his way with far too many hearts. Where do we go from here? *We fight*. We fight for more healing and restoration in our own hearts so we can be fit for the battles, trials and altercations ahead for the hearts of others—those we love and desire to protect. Mario Sepulveda, the second Chilean miner to be pulled to safety put it like this, "I have been with God and I've been with the devil. I fought between the two. I seized the hand of God, it was the best hand. I always knew God would get us out of there." We have underestimated our enemy or flat out ignored him altogether for far too long, all the while making vain attempts at life. With our new orientation, we are ready to make a difference.

> *Some people are like seed along the path, where the word is sown. As soon as they hear it Satan comes and takes away the word that was sown in them.*
>
> Mark 4:15

Satan? Really? Isn't it simply either the fault of the ground or the farmer throwing the seed? Can't the farmer have better aim or plow better rows? Realizing Satan's capability is disturbing, maybe even alarming. Oswald Chambers wrote about Satan: *"He is a defeated foe, only to God but not yet to us."* Like those warning labels the government requires on certain products that are not the best choices for us, Chambers' words are a "heads up." After all, **the thief comes only to steal and kill and destroy.** (John 10:10a emphasis added)

IT WILL GET BETTER

Living newly, we are awake, aware, tuned in and engaged with our hearts. As friends of God, we are being trained up as His partners in the great Search and Rescue mission for the hearts of others. **It is God's heart to partner with us...invite us, train us, equip us and turn us loose in power and authority to be His representatives, His ambassadors, His freedom fighters, His rescue team. Our involvement in His mission actually shapes us for our significant role in the Larger Story.**

While we take on our role here on earth, there is another mission being made ready. This one will not need our help but will complete our healing and restoration. After the final battle to end the Great Spiritual War, God will set everything right and there will be no more Satan, no more flesh, and no more fallen world. The end of our story will be better than the closing scenes of *Apollo 13*, *Titanic* and the Chilean miner's rescue. Can you imagine? Me either. The struggle will be over; the war will have been won. And we, the friends of God, will step into a great victory party, the celebration known as the Wedding Feast of the Lamb, which God has been eagerly planning and happily looking forward to (John 14:3). It will be the celebration of all time, marking the dawning of a new day, our future with Him and with each other—never to be separated again.

> *"Come!" Say the Spirit and the Bride. Whoever hears, echo, "Come!" Is anyone thirsty? Come! All who will, come and drink, drink freely of the Water of Life!*
>
> Revelation 22:17 (MSG)

We are living in the moments before the honored guest arrives at a surprise party. God has made all the arrangements, sent out the invitations, prepared the festival hall and gone to extravagant measures to show how much He loves His loved ones. Oh! How wonderful it will be when the Honored Guest arrives. But it is not yet the time. We can be assured there will be a party, one for the ages. For now, however, the questions still stand: do we have *eyes to see, ears to hear* and *hearts that are engaged?* Will we journey with understanding, participate with God, and experience firsthand *who we are, where we are* and *the good that God is up to* in our lives?

Life hangs in the balance. My friends, the invitations are out, the journey awaits us; and the great cloud of witnesses in the heavenly realm, the Spiritual Realm, is pulling for us, waiting for us to choose. Choose wisely. *Choose Life*.

www.ingramcontent.com/pod-product-compliance
Lightning Source LLC
Chambersburg PA
CBHW031100080526
44587CB00011B/759